The
~ OLD ~
TESTAMENT
EXPLAINED

Through Modern Revelation

The OLD TESTAMENT EXPLAINED

Through Modern Revelation

DAN BARKER

CFI
An imprint of Cedar Fort, Inc.
Springville, Utah

ISBN 13: 978-1-4621-1207-4

Published by CFI, an imprint of Cedar Fort, Inc., 2373 W. 700 S., Springville, UT 84663
Distributed by Cedar Fort, Inc., www.cedarfort.com

LIBRARY OF CONGRESS CATALOGING-IN-PUBLICATION DATA

Barker, Dan, 1958- author.
The Old Testament explained through modern revelation / Dan Barker.
    pages cm
Includes bibliographical references and index.
ISBN 978-1-4621-1207-4 (alk. paper)
1. Bible. Old Testament--Criticism, interpretation, etc. 2. Church of Jesus Christ of Latter-day Saints--Doctrines. I. Title.

BS1171.3.B36 2013
221.6--dc23

2013032906

Cover design by Shawnda T. Craig
Cover design © 2013 by Lyle Mortimer
Edited and typeset by Deborah Spencer

Printed in the United States of America

10 9 8 7 6 5 4 3 2 1

Printed on acid-free paper

Acknowledgments

It's my name you see on the front cover of this book, however, there should be a listing of a number of other names. It isn't just my efforts that conveys this book to you, but the combined efforts of many. First, I want to thank Catherine Christensen, acquisitions editor, at Cedar Fort for giving me the chance to compile this book in preparation for the Old Testament study year in Sunday School. Also, for her and her staff's tireless work in editing and formatting the manuscript into what you are now holding in your hands. The cover design is incredible and I also have the folks at Cedar Fort to thank for their imagination and taste. Finally, you purchased this book in a store, which, if left to me, would never have happened (you would have had to visit my garage if marketing was my responsibility). The marketing team at Cedar Fort has always done a great job of getting my books out there. I've been in little places like Palmyra and Nauvoo and have seen my books on store shelves. I have also visited the Church History Museum and noticed that my books have been for sale in the gift shop. Amazingly, I have been to my local library and have seen all three of my published books to date and do not fear that this one will also find its way to the library.

Thank you, all!

ALSO BY DAN BARKER:

Unique Stories and Facts from LDS History

Mormon History 101

Little-known Stories about the Doctrine and Covenants

Contents

Preface ix

Genesis 1

Exodus 113

Leviticus 143

Numbers 151

Deuteronomy 159

Joshua 169

Judges 181

Ruth 189

1 Samuel 191

2 Samuel 205

1 Kings 207

2 Kings 215

1 Chronicles 221

2 Chronicles 227

Ezra 239

Nehemiah 243

Esther 247

Job 249

Psalms 251

Proverbs 257

Ecclesiastes 261

Songs of Solomon 265

Isaiah 267

Jeremiah 277

Lamentations 281

Ezekiel 285

Daniel 293

Hosea 299

Joel 303

Amos 307

Obadiah 309

Jonah 311

Micah 313

Nahum 315

Habakkuk 317

Zephaniah 319

Haggai 321

Zechariah 323

Malachi 327

Sources 329

Notes 339

Preface

How Much Do You Appreciate Your Bible?

The flyleaf to Joseph Smith's King James Version of the Bible contains the following inscription, etched in Joseph Smith's handwriting:

> The Book of the Jews And the property of Joseph Smith Junior and Oliver Cowdery.
>
> Bought October the 8th 1829, at Egbert B. Grandins Book Store Palmyra Wayne County New York
>
> Price $3.75.
>
> Holiness to the Lord. (*Church History in the Fulness of Times Student Manual*, 2nd ed. [Church Educational System manual, 2003], 118)

For Joseph Smith, and the people of his era, the $3.75 Bible that he jointly purchased with Oliver Cowdery was a definite sacrifice. It translated into almost four days of labor (About $600–$800 for an average man today). Curious, I checked the price for a good Bible online at the Distribution Center and noticed that the price for the leather bound version is $40. Doing some quick calculations, I realized the average man would now only have to labor approximately two hours to acquire this rawhide bound edition.

Printing was expensive in Joseph's Smith's time, but not nearly so pricey and out of reach for those who lived in the fifteenth and sixteenth centuries. For instance, the Bible that John Wycliffe translated into English and was eventually finished by John Purvey in 1388 was worth 500 crowns at the time (Basically, $125). By 1440, this cost was drastically reduced to 5 crowns ($1.25) with the establishment of the printing press.

Even though the invention of the printing press made the Bible more affordable, it was still out of reach for the common folk. People in that age worked for 6 pennies a week. In other words, they had to labor five months to purchase a Bible, with those five months of savings devoted to nothing else but the Bible (Joseph Fielding Smith, *Doctrines of Salvation*, comp. Bruce R. McConkie, 3 vols. [1954–56], 2:185). Because of the economics of owning a Bible, few could read the Bible the way so many desperately desired.

As Latter-day Saints, we're cognizant of the fact that certain events had to take place for the reestablishment of the kingdom of God in these last days. We understand that the sailing of Columbus, the signing of the Declaration of Independence, and the placing of the Smith family in the "burnt over district" in upper State New York were all heavenly sanctioned events. What we might not recognize as part of the miracle of the Restoration of the gospel, was the fact that the Smith family had a King James Version of the Bible in their home. In 1893, B. H. Roberts, a General Authority and the author of *A Comprehensive History of the Church of Jesus Christ of Latter-day Saints*, interviewed William Smith, younger brother of the Prophet Joseph Smith. It was during this interview that William stated,

> The Reverend Mr. Lane of the Methodist church preached a sermon on the subject, "What church shall I join?" He quoted the golden text of James—
>
> *"If any of you lack wisdom, let him ask of God that giveth to all men liberally and up-braideth not, and it shall be given him."*
>
> The text made a deep impression on the mind of the Prophet. He read it on returning home, and pondered it deeply. Here was a message from the word of God. A message to all men; but to him especially, since he had been made to feel that of all men he lacked wisdom, in respect of a matter to him vital. (B. H. Roberts, *A Comprehensive History of the Church*, [1965] 1:52–53)

Without the Bible, it would not have been possible for the young Joseph Smith Jr. to read James 1:5. Without that family Bible, Joseph may never have made the short trip from the family cabin to the grove of trees on his father's farm. Miraculously, it wasn't until the turn of the century (the seventeen hundreds into the eighteen hundreds) that technology advancements were made to cheapen the cost of printing. Paper became cheaper, but the largest development had to do with the invention of power presses and stereotype printing. Added to the technological advances was the social atmosphere and attitude toward the Bible in general. Due to the religious revivals sweeping America at the time, Bible societies were popping up and distributing the Bible in large numbers. The first, the American Bible Society, began in 1816 and by the 1860s was printing and distributing one million Bibles a year, when a normal print run for most literature was two thousand books (John S. Tanner, "The King James Bible in America: Pilgrim, Prophet, President, Preacher," *BYU Studies*, vol. 50, no. 3 [2011], 13–14).

Today, we are extremely privileged to have such easy access to the scriptures, and yet so few read the Old Testament. Because of easy, inexpensive access to the Bible, much of the Christian world ignores it. I think we as Latter-day Saints have a healthy understanding of the various Bible stories, but to actually plow our way through Genesis to Malachi becomes an astronomical feat for most. So why is it like this, especially since the Old Testament is important for instruction? It was the angel Moroni who, during his tutorial session with Joseph Smith on the evening of September 21, 1823, quoted scripture from such Old Testament books as Joel, Daniel, Isaiah, and Malachi, so it must be important. Could it be because we understand the "Book of Mormon to be the most correct of all books," and "We believe the Bible to be the word of God as far as it is translated correctly" and realizing, of course, that the Bible has been translated 190 times (David Daniell, *The Bible in English: Its History and Influence* [2003]), causes us to devote our attention to more modern scripture? It was Elder Bruce R. McConkie who stated, "The brass plates that Nephi took from Jerusalem contain more of the word of the Lord for the comparable period than does our present Old Testament" (*The Millennial Messiah*, 113).

In January 1832, Joseph Smith shared the following:

> Upon my return from Amherst conference, I resumed the translation of the Scriptures. From sundry revelations which had been received, it was apparent that many important points touching the salvation of man, had been taken from the Bible, or lost before it was compiled. (In *History of the Church*, ed. B. H. Roberts [1932–51], 1:245)

Joseph Smith also taught that "Our latitude and longitude can be determined in the original Hebrew with far greater accuracy than in the English version. There is a grand distinction between the actual meaning of the prophets and the present translation" (*Teachings of the Prophet Joseph Smith*, sel. Joseph Fielding Smith [2002], 290–91).

Nevertheless, our leaders understand the value of the Old Testament. Prophets and their stories are brought to life for us from the time a young toddler enters the nursery to our high school years in seminary, and for some, into the college years with its required institute classes.

During the year 1983, designated the "Year of the Bible," the First Presidency issued a statement in support of the Bible. Among other things they wrote that when the Bible is

> read reverently and prayerfully, the Holy Bible becomes a priceless volume, converting the soul to righteousness. Principal among its virtues is the declaration that Jesus is the Christ, the Son of God, through whom eternal salvation may come to all.
>
> As we read the scriptures, we avail ourselves of the better part of this world's literature. . . . Go to the fountain of truth, searching the scriptures, reading them in our homes, and teaching our families what the Lord has said through the inspired and inspiring passages of the Holy Bible. (JoAnn Jolley, "News of the Church," *Ensign*, May, 1983, online)

Shortly after the turn of the twentieth century, it was President Joseph F. Smith who instructed,

> That which characterizes above all else the inspiration and divinity of the Scriptures is the spirit in which they are written and the spiritual wealth they convey to those who faithfully and conscientiously read them. Our attitude, therefore toward the Scriptures should be in harmony with the purposes for which they were written. They are intended to enlarge man's spiritual endowments and to reveal and intensify the bond of relationship between him and his God. The Bible, as all other books of Holy Writ, to be appreciated must be studied by those spiritually inclined and who are in quest of spiritual truths. ("Reason and the Scriptures," *Juvenile Instructor*, April 1912, 204)

President Heber J. Grant summed it up when he stated, "All my life I have been finding additional evidences that the Bible is the Book of books, and that the Book of Mormon is the greatest witness for the truth of the Bible that has ever been published" ("The President Speaks," *Improvement Era*, Nov. 1936, 660).

Just as we believe the Bible to be the word of God, so too we believe in the principle of continuing revelation. It hardly matters that the Bible has been translated almost two hundred times. What is imperative is that the heavens are open to seal the gaps created by the uninspired, conspiring, or unintentional mistakes of man. Yes, obviously it would have been better if the original translation was left intact, but this didn't happen, and continuing revelation is the safety net that keeps us in line and in tune with gospel doctrines.

The basis for most books is to instruct with the goal to provide the reader with a different perspective or present new information. The Bible is the most read book, so for me to add additional information, relying entirely on the pages of the Old Testament, is not going to happen. Nonetheless, I believe I can produce a book that will both entertain and instruct if I'm permitted to use modern revelation, or what inspired Church leaders have said, relative to this great book of scripture. For instance, it is because of revelation that we know more about the City of Enoch than what information the Old Testament provides. It was through Joseph Smith that the Lord shared where the City of Enoch was located prior to its ascension into heaven. We also understand through Joseph Smith that the Garden of Eden was not located in Mesopotamia or the Holy Land as many of our Christian friends believe. As members, we know that the Garden of Eden was located in Jackson County, Missouri. When Adam and Eve were exiled from the garden, they traveled north forty miles to present day Adam-ondi-Ahman. Again, it is through Joseph Smith that the Lord revealed the location of where Cain killed Abel. The Old Testament is not silent on the events surrounding Cain and Abel, but it does not pinpoint the exact location of where this satanic-inspired deed played out.

It was President Joseph F. Smith who taught the following about modern revelation:

> We are to understand, then, that God does not, and will not further make known his will to men; that what he has said suffices. His will to Moses and Isaiah and John is abundant for modern followers of Christ. The Latter-day Saints take issue with this doctrine, and pronounce it illogical, inconsistent, and untrue, and bear testimony to all the world that God lives and that he reveals his will to men who believe in him and who obey his commandments, as much in our day as at any time in the history of nations. The canon of scripture is not full. God has never revealed at any time that he would cease to speak forever to men. If we are permitted to believe that he has spoken, we must and do believe that he continues to speak, because he is unchangeable.
>
> His will to Abraham did not suffice for Moses, neither did his will to Moses suffice for Isaiah. Why? Because their different missions

required different instructions; and logically, that is also true of the prophets and people of today. A progressive world will never discover all truth until its inhabitants become familiar with all the knowledge of the Perfect One. How shall men become acquainted with the knowledge of the Father? Only as he reveals it to them. Now if we are permitted to believe that the Lord revealed himself to the ancients of whose deeds we read in the Holy Scriptures, it seems to me that there is no good reason for believing that it is not necessary that he should reveal himself in this day to others who desire to be guided by his Spirit and inspiration. Every new truth which grows into living action in the lives of men is a revelation in itself from God, and without the revelation of additional truth, men would not progress in this world, but, left to themselves, would retrograde, being cut off from the light and life of the great fountain of all intelligence, the Father of All.

What is revelation but the uncovering of new truths, by him who is the fountain of all Truth? To say that there is no need of new revelation, is equivalent to saying that we have no need to new truths—a ridiculous assertion. ("Modern Revelation," *Improvement Era*, Aug. 1902, 805–6)

And so, this is the premise of this book: illuminate biblical events shared from what information can be gathered in our current Old Testament, coupled with additional knowledge as a result of added heavenly manifestations to Church leaders and modern scripture. This book is not a verse-by-verse commentary but rather closes some of the gaps created by uninspired men, using information revealed through modern scripture, teachings, and thought, thus broadening our knowledge and providing us with crystal clear understanding. As such, this book is meant to be used as a companion to both your holy scriptures and a comprehensive biblical commentary (*The Old Testament Made Easier* by David J. Ridges is an excellent resource, which provides additional clarity to the Old Testament).

The Old Testament Explained through Modern Revelation is set up with each book of the Old Testament acting as the chapter heading. Within each chapter are subheadings, generally the more common biblical stories that most are familiar with (for example, The Creation, Adam and Eve, Noah, The Flood, etc.). Using these subheadings makes finding references quick and easy. I will begin by stating **"What the Book of Genesis Teaches Us,"** then give the biblical reference and quotation. To explain the scripture just given, I will then follow up with either **"What** the **Scriptures of the Restoration Teach Us,"** (These will include scriptures from the Book of Mormon, Doctrine and Covenants, Pearl of Great Price, or the Joseph Smith Translation of the Bible) or **"The Teachings of Inspired Church Leaders,"** or use combinations of both. I will also use **"Interesting Information,"** which generally is a story from our pioneer past to help explain the biblical scripture being analyzed.

With that being said, roll up your sleeves, "fresh courage take," learn and enjoy, but more important, be grateful to your loving Heavenly Father for not leaving us alone in the dark to try and figure these things out on our own. The goal of this book is to provide a renewed appreciation for the Old Testament, modern scripture, and in-tuned Church leaders who can state, "Thus saith the Lord . . ."

Genesis

The Creation

Who Created the World?

What the Book of Genesis Teaches Us

The first verse of scripture in the Old Testament reads, "In the beginning God created the heaven and the earth" (**Genesis 1:1**). Based on this statement, we can only assume that God created the world. However, **Genesis 1:26** indicates that others might have been involved with the creative process when God stated, "And God said, Let *us* make man in *our* image, after *our* likeness" (emphasis added). God, in describing the creative process, did not use *me* or *mine*, but rather *us* and *our*. Obviously, at the very least, one other individual was involved with the organization of this world, but whom? The Old Testament is silent. We, however, have been given additional insight into who the God of the Old Testament is.

What the Scriptures of the Restoration Teach Us

D&C 14:9 Behold, I am Jesus Christ, the Son of the living God, who created the heavens and the earth, a light which cannot be hid in darkness.

Mosiah 4:2 For we believe in Jesus Christ, the Son of God, who created heaven and earth, and all things: who shall come down among the children of men.

1

Abraham 3:22, 24 Jesus Christ is speaking when He states: "*We* will go down. . .," then again, "*we* will take of these materials," and finally, "*we* will make an earth" (emphasis added).

Not everyone believes that Jesus Christ is the God of the Old Testament and therefore the God spoken of in this first verse of Genesis. Once I was talking with a friend at work and we got into a discussion about religion. The conversation evolved to who created the world and who is considered the God of the Old Testament. He had a difficult time wrapping his mind around the concept of Jesus Christ as the Creator and God of the Old Testament. I could understand. It is perfectly fine as each person learns "line upon line, precept upon precept." We, as Latter-day Saints, would experience the same difficulty if our only book of scripture was the Bible. The Bible, though true, lacks clarity. It is because of modern revelation that we know who the God of the Old Testament is, as mentioned in Genesis 1:1.

The Teachings of Inspired Church Leaders

At the April 1844 conference of the Church in Nauvoo, Illinois, the Prophet Joseph Smith stated the following:

> It is necessary for us to have an understanding of God himself in the beginning. If we start right, it is easy to go right all the time; but if we start wrong we may go wrong, and it will be a hard matter to get right.
>
> There are but a very few beings in the world who understand rightly the character of God. The great majority of mankind do not comprehend anything, either that which is past, or that which is to come, as it respects their relationship to God. They do not know, neither do they understand the nature of that relationship; and consequently they know but little above the brute beast, or more than to eat, drink and sleep. This is all man knows about God or His existence, unless it is given by the inspiration of the Almighty. . . .
>
> In the beginning, the head of the Gods called a council of the Gods; and they came together and concocted [prepared] a plan to create the world and people it. When we begin to learn this way, we begin to learn the only true God, and what kind of a being we have got to worship. Having a knowledge of God, we begin to know how to approach Him, and how to ask so as to receive an answer. (In *History of the Church*, 6:303, 308)

This is consistent with President Joseph Fielding Smith's thoughts on the same subject. He too believed that there were others responsible in the creation of the world, that it was not just the responsibility of God or Jesus Christ, but definitely Adam and "perhaps Noah and Enoch; and why not Joseph Smith," and others appointed to lead or rule in this lifetime (*Doctrines of Salvation*, comp. Bruce R. McConkie, 3 vols. [1954–56], 1:74–75).

The Materials of Creation

What the Book of Genesis Teaches Us

Genesis 1:1 In the beginning God created the heaven and the earth.

What the Scriptures of the Restoration Teach Us

Moses 3:5 provides us with the following truth that the book of Genesis fails to teach:

I, the Lord God, created all things, of which I have spoken, spiritually, before they were naturally upon the face of the earth. . . . And I, the Lord God, had created all the children of men; and not yet a man to tilt the ground; for in heaven created I them.

It was Moses to whom the Lord provided one of our first recorded revelations showing the events of the creation. This revelation was given sometime between Moses's encounter with the Lord at the burning bush and the exodus of the children of Israel from Egypt (Moses 1:17, 25), and is currently known to us as the Book of Moses in the Pearl of Great Price. This scripture solidifies the fact that our Heavenly Father has a purpose and a plan for our lives. We do not merely come to this world to live and die, and that's it. But rather, the way we seek to live our lives on this earth can live on into the eternities. It gives us a goal, a purpose, and helps us strive to achieve a more Christ-centered life.

The Teachings of Inspired Church Leaders

It was during the funeral service of a Nauvoo resident, King Follet, (April 7, 1844) that Joseph Smith provided the world with the following truth:

Now, I ask all who hear me, why the learned men who are preaching salvation, say that God created the heavens and the earth out of nothing? The reason is, that they are unlearned in the things of God, and have not the gift of the Holy Ghost; they account it blasphemy in any one to contradict their idea. If you tell them that God made the world out of something, they will call you a fool. But I am learned, and know more than all the world put together. The Holy Ghost does, anyhow, and He is within me, and comprehends more than all the world: and I will associate myself with Him.

You ask the learned doctors why they say the world was made out of nothing; and they will answer, "Doesn't the Bible say He *created* the world?" And they infer, from the word create, that it must have been made out of nothing. Now, the word create came from the word *baurau* which does not mean to create out of nothing; it means to organize; the same as a man would organize materials and build a ship. Hence, we infer that God had materials to organize the world out of chaos— chaotic matter, which is element, and in which dwells all the glory. Element had an existence from the time he had. The pure principles of element are principles which can never be destroyed; they may be organized and re-organized, but not destroyed. They had no beginning, and can have no end. (*Teachings of the Prophet Joseph Smith*, sel. Joseph Fielding Smith [2002], 350–52)

President Joseph F. Smith:

Things upon the earth, so far as they have not been perverted by wickedness, are typical of things in heaven. Heaven was the prototype of this beautiful creation when it came from the hand of the Creator, and was pronounced "good." (In *Journal of Discourses*, 26 vols. [1854–86], 23:175)

President Joseph Smith:

The spirit of man is not a created being; it existed from eternity, and will exist to eternity. Anything created cannot be eternal; and earth, water, etc., had their existence in an elementary state, from eternity. (In *History of the Church*, 3:387)

The Eternal Soul

What the Book of Genesis Teaches Us

Genesis 1:27 So God created man in his own image, in the image of God created he him; male and female created he them.

The person that accepts the biblical account of the creation and the role of Adam and Eve as our first parents, also accepts the fact that he is a creation of God. However, those who believe the heavens are sealed and that God no longer speaks to prophets today generally dismiss the existence of the spirit prior to this life and fail to comprehend the eternal nature of God's plan, only because Genesis fails to acknowledge any type of premortal existence and a previous life with our Heavenly Father. The Old Testament *does* hint at a pre-mortal existence in Jeremiah 1:4 and the New Testament in John 1:1–3. Nonetheless, many of our Christian friends still fail to understand the full interpretation of these scriptures. Truths becomes blurred without access to modern scripture or revelation.

What the Scriptures of the Restoration Teach Us

Moses 3:7 And I, the Lord God, formed man from the dust of the ground, and breathed into his nostrils the breath of life; and man became a living soul, the first flesh upon the earth, the first man also; nevertheless, all things were before created; but spiritually were they created and made according to my word.

The Teachings of Inspired Church Leaders

President Joseph F. Smith clarifies man's role in the eternal scheme of the plan of salvation:

We ought to be united in all things temporal as well as spiritual. With God all things are spiritual. There is nothing temporal with Him at all, and there ought to be no distinction with us in regard to these things. Our earthly or temporal existence is merely a continuance of that which is spiritual. Every step we take in the great journey of life, the great journey of eternity, is a step in advance or in retrogression. We are here in mortality, it is true; but we are ahead of that condition we occupied before we came here and took upon us mortality. We are a step in advance of our former state. What is the body without the spirit? It is lifeless clay. What is it that affects this lifeless clay? It is the spirit, it is the immortal part, the eternal being, that existed before it came here, that exists within us, and that will continue to exist, and that by and by will redeem these tabernacles and bring them forth out of the graves. The whole mission of ours is spiritual. The work we have to do here, although we call it temporal, pertains alike to our spiritual and our temporal salvation. And the Lord has just as much right to dictate, to counsel, to direct and guide us in the manipulation and manage-ment of our temporal affairs, as we call them, as he has to say one word in relation to our spiritual affairs. So far as He is concerned there is no difference in this regard. He looks upon us as immortal beings. Our bodies are designed to become eternal and spiritual. God is spiritual Himself, although He has a body of flesh and bone as Christ has. Yet He is spiritual, and those who worship Him must do so in spirit and in truth. And when you come to separate the spiritual from the temporal, see that you do not make a mistake. (In *Journal of Discourses*, 25:250)

Joseph Smith opened the Saints' view to the possibilities of the eternities when he shared this doctrine:

God himself was once as we are now, and is an exalted man, and sits enthroned in yonder heavens! That is the great secret. If the veil were rent today, and the great God who holds this world in its orbit, and who upholds all worlds and all things by His power, was to make himself visible,—I say, if you were to see him today, you would see him like a man in form—like yourselves in all the person, image, and very form as a man; for Adam was created in the very fashion, image and likeness of God, and received instruction from, and walked, talked and conversed with Him, as one man talks and communes with another. (In *History of the Church*, 6:305)

The Length of Creation

What the Book of Genesis Teaches Us

Genesis 2:1–2 Thus the heavens and the earth were finished, and all the host of them.

And on the seventh day God ended his work which he had made; and he rested on the seventh day from all his work which he had made.

According to the book of Genesis, God took seven days to complete the earth. Think for a moment; what is a *day* as referred to in Genesis? Is it a relative term to describe some length of time and not really a twenty-four hour period? Is it based off of the Lord's day, or heaven time, in which one day to the Lord equals a thousand years to us? If this is the case, then the earth is only 13,000 years old. Or, if we are to take the scripture literally, and a day is a twenty-four hour period, then we must accept the fact that the creative process took a week, in which case we can age the earth at 6,000 years. The Old Testament is not silent on this subject, King David gives a hint that the ancients may have understood the Lord's time as opposed to man's time when he stated in **Psalm 90:4**, "For a thousand years in thy sight are but as yesterday when it is past, and as a watch in the night."

Interesting Information

As early as 1844, W. W. Phelps wrote that the text of the Book of Abraham (only a portion of which was translated, and almost none of which survived the Chicago fire of 1871) indicated that "this system" (likely the solar system) was 2.55 billion years old (*Times and Seasons* 5:758).

Again, in 1852, W. W. Phelps published the following in the Deseret Almanac:

> Time is the ocean of existence, filled with elements and life for improvement by man. The presence and absence of the sun give days and nights—and the journey of the earth in her circuit, multiplies seasons and years; and years and ages make eternity; and eternity enlarges the scope of universal pleasure amid the glory of Gods.
>
> Again, it is revealed that one of our Father's days in Kolob, is 1000 years./ It is also revealed, that his year is, as we count, 365,000 [years]./ Then a week of his years, by the count of heaven, is 2,555,000,000 [years]./ Two billions, five hundred and fifty-five millions of years! Just the length of eternity, as the martyred prophet said./ Now upon principle, suppose eternity is multiplied into itself, we shall have 6,638,020,000,000,000,000 [years]./ As the *eternity of eternities*, mentioned in the Greek version of the New Testament./ Six quintillions, six hundred and thirty-eight quadrillions, and twenty-five trillions of years for a little season of perfection among the Gods./
>
> Ho saints! is this a beginning for eternities of eternities of all the stars that now glitter in the *upper deep*? Methinks you all answer, *no*, NO NO! No man in the flesh knows the beginnings and endings of one God. (*Deseret Almanac,* 1852, 47)

The Teachings of Inspired Church Leaders

President Brigham Young:

> I am not astonished that infidelity prevails to a great extent among the inhabitants of the earth, for the religious teachers of the people advance many ideas and notions for truth which are in opposition to and contradict facts demonstrated by science, and which are generally understood. You take, for instance, our geologists, and they tell us that this

earth has been in existence for thousands and millions of years. They think, and they have good reason for their faith, that their researches and investigations enable them to demonstrate that this earth has been in existence as long as they assert it has. . . . In these respects we differ from the Christian world, for our religion will not clash with or contradict the facts of science in any particular. You may take geology, for instance, and it is true science; not that I would say for a moment that all the conclusions and deductions of its professors are true, but its leading principles are; they are facts—they are eternal; and to assert that the Lord made this earth out of nothing is preposterous and impossible. . . . How long it's been organized is not for me to say, and I do not care anything about it. As for the Bible account of the creation we may say that the Lord gave it to Moses. If we understood the process of creation there would be no mystery about it, it would be all reasonable and plain, for there is no mystery except to the ignorant. (*Discourses of Brigham Young*, comp. John A. Widtsoe [1954], 258–59)

President David O. McKay described the time surrounding the creation of the world as "The millions of years that it took to prepare the physical world" (*Gospel Ideals: Life's Surest Anchor*, BYU Devotional speech [Oct. 30, 1956]).

President Brigham Young:

[Six days] is a mere term, but it matters not whether it took six days, six months, six years, or six thousand years. The creation occupied certain periods of time. We are not authorized to say what the duration of these days was, whether Moses penned these words as we have them, or whether the translators of the Bible have given the words their intended meaning. However, God created the world. God brought forth material out of which he formed this little terra firma upon which we roam. How long had this material been in existence? Forever and forever, in some shape, in some condition. (*Discourses of Brigham Young*, 153)

Elder Bruce R. McConkie:

But first, what is a day? It is a specified time period; it is an age, an eon, a division of eternity; it is the time between two identifiable events. And each day, of whatever length, has the duration needed for its purposes. . . .

There is no revealed recitation specifying that each of the "six days" involved in the Creation was of the same duration. ("Christ and the Creation," *Ensign*, June 1982, 11)

What the Scriptures of the Restoration Teach Us

D&C 88:42–44 And again, verily I say unto you, he hath given a law unto all things, by which they move in their times and their seasons;

And their courses are fixed, even the courses of the heavens and the earth, which comprehend the earth and all the planets.

And they give light to each other in their times and in their seasons, in their minutes, in their hours, in their days, in their weeks, in their months, in their years—all these are one year with God, but not with man.

"Subdue the Earth"

What the Book of Genesis Teaches Us

Genesis 1:28 And God blessed them, and God said unto them, Be fruitful, and multiply, and replenish the earth, and subdue it: and have dominion over the fish of the sea, and over the fowl of the air, and over every living thing that moveth upon the earth.

I believe man has done well at "subduing" the earth, maybe a little too literally. Animal and plant life, along with its many natural resources have been placed for the benefit of man. If there was a fault in "subduing," it would be in the waste, allocation, greed, and speed with which man is consuming some of these God-given resources. In the past, men have polluted the skies, water, and soil of the globe, and because of poor management, have caused many species to become extinct or endangered. What is satisfying though, is man has learned from his mistakes. I wouldn't say we are perfect, but I do know that man has realized that there needs to be control, moderation, and resource management with the view of sustaining for future generations.

The Teachings of Inspired Church Leaders

President Brigham Young instructs the following:

There is a great work for the Saints to do. Progress, and improve upon, and make beautiful everything around you. Cultivate the earth and cultivate your minds. Build cities, adorn your habitations, make gardens, orchards, and vineyards, and render the earth so pleasant that when you look upon your labors you may do so with pleasure, and that angels may delight to come and visit your beautiful locations. (In *Journal of Discourses*, 8:83)

President Thomas S. Monson:

God left the world unfinished for man to work his skill upon. He left the electricity in the cloud, the oil in the earth. He left the rivers unbridged, the forests unfelled and the cities unbuilt. God gives to us the challenge of raw materials, not the ease of finished things. He leaves the pictures unpainted and the music unsung and the problems unsolved, that we might know the joys and glories of creation. ("Your Future Awaits," BYU College of Engineering and Technology Convocation, Apr. 25, 2003)

The Garden of Eden

What the Book of Genesis Teaches Us

Genesis 2:8, 10–11, 13–14 And the Lord God planted a garden eastward in Eden; and there he put the man whom he had formed.

And a river went out of Eden to water the garden; and from thence it was parted, and became into four heads.

The name of the first is Pison: that is it which compasseth the whole land of Havilah, where there is gold;

And the name of the second river is Gihon: the same is it that compasseth the whole land of Ethiopia.

And the name of the third river is Hiddekel: that is it which goeth toward the east of Assyria. And the fourth river is Euphrates.

The Teachings of Inspired Church Leaders

President Brigham Young:

In the beginning, after this earth was prepared for man, the Lord commenced his work upon what is now called the American continent, where the Garden of Eden was made. (*Discourses of Brigham Young*, 102)

As Latter-day Saints, we have been taught that the Garden of Eden is in America. We're the only people in the world that believe this. The fact that these verses of scripture name Assyria, Ethiopia, and the Euphrates River, solidifies in Christian minds the world over that the Garden of Eden was located somewhere in the Middle East.

I'm sure this doctrine was surprising to most members; Heber C. Kimball must have raised eyebrows when he pinpointed the exact location of the Garden of Eden. Imagine for a moment how it must have felt for those Saints who once resided in Jackson County to know that they lived where the Garden of Eden was once located. He stated, "The spot chosen for the garden of Eden was Jackson County, in the State of Missouri, where [the city of] Independence now stands; it was occupied in the morn of creation by Adam" (In *Journal of Discourses*, 10:235).

What the Scriptures of the Restoration Teach Us

Scripture does not reveal that the Garden of Eden was located in the vicinity of Jackson County; nonetheless, Section 116 of the Doctrine and Covenants states that Adam-ondi-Ahman was in Spring Hill, Daviess County, Missouri. This was most likely the place where Adam and Eve dwelt after exiting the Garden of Eden forty miles to the south. This revelation was given to Joseph Smith on May 19, 1838 at Spring Hill, Missouri.

> **D&C 116:1** Spring Hill is named by the Lord Adam-ondi-Ahman, because, said he, it is the place where Adam shall come to visit his people, or the Ancient of Days shall sit, as spoken of by Daniel the prophet.

Adam and Eve

Adam and Eve's Decision

What the Book of Genesis Teaches Us

> **Genesis 2:16–17** And the Lord God commanded the man, saying, Of every tree of the garden thou mayest freely eat:
>
> But of the tree of the knowledge of good and evil, thou shalt not eat of it: for in the day that thou eatest thereof thou shalt surely die.

> **Genesis 3:1–6** Now the serpent was more subtil than any beast of the field which the Lord God had made. And he said unto the woman, Yea, hath God said, Ye shall not eat of every tree of the garden?
>
> And the woman said unto the serpent, We may eat of the fruit of the trees of the garden:
>
> But of the fruit of the tree which is in the midst of the garden, God hath said, Ye shall not eat of it, neither shall ye touch it, lest ye die.
>
> And the serpent said unto the woman, Ye shall not surely die:

For God doth know that in the day ye eat thereof, then your eyes shall be opened, and ye shall be as gods, knowing good and evil.

And when the woman saw that the tree was good for food, and that it was pleasant to the eyes, and a tree to be desired to make one wise, she took of the fruit thereof, and did eat, and gave also unto her husband with her; and he did eat.

The Teachings of Inspired Church Leaders

In reference to Adam partaking of the forbidden fruit, President Joseph Fielding Smith taught, "Adam made the wise decision, in fact the only decision that he could make" ("Was the Fall of Adam Necessary?" *Improvement Era* Apr. 1962, 231).

Elder Dallin H. Oaks shared this thought:

It was Eve who first transgressed the limits of Eden in order to initiate the conditions of mortality. Her act, whatever its nature, was formally a transgression but eternally a glorious necessity to open the doorway toward eternal life. Adam showed his wisdom by doing the same. . . .

We celebrate Eve's act and honor her wisdom and courage in the great episode called the Fall. . . . Elder Joseph Fielding Smith said: "I never speak of the part Eve took in this fall as a sin, nor do I accuse Adam of a sin. . . . This was a transgression of the law, but not a sin." ("The Great Plan of Happiness," *Ensign*, Nov. 1993, 73)

It was Satan's (the serpent's) desire to throw Heavenly Father's plan into commotion. What Satan didn't know is that instead of commotion he set the plan in motion. There are those who regret that Adam and Eve sinned. Brigham Young said it best when he taught the following:

Some may regret that our first parents sinned. This is nonsense. If we had been there and they had not sinned, we should have sinned. I will not blame Adam or Eve, why? Because it was necessary that sin should enter into the world; no man could ever understand the principle of exaltation without its opposite; no one could ever receive an exaltation without being acquainted with its opposite. How did Adam and Eve sin? Did they come out in direct opposition to God and to His government? No. But they transgressed a command of the Lord, and through that transgression sin came into the world. The Lord knew they would do this, and he had designed that they should. Then came the curse upon the fruit, upon the vegetables, and upon our mother earth; and it came upon the creeping things, upon the grain in the field, the fish in the sea, and upon all things pertaining to this earth, through man's transgression. (In *Journal of Discourses*, 10:312)

Our Heavenly Father was more than aware of the implications created when Adam and Eve partook of the forbidden fruit. This was all planned out in the Council of Heaven prior to Adam and Eve being placed in the Garden of Eden. Heavenly Father's plan meant that a Savior would be provided to bring Adam and Eve and their children back to His presence. Providing a Savior for all mankind was termed the *Atonement*. Obviously, Heavenly Father and Jesus Christ would have already instructed Adam and Eve in the role that the Savior would play as far as their eternal existence in the next life. It was Eve who said, "the joy of our redemption, and the eternal life which God giveth unto all the obedient" (Moses 5:11). How could Adam and Eve possibly understand redemption and eternal life unless they were taught in Eden.

President Joseph Smith said,

> But that man was not able himself to erect a system, or plan with power sufficient to free him from a destruction which awaited him [the result of Adam and Eve partaking of the Forbidden Fruit and introducing sin into the world] is evident from the fact that God, as before remarked, prepared a sacrifice in the gift of His own Son who should be sent in due time, to prepare a way, or open a door through which through man might enter into the Lord's presence, whence he had been cast out for disobedience. From time to time these glad tidings were sounded in the ears of men in different ages of the world down to the time of Messiah's coming. (*Teachings of the Prophet Joseph Smith*, 58)

Knowing this, is it any wonder that Eve was "glad" that they had been expelled from Eden's garden temple? The "driving" of Adam and Eve from the Garden of Eden may not have been as sorrowful as one would expect.

Finally, much of the Christian world has interpreted the partaking of the fruit by Adam and Eve erroneously. There are those who believe that because our first parents sinned, by partaking of the fruit, we are born into sin and as such must be baptized as new born babies. They say babies who die prior to this baptism are exiled from God. As Latter-day Saints, we understand the plan of salvation. We know that there was a pre-earth life, and a plan was set in place to rescue us from the effects of sin that entered the world with Adam and Eve's act in the Garden of Eden. We fully understand that a Savior would be provided to bridge the chasm that had been created, provided we repent of our wrongdoings. We're also cognizant of the fact that children who die without baptism are saved.

What the Scriptures of the Restoration Teach Us

D&C 74:7 But little children are holy, being sanctified through the atonement of Jesus Christ; and this is what the scriptures mean.

D&C 68:25–27 And again, inasmuch as parents have children in Zion, or in any of her stakes which are organized, that teach them not to understand the doctrine of repentance, faith in Christ the Son of the living God, and of baptism and the gift of the Holy Ghost by the laying on of the hands, when eight years old, the sin be upon the heads of the parents.

For this shall be a law unto the inhabitants of Zion, or in any of her stakes which are organized.

And their children shall be baptized for the remission of their sins when eight years old, and receive the laying on of the hands.

Nature and Appearance of Adam and Eve

What the Book of Genesis Teaches Us

Genesis 2: 21–23 And the Lord God caused a deep sleep to fall upon Adam, and he slept: and he took one of his ribs, and closed up the flesh instead thereof;

And the rib, which the Lord God had taken from man, made he a woman, and brought her unto the man.

And Adam said, This is now bone of my bones, and flesh of my flesh: she shall be called Woman, because she was taken out of Man.

Genesis 3:20 And Adam called his wife's name Eve; because she was the mother of all living.

The book of Genesis affirms that we did have first parents. We understand that they were taught by God in the Garden of Eden and conversed with him face to face. They were intelligent individuals who could think, reason, and act for themselves. They did not originate from a germ or bacteria floating around in space. They did not crawl out of the ocean, evolve from apes or cavemen, but rather God created them in his likeness and image (Genesis 1:26). As much as I believe Adam and Eve were not far different from most people's parents, the Old Testament falls short in describing any of their physical characteristics and attributes.

The Teachings of Inspired Church Leaders

The following is from the minutes of the Salt Lake City School of the Prophets:

> Once after returning from a mission, he [Zebedee Coltrin] met Brother Joseph in Kirtland, who asked him if he did not wish to go with him to a conference at New Portage. The party consisted of Presidents Joseph Smith, Sidney Rigdon, Oliver Cowdery and myself [Zebedee Coltrin]. Next morning at New Portage, he noticed that Joseph seemed to have a far off look in his eyes, or was looking at a distance and presently he, Joseph, stepped between Brothers Cowdery and Coltrin and taking them by the arm, said, "Let's take a walk." They went to a place where there was some beautiful grass and grapevines and swampbeech interlaced. President Joseph Smith then said, "Let us pray." They all three prayed in turn—Joseph, Oliver, and Zebedee. Brother Joseph then said, "Now brethren, we will see some visions." Joseph lay down on the ground on his back and stretched out his arms and the two brethren lay on them. The heavens gradually opened, and they saw a golden throne, on a circular foundation, something like a light house, and on the throne were two aged personages, having white hair, and clothed in white garments. They were the two most beautiful and perfect specimens of mankind he ever saw. Joseph said, "They are our first parents, Adam and Eve." Adam was a large, broad-shouldered man, and Eve as a woman, was as large in proportion. (Minutes, Salt Lake City School of the Prophets, Oct. 11, 1883)

President John Taylor said, "If you were to ask Joseph what sort of a looking man Adam was, he would tell you at once; he would tell you his size and appearance and all about him" (in *Journal of Discourses*, 18:326).

But this wasn't the first time Joseph Smith saw Adam. The Prophet was able to identify Adam to both Brother Coltrin and Oliver Cowdery because he was familiar with him. Where and when did Joseph Smith have contact with our first father? Modern revelation answers this question for us.

What the Scriptures of the Restoration Teach Us

> **D&C 128:20** And again, what do we hear? Glad tidings from Cumorah! Moroni, an angel from heaven, declaring the fulfillment of the prophets—the book to be revealed. A voice of the Lord in the wilderness of Fayette, Seneca county, declaring the three witnesses to bear record of the book! The voice of Michael [Adam] on the banks of the Susquehanna, detecting the devil when he appeared as an angel of light! The voice of Peter, James, and John in the wilderness between Harmony, Susquehanna county, and Colesville, Broome county, on the Susquehanna river, declaring themselves as possessing the keys of the kingdom, and of the dispensation of the fulness of times!

Adam's Role in the Restoration

The Teachings of Inspired Church Leaders

Not only was Adam an active participant in the creation, accepting the responsibility with Eve as mankind's first parents, but he also continues to help direct the Church in the latter days. At the general conference on October 5, 1840, at Nauvoo, Illinois, an article prepared by the Prophet Joseph Smith was read indicating that Adam continues to play an active function in the establishment of the Church in the last dispensation. He said, "Adam holds the keys of the dispensation of the fullness of times" (in *History of the Church*, 4:207).

This would explain why Adam detected Satan on the banks of the Susquehanna River prior to the visitation of Peter, James, and John (D&C 128:20). Adam, known in the pre-earth life as Michael, was an active participant in the War in Heaven. Being an active participant and combating Satan, he would have the ability to recognize Satan in any situation, just as he did on the banks of the Susquehanna River.

Elder Bruce R. McConkie states, "It also could well be that Adam, who brought mortality and death into the world, was also permitted to restore the power that brings immortality and life to his descendants" (*The Millennial Messiah* [1982], 120).

What the Scriptures of the Restoration Teach Us

> **D&C 29:26** But, behold, verily I say unto you, before the earth shall pass away, Michael, mine archangel, shall sound his trump, and then

shall all the dead awake, for their graves shall be opened, and they shall come forth—yea, even all.

Adam and the Priesthood

What the Book of Genesis Teaches Us

Genesis 1:26 And God said, let us make man in our image, after our likeness: and let them have dominion over the fish of the sea, and over the fowl of the air, and over the cattle, and over all the earth, and over every creeping thing that creepeth upon the earth.

What the Scriptures of the Restoration Teach Us

It is through modern scripture, reveled to the Prophet Joseph Smith, we learn that Adam was baptized and established the Lord's church on the earth. This would also indicate that Adam held the priesthood. The words of Enoch in **Moses 6:48–52** provide this Information

Because that Adam fell, we are; and by his fall came death; and we are made partakers of misery and woe.

Behold Satan hath come among the children of men, and tempteth them to worship him; and men have become carnal, sensual, and devilish, and are shut out from the presence of God.

But God hath made known unto our fathers that all men must repent.

And he called upon our father Adam by His own voice, saying: I am God; I made the world, and men before they were in the flesh.

And he also said unto him: If thou wilt turn unto me, and hearken unto my voice, and believe, and repent of all thy transgressions, and be baptized, even in water, in the name of mine Only Begotten Son, who is full of grace and truth, which is Jesus Christ, the only name which shall be given under heaven, whereby salvation shall come unto the children of men, ye shall receive the gift of the Holy Ghost, asking all things in his name, and whatsoever ye shall ask, it shall be given you.

If Adam received the priesthood and held the authority to baptize, then who baptized Adam? Try as you may, you would fail to find the answer to this inquiry in our present Old Testament. It is through the book of Moses in the Pearl of Great Price that the above question is answered:

Moses 6:64–66 And it came to pass, when the Lord had spoken with Adam, our father, that Adam cried unto the Lord, and he was caught away by the Spirit of the Lord, and was carried down into the water, and was laid under the water, and was brought forth out of the water.

And thus he was baptized, and the Spirit of God descended upon him, and thus he was born of the Spirit, and became quickened in the inner man.

And he heard a voice out of heaven, saying: Thou are baptized with fire, and with the Holy Ghost. This is the record of the Father, and the Son, from henceforth and forever.

The Teachings of Inspired Church Leaders

According to the teachings of the Prophet Joseph Smith, Adam was given the priesthood in heaven prior to his coming to earth.

The Priesthood was first given to Adam; he obtained the First Presidency, and held the keys of it from generation to generation. He obtained it in the Creation before the world was formed. (*Teachings of the Prophet Joseph Smith*, 157)

The Righteousness of Eve

What the Book of Genesis Teaches Us

Genesis 2:21–22 And the Lord God caused a deep sleep to fall upon Adam, and he slept: and he too one of his ribs, and closed up the flesh instead thereof;

And the rib, which the Lord God had taken from man, made he a woman, and brought her unto the man.

What the Scriptures of the Restoration Teach Us

In 1918, Joseph F. Smith saw Eve in revelation:

D&C 138:38–39 Among the great and mighty ones who were assembled in this vast congregation of the righteous were Father Adam, the Ancient of Days and father of all,

And our glorious Mother Eve, with many of her faithful daughters who had lived through the ages and worshiped the true and living God.

(See also Dallin H. Oak quote on page 12).

Expulsion from the Garden

What the Book of Genesis Teaches Us

Genesis 3:22–24 And the Lord God said, Behold, the man is become as one of us, to know good and evil: and now, lest he put forth his hand, and take also of the tree of life, and eat, and live for ever:

Therefore the Lord God sent him forth from the garden of Eden, to till the ground from whence he was taken.

So he drove out the man; and he placed at the east of the garden of Eden Cherubims, and a flaming sword which turned every way, to keep the way of the tree of life.

What the Scriptures of the Restoration Teach Us

Interpretation of the account in Genesis may leave the reader cringing for Adam and Eve as they were *driven* from Eden. I think we have all seen the picture of a remorseful Adam and Eve as they exited the garden. Just moments prior to their expulsion, the Lord explained to them where there used to be a garden and fruit provided spontaneously, there would now be weeds and sweat required to obtain their daily sustenance. There would also be pain and sorrow in bringing children into the world. Nevertheless, in a careful reading of **Moses 5:10–12**, it appears that both Adam and Eve completely understood what they did when they partook of the fruit and actually rejoiced in this decision:

And in that day Adam blessed God and was filled, and began to prophesy concerning all the families of the earth, saying: Blessed be the name of God, for because of my transgression my eyes are opened, and in this life I shall have joy, and again in the flesh I shall see God.

And Eve, his wife, heard all these things and was glad, saying: Were it not for our transgression we never should have had seed, and never should have known good and evil, and the joy of our redemption, and the eternal life which God giveth unto all the obedient.

And Adam and Eve blessed the name of God, and they made all things known unto their sons and their daughters.

Motherhood

What the Book of Genesis Teaches Us

Genesis 3:16 Unto the woman he said, I will greatly multiply thy sorrow and thy conception; in sorrow thou shalt bring forth children.

Child birth is a miraculous occasion that brings great joy as a new spirit enters a physical body and joins a family. And yet, the Lord instructed Eve that sorrow would be involved in bringing children into this world. If you take a look at the word sorrow in verse 16, you will notice that a footnote is attached. The footnote tells us that sorrow does not mean sorrow literally, but rather suffering. This clarifies what a woman experiences when giving birth to a child. There is suffering, there is pain, but in the end, there is joy.

The Teachings of Inspired Church Leaders

President Gordon B. Hinckley:

Most of you are mothers, and very many of you are grandmothers and even great-grandmothers. You have walked the sometimes painful, sometimes joyous path of parenthood. You have walked hand in hand with God in the great process of bringing children into the world that they might experience this estate along the road of immortality and eternal life. It has not been easy rearing a family. Most of you have had to sacrifice and skimp and labor night and day. . . .

You [mothers] are the real builders of the nation wherever you live, for you have created homes of strength and peace and security. These become the very sinew of any nation. ("Women of the Church," *Ensign*, Nov. 1996, 67)

Righteous Presiding

What the Book of Genesis Teaches Us

Genesis 3:16 And thy desire shall be to thy husband, and he shall rule over thee.

Interesting Information

Eve is told that her desire will be to her husband and that he is to rule over her. Similar to the verse that commands man to subdue the earth, this word "rule" has also been misinterpreted. Men do not rule families; man leads his family with his wife at his side. Many men have misunderstood the use of the word *rule*, leading to many abusive, unhappy, and single-parent homes. When the Lord used the term *rule*, I think he had the following in mind. Moses Taylor, son of President John Taylor has this to say about his father:

> He had a strong desire to keep his children under the family influence and provided play grounds for us. Even when he was past seventy years of age he would join us in our games. He provided a large sand pile for the little ones and if I have ever had any better time in my life than I did digging in the sand, I have failed to recognize it. . . .
>
> I have never heard him enter into any argument with any of his family; I have never heard him and my mother contend or disagree in the presence of the children. When talking about our duties in the church, it was always in the spirit of counsel and he would frequently say, "It would please me if you are a faithful Latter-day Saint." He was held in such high esteem by his children that to please him seemed to be their greatest desire. ("Stories and Counsel of President Taylor," *Young Woman's Journal* May 1905, 219)

The Teachings of Inspired Church Leaders

President Wilford Woodruff:

When I was a boy and went to school, the schoolmaster used to come with a bundle of sticks about eight feet long, and one of the first things we expected was to get a whipping. For anything that was not pleasing to him we would get a terrible thrashing. What whipping I got then did not do me any good. . . . Kindness, gentleness and mercy are better every way. I would like this principle instilled into the minds of our young men, that they may carry it out in all their acts in life. Tyranny is not good, whether it be exercised by kings, by presidents, or by the servants of God. Kind words are far better than harsh words. If, when we have difficulties one with another, we would be kind and affable to each other, we would save ourselves a great deal of trouble. . . .

You go into a family where a man treats his wife and children kindly, and you will find that they will treat him in the same way. Complaints reach me of the treatment of men to their wives. They do not provide for them. They do not treat them kindly. All this pains me. These things should not be. . . . We should be kind to one another, do good to one another, and labor to promote the welfare, the interest and the happiness of each other, especially those of our own households.

The man stands at the head of the family. He is the patriarch of his household. . . . There is no more beautiful sight on earth than to see a man stand at the head of his family and teach them righteous principles and give them good counsel. These children honor their father, and they take consolation and joy in having a father who is a righteous man. (*Deseret Weekly*, 823)

What the Scriptures of the Restoration Teach Us

D&C 121:39–43 We have learned by sad experience that it is the nature and disposition of almost all men, as soon as they get a little authority, as they suppose, they will immediately begin to exercise unrighteous dominion.

Hence many are called, but few are chosen.

No power or influence can or ought to be maintained by virtue of the priesthood, only by persuasion, by long-suffering, by gentleness and meekness, and by love unfeigned;

By kindness, and pure knowledge, which shall greatly enlarge the soul without hypocrisy, and without guile—

Reproving betimes with sharpness, when moved upon by the Holy Ghost; and then showing forth afterwards an increase of love toward him whom though hast reproved, lest he esteem thee to be his enemy;

The Angel, Adam, and Sacrifice

What the Scriptures of the Restoration Teach Us

The book of Genesis is quiet on how Adam learned of sacrifice and the role of sacrifice in his worship. It is because of the book of Moses that we, as Latter-day Saints, have an understanding of Adam and Eve's tutorial with an angel of the Lord.

Moses 5:4–8 And Adam and Eve, his wife, called upon the name of the Lord, and they heard the voice of the Lord from the way toward the Garden of Eden, speaking unto them, and they saw him not; for they were shut out from his presence.

And he gave unto them commandments, that they should worship the Lord their God, and should offer the firstlings of their flocks, for an offering unto the Lord. And Adam was obedient unto the commandments of the Lord.

And after many days an angel of the Lord appeared unto Adam, saying: Why dost thou offer sacrifices unto the Lord? And Adam said unto him: I know not, save the Lord commanded me.

And then the angel spake, saying: This thing is a similitude of the sacrifice of the Only Begotten of the Father, which is full of grace and truth.

Wherefore, thou shalt do all that thou doest in the name of the Son, and thou shalt repent and call upon God in the name of the Son forevermore.

Interesting Information

President Heber C. Kimball:

The Prophet Joseph called upon Brother Brigham, myself and others, saying, "Brethren, come, go along with me, and I will show you something," He led us a short distance to a place where were the ruins of three altars built of stone, one above the other, and one standing a little back of the other, like unto the pulpits in the Kirtland Temple, representing the order of three grades of Priesthood; "There," said Joseph, "is the place where Adam offered up sacrifice after he was cast out of the garden." The altar stood at the highest point of the bluff. I went and examined the place several times while I remained there. (Orson F. Whitney, *Life of Heber C. Kimball* [1992], 209)

Marriage

What the Book of Genesis Teaches Us

Genesis 2:24 Therefore shall a man leave his father and his mother, and shall cleave unto his wife: and they shall be one flesh.

What the Scriptures of the Restoration Teach Us

D&C 49:15 And again, I say unto you, that whoso forbiddeth to marry is not ordained of God, for marriage is ordained of God unto man.

The Teachings of Inspired Church Leaders

Joseph F. Smith shares the following:

I desire to emphasize this. I want the young men of Zion to realize that this institution of marriage is not a man-made institution. It is of God; it is honorable, and no man who is of marriageable age is living his religion who remains single. It is not simply devised for the convenience alone of man, to suit his own notions, and his own ideas; to marry and then divorce, to adopt and then to discard, just as he pleases. There are great consequences connected with it, consequences which reach beyond this present time, into all eternity, for thereby souls are begotten into the world, and men and women obtain their being in the world. Marriage is the preserver of the human race. Without it, the purposes of God would be frustrated; virtue would be destroyed to give place to vice and corruption and the earth would be void and empty. ("Marriage God-ordained and Sanctioned," *Improvement Era*, July 1902, 713–14)

Ezra Taft Benson:

Marriage . . . is the most glorious and most exalting principle of the gospel of Jesus Christ. No ordinance is of more importance and none more sacred and more necessary to the eternal joy of man. Faithfulness to the marriage covenant brings the fullest joy here and glorious rewards hereafter. (*The Teachings of Ezra Taft Benson* [1988], 533–34)

Interesting Information

The Saints understood the marriage relationship. They took this so seriously that an instance can be found where eleven-year-old Mosiah Hancock (Born on April 9, 1834, and son of General Authority Levi Hancock) was sealed to a young girl named Mary in the Nauvoo Temple just prior to leaving Nauvoo for the west. The Saints realized that it would be many years before they would enjoy the blessings of another temple and so, in some instances, things like this happened. The following is from the autobiography of Mosiah Hancock:

On about January 10, 1846, I was privileged to go in the temple and receive my washings and anointings. I was sealed to a lovely young girl named Mary, who was about my age, but it was with the understanding that we were not to live together as man and wife until we were 16 years of age. The reason that some were sealed so young was because we knew that we would have to go West and wait many a long time for another temple." (Autobiography of Mosiah Hancock, typescript, BYU-S)

Adam and Eve's Posterity

What the Book of Genesis Teaches Us

Genesis 5:1, 4 This is the book of the generations of Adam. . . .
    And the days of Adam after he had begotten Seth were eight hundred years: and he begat sons and daughters:

What the Scriptures of the Restoration Teach Us

D&C 107:53–56 Three years previous to the death of Adam, he called

Seth, Enos, Cainan, Mahalaleel, Jared, Enoch, and Methuselah, who were all high priests, with the residue of his posterity who were righteous, into the valley of Adam-ondi-Ahman, and there bestowed upon them his last blessing.

And the Lord appeared unto them, and they rose up and blessed Adam, and called him Michael, the prince, the archangel.

And the Lord administered comfort unto Adam, and said unto him: I have set thee to be at the head; a multitude of nations shall come of thee, and thou art a prince over them forever.

And Adam stood up in the midst of the congregation; and, notwithstanding he was bowed down with age, being full of the Holy Ghost, predicted whatsoever should befall his posterity unto the latest generation.

The Teachings of Inspired Church Leaders

President Joseph Smith:

I saw Adam in the valley of Adam-ondi-Ahman. He called together his children and blessed them with a patriarchal blessing. The Lord appeared in their midst, and he (Adam) blessed them all, and foretold what should befall them to the latest generation. This is why Adam blessed his posterity; he wanted to bring them into the presence of God. (*Teachings of the Prophet Joseph Smith*, 158–59)

President Ezra Taft Benson:

How did Adam bring his descendants into the presence of the Lord?

The answer: Adam and his descendants entered into the priesthood order of God. Today we would say they went to the House of the Lord and received their blessings. ("What I Hope You Will Teach Your Children About the Temple," *Ensign*, Aug. 1985, online)

Cain and Abel

Abel

What the Book of Genesis Teaches Us

Genesis 4:2 And she [Eve] again bare his brother Abel. And Abel was a keeper of sheep, but Cain was a tiller of the ground.

From the account provided in the Old Testament, like his parents, little is known about Abel. Based on Genesis, we can only assume that Abel was a righteous man, adhering to the teachings of his parents.

> **Genesis 4:4** And Abel, he also brought of the firstlings of his flock and of the fat thereof. And the Lord had respect unto Abel and to his offering:

It's obvious that Abel understood the purpose of sacrifice. This could have only come from the righteous teaching and example of anxious parents. If Abel understood the principle of sacrifice, then it's safe to assume that he knew of Jesus Christ and his mission. Even though this is not spelled out in our current King James Version of the Old Testament, there are enough clues provided that the serious student of the Bible can read between the lines.

The Teachings of Inspired Church Leaders

President Joseph Smith:

> We read in Genesis 4:4, that Abel brought the firstlings of the flock and the fat thereof, and the Lord had respect to Abel and to his offering. And again, "By faith Abel offered unto God a more excellent sacrifice than Cain, by which he obtained witness that he was righteous, God testifying of his gifts; and by it he being dead, yet speaketh." (Hebrews 11:4) How doth he yet speak? Why he magnified the Priesthood which was conferred upon him, and died a righteous man, and therefore has become an angel of God by receiving his body from the dead, holding still the keys of his dispensation; and was sent down from heaven unto Paul to minister consoling words, and to commit unto him a knowledge of the mysteries of godliness.
>
> And if this was not the case, I would ask, how did Paul know so much about Abel, and why should he talk about his speaking after he was dead? Hence, that he spoke after he was dead must be by being sent down out of heaven to administer. (*Teachings of the Prophet Joseph Smith*, 169)

He also stated the following:

> But it is said that Abel himself obtained witness that he was righteous. Then certainly God spoke to him: indeed, it is said that God talked with him; and if He did, would He not, seeing that Abel was righteous deliver to him the whole plan of the Gospel? And is not the Gospel the news of the redemption? How could Abel offer a sacrifice and look

forward with faith on the Son of God for a remission of his sins, and not understand the Gospel? The mere shedding of the blood of beasts or offering anything else in sacrifice, could not procure a remission of sins, except it were performed in faith of something to come; if it could, Cain's offering must have been as good as Abel's. And if Abel was taught of the coming of the Son of God, was he not taught also of His ordinances? We all admit that the Gospel has ordinances, and if so, had it not always ordinances, and were not its ordinances always the same? (Joseph Smith, *Teachings of the Prophet Joseph Smith*, 59)

Cain

What the Book of Genesis Teaches Us

Genesis 4:8–9 And Cain talked with Abel his brother: and it came to pass, when they were in the field, that Cain rose up against Abel his brother, and slew him.

And the Lord said unto Cain, Where is Abel thy brother? And he said, I know not: Am I my brother's keeper?

The Teachings of Inspired Church Leaders

President Brigham Young:

Cain conversed with his God every day, and knew all about the plan of creating this earth, for his father told him. But, for the want of humility, and through jealousy, and an anxiety to possess the kingdom, and to have the whole of it under his own control, and not allow any body else the right to say one word, what did he do? He killed his brother. Then the Lord put a mark on him. (In *Journal of Discourses*, 2:142–43)

What the Scriptures of the Restoration Teach Us

Not only did Cain speak with the Lord, but He gave Cain every opportunity to learn, improve, and change. We also learn that not only Satan is known as Perdition, but Cain also.

Moses 5:22–26 And the Lord said unto Cain: Why art thou wroth? Why is thy countenance fallen?

If thou doest well, thou shalt be accepted. And if thou doest not well, sin lieth at the door, and Satan desireth to have thee; and except thou shalt hearken unto my commandments, I will deliver thee up, and it shall be unto thee according to his desire. And thou shalt rule over him;

For from this time forth thou shalt be the father of his lies; thou shalt be called Perdition; for thou wast also before the world.

And it shall be said in time to come—That these abominations were had from Cain; for he rejected the greater counsel which was had from God; and this is a cursing which I will put upon thee, except thou repent.

And Cain was wroth, and listened not any more to the voice of the Lord, neither to Abel, his brother, who walked in holiness before the Lord.

The Teachings of Inspired Church Leaders

The catalyst behind the world's first murder was Cain's inability to control his emotions. The scriptures indicate that he became "wroth." How many individuals have detoured their lives to prison because they let anger take control? Man's ability to reason is clouded once we lose control of our tempers. Brigham Young, on a few occasions, taught the Saints to place anger behind them:

> If you give way to your angry feelings, it sets on fire the whole course of nature, and is set on fire of hell; and you are then apt to set those on fire who are contending with you. When you feel as though you would burst, tell the old boiler to burst, and just laugh at the temptation to speak evil. If you will continue to do that, you will soon be masters of yourselves as to be able, if not to tame, to control your tongues—able to speak when you ought, and to be silent when you ought. (*Discourses of Brigham Young*, 269)

Interesting Information

Original member of the Quorum of the Twelve, David Patten, relates meeting "a very remarkable person who had represented himself as being Cain":

> As I was riding along the road on my mule I suddenly noticed a very strange personage walking beside me. . . . His head was about even with my shoulders as I sat in my saddle. He wore no clothing, but was covered with hair. His skin was very dark. I asked him where he dwelt and he replied that he had no home, that he was a wanderer in the earth and traveled to and fro. He said he was a very miserable creature, that he had earnestly sought death during his sojourn upon the earth,

but that he could not die, and his mission was to destroy the souls of men. About the time he expressed himself thus, I rebuked him in the name of the Lord Jesus Christ and by virtue of the Holy Priesthood, and commanded him to go hence, and he immediately departed out of my sight. (Spencer W. Kimball, *Miracle of Forgiveness* [1969], 127–28)

Birth Order and Lineage

What the Book of Genesis Teaches Us

Genesis 4:1–2 And Adam knew Eve his wife; and she conceived, and bare Cain, and said, I have gotten a man from the Lord.

And she again bare his brother Abel. And Abel was a keeper of sheep, but Cain was a tiller of the ground.

Were Cain and Abel the first born of Adam and Eve? If all we had was to rely on our current Old Testaments, one might make this assumption. Nowhere in Genesis does it indicate that Cain and Abel were the two oldest siblings in Adam and Eve's family. However, a clue is provided, hinting that maybe Cain and Abel were not the two oldest siblings.

What the Scriptures of the Restoration Teach Us

It is through modern revelation that we learn that other siblings were born prior to Cain and Abel. In fact, Moses 5 gives us every indication to believe Adam and Eve were grandparents by time Cain and Abel were born.

Moses 5:2–3, 12, 16–17 And Adam knew his wife, and she bare unto him sons and daughters, and they began to multiply and to replenish the earth.

And from that time forth, the sons and daughters of Adam began to divide two and two in the land, and to till the land, and to tend flocks, and they also begat sons and daughters.

And Adam and Eve blessed the name of God, and they made all things known unto their sons and their daughters.

And Adam and Eve, his wife, ceased not to call upon God. And Adam knew Eve his wife, and she conceived and bare Cain, and said: I have gotten a man from the Lord; wherefore he may not reject his words. But behold, Cain hearkened not, saying: Who is the Lord that I should know him?

And she again conceived and bare his brother Abel. And Abel

hearkened unto the voice of the Lord. And Abel was a keeper of sheep, but Cain was a tiller of the ground.

Seth

What the Book of Genesis Teaches Us

Genesis 4:25 And Adam knew his wife again; and she bare a son, and called his name Seth: For God, said she, hath appointed me another seed instead of Abel, whom Cain slew.

What the Scriptures of the Restoration Teach Us

D&C 107:40–43 The order of this priesthood was confirmed to be handed down from father to son, and rightly belongs to the literal descendants of the chosen seed, to whom the promises were made.

This order was instituted in the days of Adam, and came down by lineage in the following manner:

From Adam to Seth, who was ordained by Adam at the age of sixty-nine years, and was blessed by him three years previous to his (Adam's) death, and received the promise of God by his father, that his posterity should be the chosen of the Lord, and that they should be preserved unto the end of the earth;

Because he (Seth) was a perfect man, and his likeness was the express likeness of this father, insomuch that he seemed to be like unto his father in all things, and could be distinguished from him only by his age.

This scripture mentions that Seth was a perfect man, but yet we know of only one perfect being, Jesus Christ. What was meant when the Lord stated to the Prophet Joseph Smith that Seth was perfect? Seth was human like you and me and therefore subject to the weaknesses and frailties of man. No, Seth wasn't perfect the way Christ was perfect, and yet could he be perfect in different areas of his life? Of course. I know a fellow work associate that has never been late and has never called off in eighteen years of work. It could be said that he is perfect. Is it possible that Seth could have been perfect in his responsibilities in the priesthood? Again, yes, just like all worthy members in the priesthood today understand the purpose of the priesthood they hold by blessing the lives of others both in the Aaronic and Melchizedek Priesthoods.

Moses 6:3–4 And God revealed himself unto Seth, and he rebelled not, but offered an acceptable sacrifice, like unto his brother Abel. And to him also was born a son, and he called his name Enos.

And then began these men to call upon the name of the Lord, and the Lord blessed them;

The Teachings of Inspired Church Leaders

According to a speech given by President John Taylor at Ephraim, Sanpete County, on Sunday morning, April 13, 1879, it appears that the Prophet Joseph Smith saw and conversed with Seth as he did with many of the ancient patriarchs.

> The principles which he [Joseph Smith] had, placed him in communication with the Lord, and not only with the Lord, but with the ancient apostles and prophets; such men, for instance, as Abraham, Isaac, Jacob, Noah, Adam, Seth, Enoch, and Jesus and the Father, and the apostles that lived on this continent as well as those who lived on the Asiatic continent. He seemed to be as familiar with these people as we are with one another. (In *Journal of Discourses*, 21:94)

Interesting Information

> On Saturday, September 1, 1838, the First Presidency made its way from Far West toward Littlefield's halfway house—about halfway between Adam-ondi-Aham and Far West—for the purpose of appointing a city of Zion. It was named the City of Seth in honor of Adam's son. The center of this city, which could have been the site of a public square and future temple, was never established due to the expulsion of the Saints from Missouri shortly after the city was appointed. (Rick Satterfield, "Adam-ondi-Ahman Temple," http://www.ldschurchtemples.com/adamondiahman/)

While gathering information on Adam's righteous son Seth, I found it interesting that the town of Seth still exists today. While trying to determine its location, I stumbled across a real estate listing for a property in this town. There is not an actual city, but rather it is a rural area. I imagine most people, including myself, would be hard pressed to find it. Anyway, you might find the listing to be of interest:

> This farm is rich in Missouri history, the town of Seth was started in 1838, lying half way between Adam-ondi-Ahman and Far West. In

1838 the Littlefields had a dry good business and housed travelers on this site for the trip between Ahman and [Far] West. (United Country Real Estate, "LISTING #35340," American Treasures: Your Source for Missouri Historic Homes & Vintage Property for Sale, online)

Enoch

What the Book of Genesis Teaches Us

Genesis 5:23–24 And all the days of Enoch were three hundred sixty and five years:

And Enoch walked with God: and he was not; for God took him.

What the Scriptures of the Restoration Teach Us

Modern revelation provides us with the blessing God gave to Enoch. By understanding this blessing, we then can begin to understand how it is that an army set in array to destroy Enoch and his people were defeated.

Moses 6:34 Behold my Spirit is upon you [Enoch], wherefore all thy words will I justify; and the mountains shall flee before you, and the rivers shall turn from their course; and thou shalt abide in me, and I in you; therefore walk with me.

Moses 7:12–17 And it came to pass that Enoch continued to call upon all the people, save it were the people of Canaan, to repent;

And so great was the faith of Enoch that he led the people of God, and their enemies came to battle against them; and he spake the word of the Lord, and the earth trembled, and the mountains fled, even according to his command; and the rivers of water were turned out of their course; and the roar of the lions was heard out of the wilderness; and all nations feared greatly, so powerful was the word of Enoch, and so great was the power of the language which God had given him.

There also came up a land out of the depth of the sea, and so great was the fear of the enemies of the people of God, that they fled and stood afar off and went upon the land which came up out of the depth of the sea.

And the giants of the land, also, stood afar off; and there went forth a curse upon all people that fought against God;

And from that time forth there were wars and bloodshed among them; but the Lord came and dwelt with his people, and they dwelt with his people, and they dwelt in righteousness.

The fear of the Lord was upon all nations, so great was the glory of the Lord, which was upon his people. And the Lord blessed the land, and they were blessed upon the mountains, and upon the high places, and did flourish.

The Teachings of Inspired Church Leaders

President Brigham Young:

Enoch possessed intelligence and wisdom from God that few men ever enjoyed, walking and talking with God for many years; yet, according to the history written by Moses, he was a great length of time in establishing his kingdom among men. The few that followed him enjoyed the fulness of the Gospel, and the rest of the world rejected it. Enoch and his party were taken from the earth, and the world continued to ripen in iniquity until they were overthrown by the great flood in the days of Noah; and, "as it was in the days of Noah, so shall it be in the days of the coming of the Son of Man." (In *Journal of Discourses*, 9:365)

Enoch's Mission

What the Scriptures of the Restoration Teach Us

Enoch was called on a mission at the time he was sixty-five years of age. It's interesting in the account in the Book of Moses that he refers to himself as a lad and as a result, feels inadequate to the call. In fact, he provides the Lord with three excuses in one verse of scripture alone. For those who are contemplating a mission and feeling not up to the challenge due to your inability to communicate, or to open your mouth, just understand that prophets have had the same issues, and yet the Lord has made them great. I love the Lord's instruction to Enoch in verse 32. I think any missionary can apply this verse of scripture to themselves today.

> **Moses 6:27, 31–32** And he heard a voice from heaven, saying: Enoch, my son, prophesy unto this people, and say unto them—Repent, for thus saith the Lord: I am angry with this people, and my fierce anger is kindled against them; for their hearts have waxed hard, and their ears are dull of hearing, and their eyes cannot see afar off;
>
> And when Enoch had heard these words, he bowed himself to the earth, before the Lord, and spake before the Lord, saying: Why is it

that I have found favor in thy sight, and am but a lad, and all the people hate me; for I am slow of speech; wherefore am I thy servant?

And the Lord said unto Enoch: Go forth and do as I have commanded thee, and no man shall pierce thee. Open thy mouth, and it shall be filled, and I will give thee utterance, for all flesh is in my hands, and I will do as seemeth me good.

D&C 107:48, 53 Enoch was twenty-five years old when he was ordained under the hand of Adam; and he was sixty-five and Adam blessed him.

Three years previous to the death of Adam, he called Seth, Enos, Cainan, Mahalaleel, Jared, Enoch, and Methuselah, who were all high priests, with the residue of his posterity who were righteous, into the valley of Adam-ondi-Ahman, and there bestowed upon them his last blessing.

Not only was Enoch blessed under the hands of Adam at the time he received the priesthood, but also on a second occasion.

The fact that Enoch was ordained at the age of twenty-five, but also that he received the priesthood before his own father and grandfather gives us an indication of Enoch's spiritual maturity (see D&C 107).

Enoch and Spirit Prison

What the Scriptures of the Restoration Teach Us

It's highly probable that Enoch may have been the first through revelation to learn of the "spirit prison" and the purpose it will serve. While enwrapped in vision, the Lord taught Enoch the following:

Moses 7:36–39 Wherefore I can stretch forth mine hands and hold all the creations which I have made; and mine eye can pierce them also, and among all the workmanship of mine hands there has not been so great wickedness as among they brethren.

But behold, their sins shall be upon the heads of their fathers; Satan shall be their father, and misery shall be their doom; and the whole heavens shall weep over them, even all the workmanship of mine hands; wherefore should not the heavens weep, seeing these shall suffer?

But behold, these which thine eyes are upon shall perish in the floods; and behold, I will shut them up; a prison have I prepared for them.

And that which I have chosen hath pled before my face. Wherefore, he suffereth for their sins; inasmuch as they will repent in the day that my Chosen shall return unto me, and until that day they shall be in torment.

The Book of Enoch

Try as you may, you will not find in the Old Testament a Book of Enoch. It is because of modern revelation that we know that such a book did exist at one time.

What the Scriptures of the Restoration Teach Us

D&C 107:57 These things were all written in the book of Enoch, and are to be testified of in due time.

The Teachings of Inspired Church Leaders

We have often heard that there are many missing scriptures. As we read through the Old Testament, we encounter the names of books that no longer exist in our current Bible. We know that Mormon abridged many records and condensed these records into our current Book of Mormon. This would agree with Joseph Smith and Oliver Cowdery entering the Hill Cumorah and viewing stacks of records that have yet to be published and made available to us today. The same is true of the book of Enoch. Orson Pratt sheds the following light in reference to the book of Enoch:

When we get that, I think we shall know a great deal about the antediluvians [those spiritual leaders living prior to the flood], of whom at present we know so little. (In *Journal of Discourses*, 19:218)

Joseph Smith then shares the following from *History of the Church* dated December 1830:

It may be well to observe here, that the Lord greatly encouraged and strengthened the faith of His little flock, which had embraced the fulness of the everlasting Gospel, as revealed to them in the Book of Mormon, by giving some more extended information upon the Scriptures, a translation of which had already commenced. Much conjecture and conversation frequently occurred among the Saints, concerning the books mentioned, and referred to, in various places in the Old and New Testaments, which were now nowhere to be found. The common remark was, "They are lost books;" but it seems the Apostolic Church had some of these writings, as Jude mentions or quotes the Prophecy of Enoch, the seventh from Adam. To the joy of the little flock, which in all, from Colesville to Canandaigua, New York, numbered about seventy members, did the Lord reveal the following doings of olden times, from the prophecy of Enoch. (In *History of the Church*, 1:131–32)

It is here that Joseph records the seventh chapter of Moses, stating that it is "Extracts from the Prophecy of Enoch," one of the missing books of scripture to the rest of the world, but not to the Latter-day Saints.

What the Scriptures of the Restoration Teach Us

The Old Testament documents Noah, the ark, and the great flood. Many believe it is through Noah that the Lord's intention to flood the earth is first recorded. This may be true for the Bible, but the fact of the matter is that hundreds of years prior to the flood, Enoch was given a vision of this event:

> **Moses 7:43–45** Wherefore Enoch saw that Noah built an ark; and that the Lord smiled upon it, and held it in his own hand; but upon the residue of the wicked the floods came and swallowed them up.
>
> And as Enoch saw this, he had bitterness of soul, and wept over his brethren, and said unto the heavens; I will refuse to be comforted; but the Lord said unto Enoch: Lift up your heart, and be glad; and look.
>
> And it came to pass that Enoch looked; and from Noah, he beheld all the families of the earth; and he cried unto the Lord, saying; When shall the day of the Lord come? When shall the blood of the Righteous be shed, that all they that mourn may be sanctified and have eternal life?
>
> **D&C 97:21** Therefore, verily, thus saith the Lord, let Zion rejoice, for this is Zion—the pure in heart; therefore, let Zion rejoice, while all the wicked shall mourn.

Enoch Taken Up

The Teachings of Inspired Church Leaders

Brigham Young alludes to preparing a pure people, a people who are pure in heart:

> If I live as long as Enoch lived, who walked with the Lord three hundred and sixty-five years, can I then see a people prepared to enter at

once in the celestial world? No. Many may think that Enoch and his whole city were taken from the earth directly into the presence of God. That is a mistaken idea. If, within three hundred and sixty-five years, I can see a people capable of surmounting every sin, of overcoming every evil and effect of sin to such a degree as to be separated in the flesh from the sinful portion of the world and from all the effects of the fall—a great people as pure and holy as were the people of Enoch, I should not complain, and, perhaps, have no cause to. Yet, in the latter days, God will cut short his work in righteousness. (In *Journal of Discourses*, 8:134)

President Joseph Smith:

Now this Enoch God reserved unto Himself, that he should not die at that time, and appointed unto him a ministry unto terrestrial bodies, of whom there has been but little revealed. He is reserved also unto the Presidency of a dispensation, and more shall be said of him and terrestrial bodies in another treatise. He is a ministering angel, to minister to those who shall be heirs of salvation, and appeared unto Jude as Abel did unto Paul; therefore Jude spoke of him. And Enoch, the seventh from Adam, revealed these sayings: "Behold, the Lord cometh with ten thousand of His Saints."

Paul was also acquainted with this character, and received instructions from him: "By faith Enoch was translated, that he should not see death, and was not found, because God had translated him; for before his translation he had this testimony, that he pleased God; but without faith, it is impossible to please Him, for he that cometh of God must believe that He is, and that he is a revealer to those who diligently seek him" (Hebrews. 11, 5). (In *History of the Church*, 4:209)

Methuselah

What the Book of Genesis Teaches Us

Again, very little has been recorded concerning this righteous man.

Genesis 5:21, 25, 27 And Enoch lived sixty and five years, and begat Methuselah:

And Methuselah lived an hundred eighty and seven years, and begat Lamech:

And all the days of Methuselah were nine hundred sixty and nine years: and he died.

The Teachings of Inspired Church Leaders

The question that is often asked among Christians is how is it possible that these ancient patriarchs lived so long?

President Brigham Young:

This is the duty of the human family, instead of wasting their lives and the lives of their fellow beings, and the precious time God has given us to improve our minds and bodies by observing the laws of life, so that the longevity of the human family may begin to return. By and by, according to the Scriptures, the days of a man shall be like the days of a tree. But in those days people will not eat and drink as they do now; if they do their days will not be like a tree, unless it be a very short-lived tree. (In *Journal of Discourses*, 14:89)

Josephus, a first-century historian, also believed that the years of these men were literal when he wrote in the *Antiquities of the Jews*:

Let no one, upon comparing the lives of the ancients with our lives, and with the few years which we now live, think that what we have said of them is false; or make the shortness of our lives at present an argument, that neither did they attain to so long a duration of life. (*Antiquities of the Jews*, trans. William Whiston [1737], book 1, chapter 3, paragraph 9)

Interesting Information

The Egyptian papyri, which Joseph Smith obtained at the time he acquired the mummies from Michael Chandler, revealed that Methuselah was an astronomer. (Joseph Fielding Smith, *Man, His Origin and Destiny* [1969], 269, 470, 488)

What the Scriptures of the Restoration Teach Us

D&C 117:8 Is there not room enough on the mountains of Adam-ondi-Ahman, and on the plains of Olaha Shinehah, or the land where Adam dwelt, that you should covet that which is but the drop, and neglect the more weighty matters?

What are the plains of Olaha Shinehah referred to in this scripture? It is through **Abraham 3:13** that more is learned:

And he said unto me: This is Shinelah, which is the sun. And he said unto me: Kokob, which is star. And he said unto me: Olea, which is the moon. And he said unto me: Kokaubeam, which signifies stars, or all the great lights, which were in the firmament of heaven.

The Teachings of Inspired Church Leaders

President Joseph Fielding Smith, quoted in the Doctrine and Covenants Student Manual, then instructs,

Elder Janne M. Sjodahl commenting on the name, Olaha Shinehah, has said: "Shinehah means sun, and Olaha is possibly a variant of the word Olea, which is 'the moon.' If so the plains of Olaha Shine-hah would be the Plains of the Moon and the Sun, so called, perhaps because of astronomical observations there made." We learn from the writings of Moses that the Lord revealed to the ancients great knowledge concerning the stars, and Abraham by revelations and through the Urim and Thummim received wonderful information concerning the heavens and the governing planets, or stars. It was also revealed by the Prophet Joseph Smith that Methuselah was acquainted with the stars as were others of the antediluvian prophets including Adam. So it may be reasonable that here in this valley important information was made known anciently in relation to the stars of our universe. (As quoted in *Doctrine and Covenants Student Manual*, 2nd ed. [Church Educational System manual, 2001], 289–90)

Even though the Old Testament is not entirely clear on all aspects of Noah's life, surprisingly, there is much that we do know. Many verses of scripture are devoted to him and his family, allowing us to piece together the attributes and characteristics of this great prophet that are glossed over with many of the other great men spoken of in the Old Testament.

Noah's Descendants

What the Book of Genesis Teaches Us

Genesis 7:13 In the selfsame day entered Noah, and Shem, and Ham, and Japheth, the sons of Noah, and Noah's wife, and the three wives of his sons with them, into the ark.

The Teachings of Inspired Church Leaders

President Joseph Smith:

The first Sabbath after our arrival in Jackson county, Brother W. W. Phelps preached to a western audience over the boundary of the United States, wherein were present specimens of all the families of the earth; Shem, Ham and Japheth; several of the Lamanites or Indians—representative of Shem; quite a respectable number of negroes—descendants of Ham; and the balance was made up of citizens of the surrounding country, and fully represented themselves as pioneers of the West. (In *History of the Church*, 1:190–91)

What the Scriptures of the Restoration Teach Us

After the flood when Noah and his son's families exited the ark, the Lord gave a charge to the prophet similar to the one he gave to Adam and Eve while in the Garden of Eden. It is found in **Genesis 9:1**, "And God blessed Noah and his sons, and said unto them, Be fruitful, and multiply, and replenish the earth."

Noah and the Priesthood

What the Book of Genesis Teaches Us

Genesis 6:9 These are the generations of Noah: Noah was a just man and perfect in his generations, and Noah walked with God.

The Teachings of Inspired Church Leaders

Not only did Noah walk with God, but he was also second only to Adam in priesthood hierarchy and third from God.

President Joseph Smith:

He [Adam] is Michael the Archangel, spoken of in the Scriptures. Then to Noah who is Gabriel; he stands next in authority to Adam in the Priesthood; he was called of God to this office, and was the father of all living in his day, and to him was given the dominion. These men held keys first on earth, and then in heaven. (In *History of the Church*, 3:386)

President Joseph Smith also stated the following:

Now taking it for granted that the scriptures say what they mean, and mean what they say, we have sufficient grounds to go on and prove from the Bible that the gospel has always been the same; the ordinances to fulfill its requirements, the same; and the officers to officiate, the same; and the signs and fruits resulting from the promises, the same: therefore, as Noah was a preacher of righteousness he must have been baptized and ordained to the priesthood by the laying on of the hands, etc. For no man taketh this honor upon himself except he be called of God as was Aaron [Hebrew 5:4]. (*Teachings of the Prophet Joseph Smith*, 264)

What the Scriptures of the Restoration Teach Us

Not only was Noah perfect (perfect in his calling), but according to modern revelation in the Doctrines and Covenants, he received the priesthood at an extremely young age.

D&C 107:52 Noah was ten years old when he was ordained under the hand of Methuselah.

Noah's Mistake and Forgiveness

What the Book of Genesis Teaches Us

Genesis 9:20–27 And Noah began to be an husbandman, and he planted a vineyard:

And he drank of the wine, and was drunken; and he was uncovered within his tent.

And Ham, the father of Canaan, saw the nakedness of his father, and told his two brethren without.

And Shem and Japheth took a garment, and laid it upon both their shoulders, and went backward, and covered the nakedness of their father; and their faces were backward, and they saw not their father's nakedness.

And Noah awoke from his wine, and knew what his younger son had done unto him.

And he said, Cursed be Canaan; a servant of servants shall he be unto his brethren.

And he said, Blessed be the Lord God of Shem; and Canaan shall be his servant.

God shall enlarge Japheth, and he shall dwell in the tents of Shem; and Canaan shall be his servant.

The Teachings of Inspired Church Leaders

President Joseph Smith:

I charged the Saints not to follow the example of the adversary in accusing the brethren, and said, "If you do not accuse each other, God will not accuse you. If you have no accuser you will enter heaven, and if you will follow the revelations and instructions which God gives you through me, I will take you into heaven as my back load. If you will not accuse me, I will not accuse you. If you will throw a cloak of charity over my sins, I will over yours—for charity covereth a multitude of sins. What many people call sin is not sin; I do many things to break down superstition, and I will break it down"; I referred to the curse of Ham for laughing at Noah, while in his wine, but doing no harm. Noah was a righteous man, and yet he drank wine and became intoxicated; the Lord did not forsake him in consequence thereof, for he retained all the power of his Priesthood, and when he was accused by Canaan, he cursed him by the Priesthood which he held, and the Lord had respect to his work, and the Priesthood which he held, notwithstanding he was drunk, and the curse remains upon the posterity of Canaan until the present day. (*Teachings of the Prophet Joseph Smith*, 193–94)

Elder Mark E. Petersen:

Let no one downgrade the life and mission of this great prophet. Noah was so near perfect in his day that he literally walked and talked with God. . . .

Few men in any age were as great as Noah. In many respects he was like Adam, the first man. Both had served as ministering angels in the presence of God even after their mortal experience. Adam was Michael, the archangel, but Noah was Gabriel, one of those nearest to God. Of all the hosts of heaven, he was chosen to open the Christian era by announcing to Mary that she would become the mother of the Savior, Jesus Christ. He even designated the name by which the Redeemer should be known here on earth, saying he would be the Son of God. . . .

The Lord decreed that [the earth would be cleansed] by water, a worldwide deluge. Therefore, from among his premortal spirit children, God chose another great individual—His third in line, Gabriel—to resume the propagation of mankind following the flood. (*Noah and the Flood* [1982], 1–4)

The Angel Gabriel

The Old Testament does not indicate that Noah and the angel Gabriel are the same person. It is through modern revelation that we learn the connection.

What the Scriptures of the Restoration Teach Us

Not only was the angel Gabriel (Noah) permitted to make the heavenly announcement to Elizabeth, the mother of John the Baptist, and Mary, the mother of Jesus Christ, but he also appeared to the prophet Daniel and the Prophet Joseph Smith.

> **D&C 128:21** And again, the voice of God in the chamber of old Father Whitmer, in Fayette, Seneca county, and at sundry times, and in divers places through all the travels and tribulations of this Church of Jesus Christ of Latter-day Saints! And the voice of Michael, the archangel; the voice of Gabriel, and of Raphael, and of divers angels, from Michael or Adam down to the present time, all declaring their dispensation, their rights, their keys, their honors, their majesty and glory, and the power of their priesthood; giving line upon line, precept upon precept; here a little, and there a little; giving us consolation by holding forth that which is to come, confirming our hope!

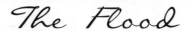

The Flood

Baptism of the Earth

What the Book of Genesis Teaches Us

> **Genesis 6:11–13** The earth also was corrupt before God, and the earth was filled with violence.
>
> And God looked upon the earth, and, behold, it was corrupt; for all flesh had corrupted his way upon the earth.
>
> And God said unto Noah, The end of all flesh is come before me; for the earth is filled with violence through them; and, behold, I will destroy them with the earth.

According to the Old Testament, the Lord's purpose for the flood was to destroy the wickedness from before his sight. This is true, but according to inspired Church leaders, we do know that the flood served another purpose.

The Teachings of Inspired Church Leaders

Elder Orson Pratt:

The first ordinance instituted for the cleansing of the earth, was that of immersion in water; it was buried in the liquid element, and all things sinful upon the face of [the earth] were washed away. As it came forth from the ocean flood, like the new-born child, it was innocent, it arose to newness of life; it was its second birth from the womb of mighty waters—a new world issuing from the ruins of the old, clothed with all the innocency of its first creation. (In *Journal of Discourses*, 1:331)

President Brigham Young:

This earth, in its present condition and situation, is not a fit habitation for the sanctified; but it abides the law of its creation, has been baptized with water [At the time of the flood], will be baptized by fire [At Christ's second coming] and the Holy Ghost, and by-and-by will be prepared for the faithful to dwell upon. (In *Journal of Discourses*, 8:83)

Great Wickedness on the Earth

What the Book of Genesis Teaches Us

Genesis 6:5–6, 11 And God saw that the wickedness of man was great in the earth, and that every imagination of the thoughts of his heart was only evil continually.

And it repented the Lord that he had made man on the earth, and it grieved him at his heart.

The earth also was corrupt before God, and the earth was filled with violence.

What the Scriptures of the Restoration Teach Us

It is through modern revelation that the above scripture is clarified. The Lord was not grieved, but rather Noah, as stated in **Moses 8:25–26**:

And it repented Noah, and his heart was pained that the Lord had made man on the earth, and it grieved him at the heart.

And the Lord said: I will destroy man whom I have created, from the face of the earth, both man and beast, and the creeping things, and the fowls of the air; for it repenteth Noah that I have created them, and that I have made them; and he hath called upon me; for they have sought his life.

What the Scriptures of the Restoration Teach Us

Nevertheless, as much as Noah grieved, he must have been consoled in the fact that as part of the plan of salvation, a Savior would be provided. Noah was sent to preach and give the people a chance. The destruction was not imminent; in fact, they were given 120 years to repent, but when all was said and done, not even Noah could change attitudes or behaviors. From a revelation given to Enoch, we learn the following:

> **Moses 7:38–39** But behold, these which thine eyes are upon shall perish in the floods; and behold, I will shut them up; a prison have I prepared for them.
>
> And That which I have chosen hath pled before my face. Wherefore, he suffereth for their sins; inasmuch as they will repent in the day that my Chosen shall return unto me, and until that day they shall be in torment;

It becomes obvious in the Doctrine and Covenants that one of the prophets referenced is Noah when the scripture states "the rebellious who rejected the testimonies and the warnings of the ancient prophets." Since our days in Primary, we have been taught that Noah preached to a hard-hearted and an uncaring people, that his warning of destruction by deluge fell on deaf ears.

> **D&C 138:20–22, 57–59** But unto the wicked he did not go, and among the ungodly and the unrepentant who had defiled themselves while in the flesh, his voice was not raised;
>
> Neither did the rebellious who rejected the testimonies and the warnings of the ancient prophets behold his presence, nor look upon his face.
>
> Where these were, darkness reigned, but among the righteous there was peace;
>
> I beheld that the faithful elders of this dispensation, when they depart from mortal life, continue their labors in the preaching of the gospel of repentance and redemption, through the sacrifice of the Only Begotten Son of God, among those who are in darkness and under the bondage of sin in the great world of the spirits of the dead.

The dead who repent will be redeemed, through obedience to the ordinances of the house of God,

And after they have paid the penalty of their transgressions, and are washed clean, shall receive a reward according to their works, for they are heirs of salvation.

The Teachings of Inspired Church Leaders

How is it that a prophet of God can forewarn a people for 120 years, and yet they fail to repent? Brigham Young helps answer this inquiry:

You are aware that many think that the devil has rule and power over both body and spirit. Now, I want to tell you that he does not hold any power over man, only so far as the body overcomes the spirit that is in a man, through yielding to the spirit of evil. The spirit that the Lord puts into a tabernacle of flesh, is under the dictation of the Lord Almighty; but the spirit and body are united in order that the spirit may have a tabernacle, and be exalted; and the spirit is influenced by the body, and the body by the spirit.

In the first place the spirit is pure, and under the special control and influence of the Lord, but the body is of the earth, and is subject to the power of the devil, and is under the mighty influence of that fallen nature that is of the earth. If the spirit yields to the body, the devil then has power to overcome both the body and spirit of that man, and he loses both.

Recollect, brethren and sisters, every one of you, that when evil is suggested to you, when it arises in your hearts, it is through the temporal organization. When you are tempted, buffeted, and step out of the way inadvertently: when you are overtaken in a fault, or commit an overt act unthinkingly; when you are full of evil passion, and wish to yield to it, then stop and let the spirit, which God has put into your tabernacles, take the lead. If you do that, I will promise that you will overcome all evil, and obtain eternal lives. But many, very many, let the spirit yield to the body, and are overcome and destroyed. (In *Journal of Discourses*, 2:255)

The Teachings of Inspired Church Leaders

President Taylor shares his understanding of why the Lord permitted the flood:

Now I will go back to show you how the Lord operates. He destroyed a whole world at one time save a few, whom he preserved for his own special purpose. And why? He had more than one reason for doing so. This antediluvian people were not only very wicked themselves, but having the power to propagate their species, they transmitted their unrighteous natures and desires to their children, and brought them up to indulge in their own wicked practices. And the spirits that dwelt in the eternal worlds knew this, and they knew very well that to be born of such parentage would entail upon themselves an infinite amount of trouble, misery and sin. . . . But, says the caviller, is it right that a just God should sweep off so many people? Is that in accordance with mercy? Yes, it was just to those spirits that had not received their bodies, and it was just and merciful too to those people guilty of the iniquity. Why? Because by taking away their earthly existence he prevented them from entailing their sins upon their posterity and degenerating them, and also prevented them from committing further acts of wickedness. (In *Journal of Discourses*, 19:158–59)

Not All Were Wicked

What the Scriptures of the Restoration Teach Us

It is also through modern revelation that we learn that not everyone rejected Noah's words as may be assumed through the account written in the Old Testament. Enoch saw in vision, as stated in **Moses 7:27**, that Noah and others were successful in calling some people to repentance:

> And Enoch beheld angels descending out of heaven, bearing testimony of the Father and Son; and the Holy Ghost fell on many, and they were caught up by the powers of heaven into Zion.

In other words, those that accepted Noah's words and repented were translated into heaven, similar to the city and people of Enoch.

The Rains Came Down

What the Book of Genesis Teaches Us

> **Genesis 7:11, 19–20** In the six hundredth year of Noah's life, in the second month, the seventeenth day of the month, the same day were all the fountains of the great deep broken up, and the windows of heaven were opened.
>
> And the waters prevailed exceedingly upon the earth; and all the

high hills, that were under the whole heaven, were covered.

Fifteen cubits upward did the waters prevail; and the mountains were covered.

The Teachings of Inspired Church Leaders

President John Taylor:

I would like to know by what known law the immersion of the globe could be accomplished. It is explained here in a few words: "The windows of heaven were opened"—that is, the waters that exist throughout the space surrounding the earth from whence come these clouds from which the rain descends. That was one cause. Another cause was "the fountains of the great deep were broken up"—that is something beyond the oceans, something outside of the seas, some reservoirs of which we have no knowledge, were made to contribute to this event, and the waters were let loose by the hand and by the power of God; for God said He would bring a flood upon the earth and He brought it, but He had to let loose the fountains of the great deep, and pour out the waters from there, and when the flood commenced to subside, we are told "that the fountains also of the deep and the windows of heaven were stopped, and the rain from heaven was restrained, and the waters returned from off the earth." Where did they go to? From whence they came. Now, I will show you something else on the back of that. Some people talk very philosophically about tidal waves coming along. But the question is—How could you get a tidal wave out of the Pacific ocean, say, to cover the Sierra Nevadas? But the Bible does not tell us it was a tidal wave. It simply tells that "all the high hills that were under the whole heaven were covered. Fifteen cubits upwards did the waters prevail; and the mountains were covered." That is, the earth was immersed. It was a period of baptism. (In *Journal of Discourses*, 26:74–75)

The Rainbow

What the Book of Genesis Teaches Us

Genesis 9:8–17 And God spake unto Noah, and to his sons with him, saying,

And I, behold, I establish my covenant with you, and with your seed after you;

And with every living creature that is with you, of the fowl, of the cattle, and of every beast of the earth with you; from all that go out of the ark, to every beast of the earth.

And I will establish my covenant with you; neither shall all flesh be cut off any more by the waters of a flood; neither shall there any more be a flood to destroy the earth.

And God said, This is the token of the covenant which I make between me and you and every living creature that is with you, for perpetual generations:

I do set my bow in the cloud, and it shall be for a token of a covenant between me and the earth.

And it shall come to pass, when I bring a cloud over the earth, that the bow shall be seen in the cloud:

And I will remember my covenant, which is between me and you and every living creature of all flesh; and the waters shall no more become a flood to destroy all flesh.

And the bow shall be in the cloud; and I will look upon it, that I may remember the everlasting covenant between God and every living creature of all flesh that is upon the earth.

And God said unto Noah, This is the token of the covenant, which I have established between me and all flesh that is upon the earth.

The Teachings of Inspired Church Leaders

President Joseph Smith:

I have asked of the Lord concerning His coming; and while asking the Lord, He gave a sign and said, "In the days of Noah I set a bow in the heavens as a sign and token that in any year that the bow should be seen the Lord would not come; but there should be seed time and harvest during that year; but whenever you see the bow withdrawn, it shall be a token that there shall be famine, pestilence, and great distress among the nations, and that the coming of the Messiah is not far distant." (In *History of the Church*, 6:254)

The Life of Man

What the Book of Genesis Teaches Us

It isn't long after the story of the flood in Genesis 8 that a genealogy of a number of generations of Shem's line is given. The most notable difference is the reduction in years of the life of a man. The following verses are from **Genesis 11:10–25**:

These are the generations of Shem: Shem was an hundred years old, and begat Arphaxad two years after the flood:

And Shem lived after he begat Arphaxad five hundred years, and begat sons and daughters.

And Arphaxad lived five and thirty years, and begat Salah:

And Arphaxad lived after he begat Salah four hundred and three years, and begat sons and daughters.

And Salah lived thirty years, and begat Eber:

And Salah lived after he begat Eber four hundred and three years, and begat sons and daughters.

And Eber lived four and thirty years, and begat Peleg:

And Eber lived after he begat Peleg four hundred and thirty years, and begat sons and daughters.

And Peleg lived thirty years, and begat Reu:

And Peleg lived after he begat Reu two hundred and nine years, and begat sons and daughters.

And Reu lived two and thirty years, and begat Serug:

And Reu lived after he begat Serug two hundred and seven years, and begat sons and daughters.

And Serug lived thirty years, and begat Nahor:

And Serug lived after he begat Nahor two hundred years, and begat sons and daughters.

And Nahor lived nine and twenty years, and begat Terah:

And Nahor lived after he begat Terah an hundred and nineteen years, and begat sons and daughters.

The Teachings of Inspired Church Leaders

President Brigham Young gives us an idea why the lives of men had been shortened:

> The fathers and mothers have laid the foundation for many of these diseases, from generation to generation, until the people are reduced to their present condition. True, some live to from fifty to ninety years of age, but it is an unusual circumstance to see a man an hundred years old, or a woman ninety. The people have laid the foundation of short life through their diet, their rest, their labor, and their doing this, that, and the other in a wrong manner, with improper motives, and at improper times. (In *Journal of Discourses*, 2:269)

President Brigham Young also shared this concept:

Instead of doing two days' work in one day, wisdom would dictate to our sisters, and to every other person, that if they desire long life and good health, they must, after sufficient exertion, allow the body to rest before it is entirely exhausted. When exhausted, some argue that they need stimulants in the shape of tea, coffee, spirituous liquors, tobacco, or some of those narcotic substances which are often taken to goad on the lagging powers to greater exertions, but instead of these kind of stimulants they should recruit by rest. Work less, wear less, eat less, and we shall be a great deal wiser, healthier, and wealthier people than by taking the course we now do. . . . It is difficult to find anything more healthy to drink than good cold water, such as flows down to us from springs and snows of our mountains. This is the beverage we should drink. It should be our drink at all times. If we constantly drink even malt liquor made from our barley and wheat, our health would be injured more or less thereby. It may be remarked that some men who use spirituous liquors and tobacco are healthy, but I argue that they would be much more healthy if they did not use it, and then they are entitled to the blessings promised to those who observe the advice given in the "Word of Wisdom." Some few persons who have been addicted to the use of hot drinks, etc., have reached the age of eighty, eighty-three, and eighty-four years, but had they not been addicted to such habits of living they might have reached the age of a hundred or a hundred and five years. (In *Journal of Discourses*, 12:122)

The Dividing of the Earth

What the Book of Genesis Teaches Us

Genesis 10:25 And unto Eber were born two sons: the name of one was Peleg; for in his days was the earth divided; and his brother's name was Joktan.

Many biblical scholars have dismissed this as meaning nothing more than political or cultural divisions. Since the actual event takes place close, time wise, to the Tower of Babel, it is easy to understand how one could say it was a division of languages or tribes. Nevertheless, through inspired Church leaders, we learn that the Bible means what it says, that it is to be taken literally.

What the Scriptures of the Restoration Teach Us

It is generally believed that at one time the entire earth surface was made up of one landmass. I'm sure you have at one time or another looked at the shapes of the seven continents and been able to see how western Africa easily forms to eastern South America, and how Indonesia fits like a glove into northern Australia, and how Australia conforms to the coast line of eastern Africa. Modern revelation supports the idea of one continent that divided into the present globe.

> **D&C 133:23–24** He shall command the great deep, and it shall be driven back into the north countries, and the islands shall become one land;
>
> And the land of Jerusalem and the land of Zion shall be turned back into their own place, and the earth shall be like as it was in the days before it was divided.

The Teachings of Inspired Church Leaders

President Joseph Smith:

> The Eternal God hath declared that the great deep shall roll back into the north countries and that the land of Zion and the land of Jerusalem shall be joined together, as they were before they were divided in the days of Peleg. No wonder the mind starts at the sound of the last days! ("The Last Days" *The Evening and Morning Star*, Feb 1833. 129)

Interesting Information

Peleg is the great-great-grandson of Shem, who was the son of Noah. *Peleg* is a Hebrew word meaning division.

As early as November 1, 1831, Joseph Smith understood the land masses were fused as one, or one giant supercontinent (Section 133). In 1885, the remainder of the world came on board when Austrian geologist Eduard Suess theorized the world as one supercontinent, which he termed *Gondwanaland* (Jay M. Todd, "Gondwanaland: What It Means to Latter-day Saints," *New Era*. Mar. 1971, online).

A scientist writes the following in reference to continental drift:

> Formerly, most scientists regarded the earth as rigid and the continents as fixed, but now the surface of the earth is seen as slowly deformable and the continents as "rafts" floating on a "sea" of denser rock. The continents have repeatedly collided and joined, repeatedly broken and separated in different patterns, and, very likely, they have grown larger in the process.
>
> This scientific revolution, as others before it, was long in the

making, but it was not until the late 1960s that it began to succeed. At a meeting of the world's geophysicists in August of 1971, it was made clear that the notion of continental drift, which had been heresy only a few years before, had become the orthodoxy of the great majority. (In J. Tuzo Wilson, comp., *Continents Adrift: Readings from Scientific American*, preface)

The theory of plate tectonics states that the earth is set on massive plates and that these plates are constantly in motion. Where two plates collide, one plate will slip under or go above another. It is the colliding of the plates that result in the formation of mountains and the earthquakes that are so prevalent in the world. This also explains why entire continents are on the move and move up to a few inches a year. It also helps explain the days of Peleg when the earth was divided.

The Tower of Babel

Nimrod and "a Tower, Whose Top May Reach into Heaven"

What the Book of Genesis Teaches Us

Genesis 11:1–9 And the whole earth was of one language, and of one speech.

And it came to pass, as they journeyed from the east, that they found a plain in the land of Shinar; and they dwelt there.

And they said one to another, Go to, let us make brick, and burn them thoroughly. And they had brick for stone, and slime had they for mortar.

And they said, Go to, let us build us a city and a tower, whose top may reach unto heaven; and let us make us a name, lest we be scattered abroad upon the face of the whole earth.

And the Lord came down to see the city and the tower, which the children of men builded.

And the Lord said, Behold, the people is one, and they have all one language; and this they begin to do: and now nothing will be restrained from them, which they have imagined to do.

Go to, let us go down, and there confound their language, that they may not understand one another's speech.

So the Lord scattered them abroad from thence upon the face of all the earth: and they left off to build the city.

Therefore is the name of it called Babel; because the Lord did there confound the language of all the earth: and from thence did the Lord scatter them abroad upon the face of all the earth.

Lee Donaldson and his coauthors, answering questions in a February 1994 *Ensign* article, suggest that the tower could have reached a height of nearly three hundred feet. This, in large part, was the end result of new technology: oven baked bricks. Prior to this, sun baked bricks were the method of construction ("I Have a Question," 60–61).

Interesting Information

George Laub quotes Joseph Smith in his Nauvoo journal:

Now I will tell the designs of building the tower of Babel. It was designed to go to the city of Enoch, for the veil was not yet so thick that it hid it from their Sight. So they concluded to go to the City of Enoch, for God gave him place above this impure Earth. For he could breath a pure air & him and his City was taken, for God provided a better place for him for they was pure in heart. For it is the pure in heart that causes Zion to be & the time will come again to meet, that Enoch and his city will come again to meet our city & his people, our people, & the Air will be pure & the Lord will be in our midst for Ever. (Eugene England, "George Laub's Nauvoo Journal," *BYU Studies* vol. 18, no. 2 [1978], 25)

It was Nimrod who was the force behind the building of a tower to reach to heaven. The motivation for this tower was twofold. First, to "make us a name," even though in the process of making that name, gospel covenants would not be involved. And second, so that they would not be scattered (Lee Donaldson, et al., "I Have a Question," *Ensign*, Feb. 1994, 60–61).

What the Scriptures of the Restoration Teach Us

D&C 2:1–3 Behold, I will reveal unto you the Priesthood, by the hand of Elijah the prophet, before the coming of the great and dreadful day of the Lord.

And he shall plant in the hearts of the children the promises made to the fathers, and the hearts of the children shall turn to their fathers.

If it were not so, the whole earth would be utterly wasted at his coming.

One meaning of the word *wasted* in Joseph Smith's day was "destroyed by scattering" (*Webster's Dictionary*, 1828, in Lee Donaldson, et al., "I Have a Question," *Ensign*, Feb. 1994).

Genesis 11:1–9 is an example of God's children turning their backs on the teachings of their fathers and substituting a true temple with an imitation temple based off of pagan ideals. The "temple" would take the form of a tower as conceived by their leader, Nimrod. Nevertheless, what Nimrod did not understand is the necessity of divine priesthood authority. Neither Nimrod, nor any of his followers received priesthood investiture to perform temple functions; they were simply going through the motions, only an artificial mock of what true worship meant or looked like.

The events surrounding the Tower of Babel redirected the history of the world. It was here that the Lord instituted the confusion of tongues. The building of the tower came to an immediate halt. It was from here that groups of individuals were led to other places of the world, like the Jaredites. Noah was still alive at this time and obviously other righteous individuals such as Jared and the brother of Jared.

For the rest of the world, these stories may be difficult to fathom; however, we, as Latter-day Saints, have more than just the Bible to confirm the truth of what we read in the Old Testament.

The Adamic Language

What the Book of Genesis Teaches Us

Genesis 11:1 And the whole earth was of one language, and of one speech.

The inquisitive mind could ask the question, what was the one language that the whole earth spoke at the time of the confounding of tongues? It is through modern revelation that we discover the tongue all men spoke from Adam to the Tower of Babel.

What the Scriptures of the Restoration Teach Us

Moses 6:5–6, 57 And a book of remembrance was kept, in the which was recorded, in the language of Adam, for it was given unto as many as called upon God to write by the spirit of inspiration;

And by them their children were taught to read and write, having a language which was pure and undefiled.

Wherefore teach it unto your children, that all men, everywhere, must repent, or they can in nowise inherit the kingdom of God, for no unclean thing can dwell there, or dwell in his presence; for, in the language of Adam, Man of Holiness is his name, and the name of his Only Begotten is the Son of Man, even Jesus Christ, a righteous Judge, who shall come in the meridian to time.

In the Book of Mormon, we learn that Jared prayed to the Lord that his family's language would not become confused at the building of the tower. The Lord granted Jared his request. If what the people spoke prior to the flood was the Adamic language, then it can only be assumed that by the Lord not confusing Jared and his family's language that they continued to speak the Adamic language. Of course this is me speaking.

Ether 1:34–37 And the brother of Jared being a large and mighty man, and a man highly favored of the Lord, Jared, his brother, said unto him: Cry unto the Lord, that he will not confound us that we may not understand our words.

And it came to pass that the brother of Jared did cry unto the Lord, and the Lord had compassion upon Jared; therefore he did not confound the language of Jared and Jared and his brother were not confounded.

Then Jared said unto his brother: Cry again unto the Lord and it may be that he will turn away his anger from them who are our friends, that he confound not their language.

And it came to pass that the brother of Jared did cry unto the Lord, and the Lord had compassion upon their friends and their families also, that they were not confounded.

Ether 3:22–24 And behold, when ye shall come unto me, ye shall write them and shall seal them up, that no one can interpret them; for ye shall write them in a language that they cannot be read.

And behold, these two stones will I give unto thee, and ye shall seal them up also with the things which ye shall write.

For behold, the language which ye shall write I have confounded; wherefore I will cause in my own due time that these stones shall magnify to the eyes of men these things which ye shall write.

The Teachings of Inspired Church Leaders

Brigham Young shares the following event shortly after his baptism on 14 April, 1832, in Mendon, New York. After his baptism, he desired to meet the Prophet Joseph Smith and soon traveled to Kirtland, Ohio. It was at the meeting of Brigham Young and Joseph Smith that Joseph revealed the name of the language which Adam and his posterity spoke. Brigham Young tells the story:

> We went to his father's house and learned that he was in the woods, chopping. We immediately repaired to the woods, where we found the Prophet, and two or three of his brothers, chopping and hauling wood. Here my joy was full at the privilege of shaking the hand of the Prophet of God, and received the sure testimony, by the Spirit of prophecy, that he was all that any man could believe him to be, as a true Prophet. He was happy to see us, and bid us welcome. We soon returned to his house, he accompanying us.
>
> In the evening a few of the brethren came in, and we conversed together upon the things of the kingdom. He called upon me to pray; in my prayer I spoke in tongues. As soon as we arose from our knees the brethren flocked around him, and asked his opinion concerning the gift of tongues that was upon me. He told them it was the pure Adamic language. Some said to him they expected he would condemn the gift brother Brigham had, but he said, "No, it is of God, and the time will come when brother Brigham Young will preside over this Church." The latter part of this conversation was in my absence. (*Manuscript History of Brigham Young*, 1847–1850, ed. William S. Harwell [1997], 4–5)

What the Book of Zephaniah Teaches Us

We know that at the Second Coming of the Savior during the millennium, there will be many changes. One of which will be the language that is spoken as prophesied by the prophet Zephaniah.

Zephaniah 3:9 For then will I turn to the people a pure language, that they may all call upon the name of the Lord, to serve him with one consent.

Interesting Information

W. W. Phelps:

The English language is used by nearly 60,000,000 of people; that of China by 600,000,000. The Chinese must be the oldest known language spoken on the globe. The English is about as young as any, but as the Lord has seen fit to "reveal-" the Book of Mormon, and the fullness of the everlasting gospel in English, the day is not far distant, when

every saint must learn to speak English, in order to understand the keys
of the holy priesthood. In this light, the English bids fair to become the
great, last, and best, till the Lord restores a "pure language," even the
one that Adam brought from Kolob, or the celestial garden, when he
came to this globe and gave names to all,—according to the council of
the Gods in the "elder world." (*Deseret Almanac*, 1853, 14)

Abraham

Leaving His Home

What the Book of Genesis Teaches Us

Genesis 12:1 Now the Lord had said unto Abram, Get thee out of thy
country, and from thy kindred, and from they father's house, unto a
land that I will shew thee.

Why did the Lord command Abram to leave his father's house? Obviously, we are not able to answer this inquiry by using the Old Testament
alone; however, we learn more, much more because of scripture translated
by Joseph Smith.

What the Scriptures of the Restoration Teach Us

Abraham 1:1–2, 5–12 In the land of the Chaldeans, at the residence
of my fathers, I, Abraham, saw that it was needful for me to obtain
another place of residence;
    And, finding there was greater happiness and peace and rest for
me, I sought for the blessings of the fathers, and the right whereunto
I should be ordained to administer the same; having been myself a
follower of righteousness, desiring also to be one who possessed great
knowledge, and to be a greater follower of righteousness, and to possess
a greater knowledge, and to be a father of many nations, a prince of
peace, and desiring to receive instructions, and to keep the commandments of God, I became a rightful heir, a High Priest, holding the right
belonging to the fathers.
    My fathers, having turned from their righteousness, and from the
holy commandments which the Lord their God had given unto them,
unto the worshiping of the gods of the heathen, utterly refused to hearken to my voice;

For their hearts were set to do evil, and were wholly turned to the god of Elkenah, and the god of Libnah, and the god of Mahmackrah, and the god of Korash, and the god of Pharaoh, king of Egypt;

Therefore they turned their hearts to the sacrifice of the heathen in offering up their children unto these dumb idols, and hearkened not unto my voice, but endeavored to take away my life by the hand of the priest of Elkenah. The priest of Elkenah was also the priest of Pharaoh.

Now, at this time it was the custom of the priest of Pharaoh, the king of Egypt, to offer up upon the altar which was built in the land of Chaldea, for the offering unto these strange gods, men, women, and children.

And it came to pass that the priest made an offering unto the god of Pharaoh, and also unto the god of Shagreel, even after the manner of the Egyptians. Now the god of Shagreel was the sun.

Even the thank-offering of a child did the priest of Pharaoh offer upon the altar which stood by the hill called Potiphar's Hill, at the head of the plain of Olishem.

Now, this priest had offered upon this altar three virgins at one time, who were the daughters of Onitah, one of the royal descent directly from the loins of Ham. These virgins were offered up because of their virtue; they would not bow down to worship gods of wood or of stone, therefore they were killed upon this altar, and it was done after the manner of the Egyptians.

And it came to pass that the priests laid violence upon me, that they might slay me also, as they did those virgins upon this altar; and that you may have a knowledge of this altar, I will refer you to the representation at the commencement of this record.

Abraham in Egypt

What the Book of Genesis Teaches Us

Genesis 12:10 And there was a famine in the land: and Abram went down into Egypt to sojourn there; for the famine was grievous in the land.

What the Scriptures of the Restoration Teach Us

The Genesis account gives very little knowledge or understanding of what happened as Abraham resided in Egypt with his family. The only story that Genesis shares is the account of Abraham asking Sarai, his wife, to tell the Egyptians that she is his sister so that they would not kill him.

However, much more took place in Egypt as the Lord took the opportunity to reveal to Abraham the following:

> **Abraham 3:1–4** And I, Abraham, had the Urim and Thummim, which the Lord my God had given unto me, in Ur of the Chaldees;
>
> And I saw the stars, that they were very great, and that one of them was nearest unto the throne of God; and there were many great ones which were near unto it;
>
> And the Lord said unto me: These are the governing ones; and the name of the great one is Kolob, because it is near unto me, for I am the Lord thy God: I have set this one to govern all those which belong to the same order as that upon which thou standest.
>
> And the Lord said unto me, by the Urim and Thummim, that Kolob was after the manner of the Lord, according to its times and seasons in the revolutions thereof; that one revolution was a day unto the Lord, after his manner of reckoning, it being one thousand years according to the time appointed unto that whereon thou standest. This is the reckoning of the Lord's time, according to the reckoning of Kolob.

The Teachings of Inspired Church Leaders

President Joseph Smith:

> The learning of the Egyptians, and their knowledge of astronomy was no doubt taught them by Abraham and Joseph, as their records testify, who received it from the Lord. (*Teachings of the Prophet Joseph Smith*, 251)

Interesting Information

Because of the scriptures of the restoration, in combination with the Old Testament, we know of at least two or three Urim and Thummim that have existed over time. It is through D&C 17:1 that we understand the first Urim and Thummim was possessed by the brother of Jared. This is the same Urim and Thummim that passed down through various Book of Mormon prophets until it was delivered to Joseph Smith. In Abraham 3:1, we learn that Abraham was also given a Urim and Thummim. Possibly, this same Urim and Thummim was given to Moses, or, more likely, Moses received a third one as mentioned in Exodus 28:30.

Joseph Smith gives the following description of the Urim and Thummim that he possessed:

Also that there were two stones in silver bows—and these stones, fastened to a breastplate, constituted what is called the Urim and Thummim—deposited with the plates; and the possession and use of these stones were what constituted "Seers" in ancient or former times; and that God had prepared them for the purpose of translating the book. (In *History of the Church*, 1:12)

The Sister Lie

What the Book of Genesis Teaches Us

Genesis 12:10–20 And there was a famine in the land: and Abram went down into Egypt to sojourn there; for the famine was grievous in the land.

And it came to pass, when he was come near to enter into Egypt, that he said unto Sarai his wife, Behold now, I know that thou are a fair woman to look upon:

Therefore it shall come to pass, when the Egyptians shall see thee, that they shall say, This is his wife: and they will kill me, but they will save thee alive.

Say, I pray thee, thou are my sister: that it may be will with me for thy sake; and my soul shall live because of thee.

And it came to pass, that, when Abram was come into Egypt, the Egyptians beheld the woman that she was very fair.

The princes also of Pharaoh saw her, and commended her before Pharaoh: and the woman was taken into Pharaoh's house.

And he entreated Abram well for her sake: and he had sheep, and oxen, and he asses, and menservants, and maidservants, and she asses, and camels.

And the Lord plagued Pharaoh and his house with great plagues because of Sarai Abram's wife.

And Pharaoh called Abram, and said, What is this that thou hast done unto me? Why didst thou not tell me that she was thy wife?

Why saidst thou, She is my sister? so I might have taken her to me to wife: now therefore behold thy wife, take her, and go thy way.

And Pharaoh commanded his men concerning him: and they sent him away, and his wife, and all that he had.

What the Scriptures of the Restoration Teach Us

From Genesis, we can only assume that Abram (Abraham) "lied" to save his life. It can be uncomfortable to think that a man chosen of God would consider "lying." If Abraham had such great faith, then why did he feel the need to deceive Pharaoh? The book of Abraham in the Pearl of Great Price discusses the situation, and the words of Joseph Smith may help answer the Lord's reasoning for having Abraham act the way he did.

> **Abraham 2:22–25** And it came to pass when I was come near to enter into Egypt, the Lord said unto me: Behold, Sarai, thy wife, is a very fair woman to look upon;
>
> Therefore it shall come to pass, when the Egyptians shall see her, they will say—She is his wife; and they will kill you, but they will save her alive; therefore see that ye do on this wise:
>
> Let her say unto the Egyptians, she is thy sister, and thy soul shall live.
>
> And it came to pass that I, Abraham, told Sarai, my wife, all that the Lord had said unto me—Therefore say unto them, I pray thee, thou art my sister, that it may be well with me for thy sake, and my soul shall live because of thee.

The Teachings of Inspired Church Leaders

President Joseph Smith:

> That which is wrong under one circumstance, may be, and often is, right under another.
>
> God said, "Thou shalt not kill;" at another time He said, "Thou shalt utterly destroy." This is the principle on which the government of heaven is conducted—by revelation adapted to the circumstances in which the children of the kingdom are placed. Whatever God requires is right, no matter what it is, although we may not see the reason thereof till long after the events transpire. (*Teachings of the Prophet Joseph Smith*, 256)

What the Scriptures of the Restoration Teach Us

Parallel to Abraham being commanded to lie, Nephi was also commanded to "break" a commandment for a specific circumstance:

> **1 Nephi 4:10–18** And it came to pass that I was constrained by the Spirit that I should kill Laban; but I said in my heart: Never at any time have I shed the blood of man. And I shrunk and would that I might not slay him.
>
> And the Spirit said unto me again: Behold the Lord hath delivered him into thy hands. Yea, and I also knew that he had sought to take

away mine own life; yea, and he would not hearken unto the commandments of the Lord; and he also had taken away our property.

And it came to pass that the Spirit said unto me again: Slay him, for the Lord hath delivered him into thy hands;

Behold the Lord slayeth the wicked to bring forth his righteous purposes. It is better that one man should perish than that a nation should dwindle and perish in unbelief.

And now, when I, Nephi, had heard these words, I remembered the words of the Lord which he spake unto me in the wilderness, saying that: Inasmuch as thy seed shall keep my commandments, they shall prosper in the land of promise.

Yea, and I also thought that they could not keep the commandments of the Lord according to the law of Moses, save they should have the law.

And I also knew that the law was engraven upon the plates of brass.

And again, I knew that the Lord had delivered Laban into my hands for this cause—that I might obtain the records according to his commandments.

Therefore I did obey the voice of the Spirit, and took Laban by the hair of the head, and I smote off his head with his own sword.

Interesting Information

Hugh Nibley shares the following:

Pharaoh's recognition of Abraham's priesthood was unknown in any other ancient source until the 1947 discovery of the Genesis Apocryphon, purporting, like the book of Abraham, to contain an autobiographical account of Abraham but continuing the narrative into Egypt (*Genesis Apocryphon* 20:8–34): When Pharaoh took Sarah to the palace, Abraham tearfully appealed to God, who immediately protected her by afflicting Pharaoh. The affliction worsened, but Pharaoh finally had a dream of Abraham healing him; the patriarch was then summoned and, laying hands on Pharaoh's head, restored him to health. This is the only known instance in the Old Testament or related pseudepigrapha of a healing by Laying on the Hands, and it sets the stage for the book of Abraham's encounter with Pharaoh "a crucial event in the history of mankind." (*Abraham in Egypt* [1981], 63)

The fact that Pharaoh desired Sarai as one of his wives was not uncommon at the time of Abraham. However, Pharaoh's actions were not indicative of the way things always were in Egypt. When the country was first founded, it was a righteous nation. In fact, it is in the Book of Abraham that Abraham gives a brief history of this country.

> **Abraham 1:23–27** The land of Egypt being first discovered by a woman, who was the daughter of Ham, and the daughter of Egyptus, which in the Chaldean signifies Egypt, which signifies that which is forbidden;
>
> When this woman discovered the land it was under water, who afterward settled her sons in it; and thus, from Ham, sprang that race which preserved the curse in the land.
>
> Now the first government of Egypt was established by Pharaoh, the eldest son of Egyptus, the daughter of Ham, and it was after the manner of the government of Ham, which was patriarchal.
>
> Pharaoh, being a righteous man, established his kingdom and judged his people wisely and justly all his days, seeking earnestly to imitate that order established by the fathers in the first generations, in the days of the first patriarchal reign, even in the reign of Adam, and also of Noah, his father, who blessed him with the blessings of the earth, and with the blessings of wisdom, but cursed him as pertaining to the Priesthood.
>
> Now, Pharaoh being of that lineage by which he could not have the right of Priesthood, notwithstanding the Pharaohs would fain claim it from Noah, through Ham, therefore my father was led away by their idolatry;

Abraham's Priesthood

What the Book of Genesis Teaches Us

> **Genesis 14:18–20** And Melchizedek king of Salem brought forth bread and wine: and he was the priest of the most high God.
>
> And he blessed him, and said, Blessed be Abram of the most high God, possessor of heaven and earth:
>
> And blessed be the most high God, which hath delivered thine enemies into thy hand. And he gave him tithes of all.

What the Scriptures of the Restoration Teach Us

> **Joseph Smith Translation—Genesis 14:17–19** And Melchizedek, king of Salem, brought forth bread and wine; and he brake bread and

blest it; and he blest the wine, he being the priest of the most high God,

And he gave to Abram, and he blessed him, and said, Blessed Abram, thou are a man of the most high God, possessor of heaven and of earth;

And blessed is the name of the most high God, which hath delivered thine enemies into thine hand. And Abram gave him tithes of all he had taken.

D&C 84:14 Which Abraham received the priesthood from Melchizedek, who received it through the lineage of his fathers, even till Noah.

The Teachings of Inspired Church Leaders

President John Taylor:

In this action of Melchizedek, in administering the bread and wine, by virtue of his priestly office, is there not a representation of the body and blood of our Lord and Savior Jesus Christ, as also indicated by the Messiah Himself when He partook of the passover with His disciples? (*The Mediation and Atonement* [1882], 83)

President Joseph Smith:

Abraham says to Melchizedek, I believe all that thou hast taught me concerning the priesthood and the coming of the Son of Man; so Melchizedek ordained Abraham and sent him away. Abraham rejoiced, saying, Now I have a priesthood. (*Teachings of the Prophet Joseph Smith*, 322–23)

President Brigham Young:

Abraham was faithful to the true God, he overthrew the idols of his father and obtained the Priesthood after the order of Melchesidek, which is after the order of the Son of God, and a promise that of the increase of his seed there should be no end. (In *Journal of Discourses*, 11:118)

Abraham and Joseph Smith

What the Book of Genesis Teaches Us

Genesis 15:12 And when the sun was going down, a deep sleep fell upon Abram; and, lo, an horror of great darkness fell upon him.

Abraham's vision of the Lord is reminiscent of Joseph Smith's first vision. Satan recognizes those who will build the kingdom of God and intends to slow this growth by instilling confusion and deception in this world.

What the Scriptures of the Restoration Teach Us

Joseph Smith—History 1:15 After I had retired to the place where I had previously designed to go, having looked around me, and finding myself alone, I kneeled down and began to offer up the desires of my heart to God. I had scarcely done so, when immediately I was seized upon by some power which entirely overcame me, and had such an astonishing influence over me as to bind my tongue so that I could not speak. Thick darkness gathered around me, and it seemed to me for a time as if I were doomed to sudden destruction.

Polygamy

What the Book of Genesis Teaches Us

Genesis 16:1–3 Now Sarai Abram's wife bare him no children: and she had an handmaid, an Egyptian, whose name was Hagar.

And Sarai said unto Abram, Behold now, the Lord hath restrained me from bearing: I pray thee, go in unto my maid; it may be that I may obtain children by her. And Abram hearkened to the voice of Sarai.

And Sarai Abram's wife took Hagar her maid the Egyptian, after Abram had dwelt ten years in the land of Canaan, and gave her to her husband Abram to be his wife.

What the Scriptures of the Restoration Teach Us

D&C 132:1–2, 29–30, 34–35 Verily, thus saith the Lord unto you my servant Joseph, that inasmuch as you have inquired of my hand to know and understand wherein I, the Lord, justified my servants Abraham, Isaac, and Jacob, as also Moses, David and Solomon, my servants, as touching the principle and doctrine of their having many wives and concubines—

Behold, and lo, I am the Lord thy God, and will answer thee as touching this matter.

Abraham received all things, whatsoever he received, by revelation and commandment, by my word, saith the Lord, and hath entered into his exaltation and sitteth upon his throne.

Abraham received promises concerning his seed, and of the fruit of his loins—from whose loins ye are, namely, my servant Joseph—which were to continue so long as they were in the world; and as touching Abraham and his seed, out of the world they should continue; both in the world and out of the world should they continue as innumerable as the stars; or, if ye were to count the sand upon the seashore ye could not number them.

God commanded Abraham, and Sarah gave Hagar to Abraham to wife. And why did she do it? Because this was the law; and from Hagar sprang many people. This, therefore, was fulfilling, among other things, the promises.

Was Abraham, therefore, under condemnation? Verily I say unto you, Nay; for I, the Lord, commanded it.

The Teachings of Inspired Church Leaders

President Joseph Smith:

October 5, 1843: In the afternoon, rode to the prairie to show some of the brethren some land. Evening, at home, and walked up and down the streets with my scribe. Gave instructions to try those persons who were preaching, teaching, or practicing the doctrine of plurality of wives; for, according to the law, I hold the keys of this power in the last days; for there is never but one on earth at a time on whom the power and its keys are conferred; and I have constantly said no man shall have but one wife at a time, unless the Lord directs otherwise. (In *History of the Church*, 6:46)

Interesting Information

The St. Louis Luminary:

The *Luminary* printed the following report from the *New York City Nichol's Journal*:

"The House of Representatives spent two whole days not long since, in debating that most amusing of modern bugaboos, the Polygamy of Utah. . . .

"We cannot help thinking that a Mormon, who in good faith takes two or three wives, and maintains them, may be a better man than a good many other sort of Christians we know of, in Congress and out.

"Everybody thinks Abraham, and Jacob, and the Patriarchs were good men. Why not the Mormons, who believe as they did? Would Congress punish Abraham? . . .

"People are predicting that we shall have trouble about Utah. So we shall, and shall deserve to have it, if we meddle with what don't concern us. What possible business is it to any citizen of New York, how many wives some man has in the City of the Salt Lake?" (Susan Easton Black, "St. Louis Luminary: The Latter-day Saint Experience at the Mississippi River, 1854–1855," *BYU Studies* vol. 49 no. 4, 165–66)

Circumcision

What the Book of Genesis Teaches Us

Genesis 17:1–2, 9–12 And when Abram was ninety years old and nine, the Lord appeared to Abram, and said unto him, I am the Almighty God; walk before me, and be thou perfect.

And I will make my covenant between me and thee, and will multiply thee exceedingly.

And God said unto Abraham, Thou shalt keep my covenant therefore, thou, and thy seed after thee in their generations.

This is my covenant, which ye shall keep, between me and you and thy seed after thee; . . . every man child among you shall be circumcised.

And ye shall circumcise the flesh of your foreskin; and it shall be a token of the covenant betwixt me and you.

And he that is eight days old shall be circumcised among you, every man child in your generations, he that is born in the house, or bought with money of any stranger, which is not of thy seed.

What the Scriptures of the Restoration Teach Us

Scriptures teach that the circumcision a male receives at the age of eight days old is symbolic of the baptism of children at the age of eight years old.

Joseph Smith Translation—Genesis 17:11–12 And I will establish a covenant of circumcision with thee, and it shall be my covenant between me and thee, and they seed after thee, in their generations; that thou mayest know for ever that children are not accountable before me until they are eight years old.

And thou shalt observe to keep all my covenants wherein I covenanted with thy fathers; and thou shalt keep the commandments which I have given thee with mine own mouth, and I will be a God unto thee and thy seed after thee.

D&C 74:1–7 For the unbelieving husband is sanctified by the wife, and the unbelieving wife is sanctified by the husband; else were your children unclean, but now are they holy.

Now, in the days of the apostles the law of circumcision was had among all the Jews who believed not in the gospel of Jesus Christ.

And it came to pass that there arose a great contention among the people concerning the law of circumcision, for the unbelieving husband was desirous that his children should be circumcised and become subject to the law of Moses, which law was fulfilled.

And it came to pass that the children, being brought up in subjection to the law of Moses, gave heed to the traditions of their fathers and believed not the gospel of Christ, wherein they became unholy.

Wherefore, for this cause the apostle wrote unto the church, giving unto them a commandment, not of the Lord, but of himself, that a believer should not be united to an unbeliever; except the law of Moses should be done away among them,

That their children might remain without circumcision; and that the tradition might be done away, which saith that little children are unholy; for it was had among the Jews;

But little children are holy, being sanctified through the atonement of Jesus Christ; and this is what the scriptures mean.

God appears to Abraham

What the Book of Genesis Teaches Us

Genesis 18:1–3 And the Lord appeared unto him in the plains of Mamre: and he sat in the tent door in the heat of the day;

And he lift up his eyes and looked, and, lo, three men stood by him: and when he saw them, he ran to meet them from the tent door, and bowed himself toward the ground,

And said, My Lord, if now I have found favour in thy sight, pass not away, I pray thee, from thy servant.

The Teachings of Inspired Church Leaders

President Joseph Fielding Smith:

We are not justified in teaching that our Heavenly Father, with other heavenly persons, came down, dusty and weary, and ate with Abraham. This is not taught in the 18th chapter of Genesis. The first verse of that chapter should read as follows: "And the Lord appeared unto him in the plains of Mamre." That is a complete thought. The second part of this paragraph has nothing to do with the Lord's appearing to Abraham . . . : "And he sat in the tent door in the heat of the day; and he lifted up his eyes and looked, and, lo, three men stood by him." These three men were mortals. They had bodies and were able to eat, to bathe, and sit and rest from their weariness. Not one of these three was the Lord. (*Doctrines of Salvation*, 1:16)

Elias

What the Book of Genesis Teaches Us

Genesis is quiet on Elias and his mission. It's only because of the New Testament and modern revelation that we know anything about this prophet.

Bible Dictionary:

A man called Elias apparently lived in mortality in the days of Abraham, who committed the dispensation of the gospel of Abraham to Joseph Smith and Oliver Cowdery in the Kirtland (Ohio) Temple on April 3, 1836 (D&C 110:12). We have no specific information as to the details of his mortal life or ministry.

Thus the word *Elias* has many applications and has been placed upon many persons as a title pertaining to both preparatory and restorative functions. It is evident from the questions they asked that both the Jewish leaders and the disciples of Jesus knew something about the doctrine of Elias, but the fragmentary information in our current Bibles is not sufficient to give an adequate understanding of what was involved in use of the term. Only by divine revelation to the Prophet Joseph Smith is this topic brought into focus for us who live in the last days. ("Elias")

What the Scriptures of the Restoration Teach Us

D&C 110:12 After this, Elias appeared, and committed the dispensation of the gospel of Abraham, saying that in us and our seed all generations after us should be blessed.

The Teachings of Inspired Church Leaders

President Joseph Smith, on March 10, 1844:

There is a difference between the spirit and office of Elias and Elijah. It is the spirit of Elias I wish first to speak of; and in order to come at the subject, I will bring some of the testimony from the Scripture and give my own.

In the first place, suffice it to say, I went into the woods to inquire of the Lord, by prayer, His will concerning me, and I saw an angel, and he laid his hands upon my head, and ordained me to a Priest after the order of Aaron, and to hold the keys of this Priesthood, which office was to preach repentance and baptism for the remission of sins, and also to baptize. But I was informed that this office did not extend to the laying on of hands for the giving of the Holy Ghost; that that office was a greater work, and was to be given afterward; but that my ordination was a preparatory work, or a going before, which was the spirit of Elias; for the spirit of Elias was a going before to prepare the way for the greater, which was the case with John the Baptist. He came crying through the wilderness, "Prepare ye the way of the Lord, make his paths straight." And they were informed, if they could receive it, it was the spirit of Elias; and John was very particular to tell the people, he was not that Light, but was sent to bear witness of that Light.

He told the people that his mission was to preach repentance and baptize with water; but it was He that should come after him that should baptize with fire and the Holy Ghost.

If he had been an imposter, he might have gone to work beyond his bounds, and undertook to have performed ordinances which did not belong to that office and calling, under the spirit of Elias.

The spirit of Elias is to prepare the way for a greater revelation of God, which is the Priesthood of Elias, or the Priesthood that Aaron was ordained unto. And when God sends a man into the world to prepare for a greater work, holding the keys of the power of Elias, it was called the doctrine of Elias, even from the early ages of the world.

John's mission was limited to preaching and baptizing: but what he did was legal; and when Jesus Christ came to any of John's disciples, He baptized them with fire and the Holy Ghost.

We find the apostles endowed with greater power than John: their office was more under the spirit and power of Elijah than Elias.

In the case of Phillip when he went down to Samaria, when he was under the spirit of Elias, he baptized both man and women. When Peter and John heard of it, they went down and laid hands upon them, and they received the Holy Ghost. This shows the distinction between the two powers.

When Paul came to certain disciples, he asked if they had received the Holy Ghost? They said, No. Who baptized you, then? We were baptized unto John's baptism. No, you were not baptized unto John's baptism, or you would have been baptized by John. And so Paul went and baptized them, for he knew what the true doctrine was, and he knew that John had not baptized them. And these principles are strange to me, that men who have read the Scriptures of the New Testament are so far from it.

What I want to impress upon your minds is the difference of power in the different parts of the Priesthood, so that when any man come among you, saying, "I have the spirit of Elias," you can know whether he be true or false; for any man that comes, having the spirit and power of Elias, he will not transcend his bounds.

John did not transcend his bounds, but faithfully performed that part belonging to his office; and every portion of the great building should be prepared right and assigned to its proper place; and it is necessary to know who holds the keys of power, and who does not, or we may be likely to be deceived.

That person who holds the keys of Elias hath a preparatory work. . . .

This is the Elias spoken of in the last days, and here is the rock upon which many split, thinking the time was past in the days of John and Christ, and no more to be. But the spirit of Elias was revealed to me, and I know it is true; therefore I speak with boldness, for I know verily my doctrine is true. (In *History of the Church*, 6:249–51)

President Joseph Fielding Smith:

Joseph Smith was chosen to stand at the head of the work of the Lord in the last days, and his work was assigned to him through the foreknowledge of our Eternal Father in the eternities before he was born. He came in the spirit of Elias to prepare the way for the coming of our Lord. No prophet since the days of Adam, save, of course, our Redeemer, has been given a greater mission. (*Improvement Era*, 717)

Melchizedek

What the Book of Genesis Teaches Us

Genesis 14:18 And Melchizedek king of Salem brought forth bread and wine: and he was the priest of the most high God.

What the Scriptures of the Restoration Teach Us

It is interesting that Melchizedek shares some of the same titles as Jesus Christ:

Joseph Smith Translation—Genesis 14:33, 36 And now, Melchizedek was a priest of this order; therefore he obtained peace in Salem, and was called the Prince of peace.

And this Melchizedek, having thus established righteousness, was called the king of heaven by his people, or, in other words, the King of Peace.

D&C 107:2–4 Why the first is called the Melchizedek Priesthood is because Melchizedek was such a great high priest.

Before his day it was called the Holy Priesthood, after the order of the Son of God.

But out of respect or reverence to the name of the Supreme Being, to avoid the too frequent repetition of his name, they, the church, in ancient days, called that priesthood after Melchizedek, or the Melchizedek Priesthood.

Alma 13:14–19 Yea, humble yourselves even as the people in the days of Melchizedek, who was also a high priest after this same order which I have spoken, who also took upon him the high priesthood forever.

And it was this same Melchizedek to whom Abraham paid tithes; yea, even our father Abraham paid tithes of one-tenth part of all he possessed.

Now these ordinances were given after this manner, that thereby the people might look forward on the Son of God, it being a type of his order, or it being his order, and this that they might look forward to him for a remission of their sins, that they might enter into the rest of the Lord.

Now this Melchizedek was a king over the land of Salem; and his people had waxed strong in iniquity and abomination; yea, they had all gone astray; they were full of all manner of wickedness;

But Melchizedek having exercised mighty faith, and received the office of the high priesthood according to the holy order of God, did preach repentance unto his people. And behold, they did repent; and Melchizedek did establish peace in the land in his days; therefore he was called the prince of peace, for he was the king of Salem; and he did reign under his father.

Now, there were many before him, and also there were many

afterwards, but none were greater; therefore, of him they have more particularly made mention.

Joseph Smith Translation—Genesis 14:26 Now Melchizedek was a man of faith, who wrought righteousness; and when a child he feared God, and stopped the mouths of lions, and quenched the violence of fire.

It is also interesting that Paul uses this same verse in Hebrews, yet does not identify the individual that he is speaking about. Obviously it was Melchizedek that he was making reference to.

Hebrews 11:33–34 Who through faith subdued kingdoms, wrought righteousness, obtained promises, stopped the mouths of lions,
Quenched the violence of fire, escaped the edge of the sword, out of weakness were made strong, waxed valiant in fight, turned to flight the armies of the aliens.

Interesting Information

"The Old Testament high priest was an office in the Aaronic Priesthood, not an office in the Melchizedek Priesthood as it is today. The high priest was the presiding priest, or head, of the Aaronic Priesthood. Today the presiding bishop holds that position" (*Old Testament Student Manual: Genesis–2 Samuel*, 3rd ed. [Church Educational System manual, 2003], 187).

Mystery enshrouds Melchizedek's lineage. As stated earlier, Genesis tells us that "he was the priest of the most high God." We learn the following in the Doctrine and Covenants:

D&C 84:14 Which Abraham received the priesthood from Melchizedek, who received it through the lineage of his fathers, even till Noah.

Because so little is known of him, there are those who have theorized that Melchizedek is actually Shem, Noah's son. The argument is compelling and an individual could be easily swayed in their belief one way or another. Alma Gygi discusses in the November 1973 *Ensign* the possibility of Melchizedek as Shem:

1. The inheritance given to Shem included the land of Salem. Melchizedek appears in scripture as the king of Salem, who reigns over this area.
2. Shem, according to later revelation, reigned in righteousness

and the priesthood came through him. Melchizedek appears on the scene with a title that means "king of righteousness."

3. Shem was the great high priest of his day. Abraham honored the high priest Melchizedek by seeking a blessing at his hands and paying him tithes.

4. Abraham stands next to Shem in the patriarchal order of the priesthood and would surely have received the priesthood from Shem; but D&C 84:5–17 says Abraham received the priesthood from Melchizedek.

5. Jewish tradition identifies Shem as Melchizedek.

6. President Joseph F. Smith's remarkable vision names Shem among the great patriarchs, but no mention is made of Melchizedek.

7. *Times and Seasons* (vol. 6, p. 746) speaks of "Shem, who was Melchizedek. . . ."

("Is It Possible That Shem and Melchizedek Are the Same Person?," *Ensign*, Nov. 1973, 15–16)

The Lord's Promises

"Is Anything too Hard for the Lord?"

What the Book of Genesis Teaches Us

Genesis 18: 9–14 And they said unto him, Where is Sarah thy wife? And he said, Behold, in the tent.

And he said, I will certainly return unto thee according to the time of life; and, lo, Sarah thy wife shall have a son. And Sarah heard it in the tent door, which was behind him.

Now Abraham and Sarah were old and well stricken in age; and it ceased to be with Sarah after the manner of women.

Therefore Sarah laughed within herself, saying, After I am waxed old shall I have pleasure, my lord being old also?

And the Lord said unto Abraham, Wherefore did Sarah laugh, saying, Shall I of a surety bear a child, which am old?

Is any thing too hard for the Lord? At the time appointed I will return unto thee, according to the time of life, and Sarah shall have a son.

What the Scriptures of the Restoration Teach Us

Is anything too hard for the Lord? He provided the plagues in Egypt that would free the children of Israel from the iron yoke they were under, he split the Red Sea, he caused the walls of Jericho to tumble, and he provided a desperately desired son to an aged couple. No, there is nothing too hard for the Lord. In more modern times, he gives the following commandment in **D&C 94:1**:

> And again, verily I say unto you, my friends, a commandment I give unto you, that ye shall commence a work of laying out and preparing a beginning and foundation of the city of the stake of Zion, here in the land of Kirtland, beginning at my house.

This revelation is dated May 6, 1833. Another revelation was provided to the Saints three weeks later on June 1, reprimanding them for their failed attempt at starting the temple in Kirtland. The Lord knew what the Saints were up against. He had given the dimensions of the structure and all knew it would be an expensive endeavor. The Lord knew the Saints were in their poverty, but the Lord also knew "that nothing is too hard for the Lord." He was just waiting for them to make the first move, so that he could begin to rain down blessings from heaven, signifying that he was there to help, that this was his temple, and that he would not let them fail. All the Lord asks of us is our faith, he just wants us to make the first move, and then he will step in, picking up the loose ends and make it all work.

> **D&C 95:1, 8, 11** Verily, thus saith the Lord unto you whom I love, and whom I love I also chasten that their sins may be forgiven, for with the chastisement I prepare a way for their deliverance in all things out of temptation, and I have loved you—
>
> Yea, verily I say unto you, I gave unto you a commandment that you should build a house, in the which house I design to endow those whom I have chosen with power from on high;
>
> Verily I say unto you, it is my will that you should build a house. If you keep my commandments you shall have power to build it.

The Teachings of Inspired Church Leaders

President James E. Faust, in the manual, *Teaching, No Greater Call*, makes this statement:

> The Lord has a great work for each of us to do. You may wonder how

this can be. You may feel there is nothing special or superior about you or your ability. . . .

The Lord can do remarkable miracles with a person of ordinary ability who is humble, faithful, and diligent in serving the Lord and seeks to improve himself. This is because God is the ultimate source of power. (*Teaching, No Greater Call: A Resource Guide for Gospel Teaching* [1999], 21)

Interesting Information

Eli H. Peirce was a less active individual, who, whether he knew it or not, understood that nothing is too hard for the Lord.

Eli H. Peirce recorded his feelings of a mission call he received:

On the fifth day of October, 1875, at the Semi-annual conference . . . I was called to perform a mission to the United States.

Just why my name was suggested as a candidate for this mission, and presented at conference for approval or rejection by the people, I cannot say. My mind prior to that time had been entirely given up to temporalities. I had never read to exceed a dozen chapters of the Bible in my life, and little more than that from either the Book of Mormon or Doctrine and Covenants. . . .

One of my fellow employees was at the conference; I was not, because I did not care to be. He heard my name called, abruptly left the meeting, and ran over to the telegraph office to call and tell me the startling news. . . .

As soon as I had been informed of what had taken place, I threw the novel in the waste basket, the pipe in a corner. . . . [I] Have never read a novel nor smoked a pipe from that hour. . . .

Remarkable as it may seem . . . a thought of disregarding the call, or of refusing to comply with the requirement, never once entered my mind. . . .

I was rebaptized, confirmed, set apart, ordained a Seventy, and started on my mission, all within a month from the time I was called. Went direct to New York City. (Eliza R. Snow Smith, comp., *Biography and Family Record of Lorenzo Snow: One of the Twelve Apostles of the Church of Jesus Christ of Latter-Day Saints* [1884], 407–9)

The Lord blessed Eli richly for his act of faith. In fact, he would go on to serve two more missions. How successful was Eli? Baptisms, 108; ordinations, 11; children blessed, 37; branches organized, 5; branches reorganized, 1; marriages, 1; meetings held, 249; miles traveled, 9,870; total cost, $1,320 (Snow Smith, comp., *Biography and Family Record*, 421).

Elect Women of the Lord

What the Book of Genesis Teaches Us

Genesis 23:1–2 And Sarah was an hundred and seven and twenty years old: these were the years of the life of Sarah.

And Sarah died in Kirjath-arba; the same is Hebron in the land of Canaan: and Abraham came to mourn for Sarah, and to weep for her.

Sarah was an "elect" lady of the Lord. She stood by her husband through all of their trials and was a strength to Abraham.

What the Scriptures of the Restoration Teach Us

D&C 25:1–4 Hearken unto the voice of the Lord your God, while I speak unto you, Emma Smith, my daughter; for verily I say unto you, all those who receive my gospel are sons and daughters in my kingdom.

A revelation I give unto you concerning my will; and if thou art faithful and walk in the paths of virtue before me, I will preserve thy life, and thou shalt receive an inheritance in Zion.

Behold, they sins are forgiven thee, and thou art an elect lady, whom I have called.

Murmur not because of the things which thou hast not seen, for they are withheld from thee and from the world, which is wisdom in me in a time to come.

Interesting Information

Lucy Mack Smith shares the following insight into the life of Emma Smith and what she had to endure:

And, although her [Emma Smith's] strength was exhausted, still her spirits were the same, which, in fact, was always the case with her, even under the most trying circumstances. I have never seen a woman in my life, who would endure every species of fatigue and hardship, from month to month, and from year to year, with that unflinching courage, zeal, and patience, which she has ever done; for I know that which she has had to endure—she has been tossed upon the ocean of uncertainty—she has breasted the storms of persecution, and buffeted the rage of men and devils, which would have borne down almost any other woman. (*History of Joseph Smith by His Mother*, ed. Scot Facer Proctor and Maurine Jensen Proctor [1996], 248)

Sodom and Gomorrah

What the Book of Genesis Teaches Us

Genesis 18:20–26 And the Lord said, Because the cry of Sodom and Gomorrah is great, and because their sin is very grievous;

I will go down now, and see whether they have done altogether according to the cry of it, which is come unto me; and if not, I will know.

And the men turned their faces from thence, and went toward Sodom: but Abraham stood yet before the Lord.

And Abraham drew near, and said, Wilt thou also destroy the righteous with the wicked?

Peradventure there be fifty righteous within the city; Wilt thou also destroy and not spare the place for the fifty righteous that are therein?

That be far from thee to do after this manner, to slay the righteous with the wicked: and that the righteous should be as the wicked, that be far from thee: Shall not the Judge of all the earth do right?

And the Lord said, If I find in Sodom fifty righteous within the city, then I will spare all the place for their sakes.

Abraham continues to question the Lord and is able to get God's promise that he will not destroy the city of Sodom and Gomorrah if there were as few as ten righteous individuals. This situation is similar to the Book of Mormon city of Ammonihah.

What the Scriptures of the Restoration Teach Us

Alma 10:22–23 Yea, and I say unto you that if it were not for the prayers of the righteous, who are now in the land, that ye would even now be visited with utter destruction; yet it would not be by flood, as were the people in the days of Noah, but it would be by famine, and by pestilence, and the sword.

But it is by the prayers of the righteous that ye are spared; now therefore, if ye will cast out the righteous from among you then will not the Lord stay his hand; but in his fierce anger he will come out against you; then ye shall be smitten by famine, and by pestilence, and by the sword; and the time is soon at hand except ye repent.

Unfortunately, like Sodom, the righteous were either killed or removed, and the great city of Ammonihah was destroyed in one day.

Alma 14:9–11 And it came to pass that they took Alma and Amulek, and carried them forth to the place of martyrdom, that they might witness the destruction of those who were consumed by fire.

And when Amulek saw the pains of the women and children who were consuming in the fire, he also was pained; and he said unto Alma: How can we witness this awful scene? Therefore let us stretch forth our hands, and exercise the power of God which is in us, and save them from the flames.

But Alma said unto him: The Spirit constraineth me that I must not stretch forth mine hand; for behold the Lord receiveth them up unto himself, in glory; and he doth suffer that they may do this thing, or that the people may do this thing unto them, according to the hardness of their hearts, that the judgments which he shall exercise upon them in his wrath may be just; and the blood of the innocent shall stand as a witness against them, yea, and cry mightily against them at the last day.

Alma 15:1 And it came to pass that Alma and Amulek were commanded to depart out of that city; and they departed, and came out even into the land of Sidom; and behold, there they found all the people who had departed out of the land of Ammonihah, who had been cast out and stoned, because they believed in the words of Alma.

Alma 16:9–10 And thus ended the eleventh year of the judges, the Lamanites having been driven out of the land, and the people of Ammonihah were destroyed; yea, every living soul of the Ammoni-hahites was destroyed, and also their great city, which they said God could not destroy, because of its greatness.

But behold, in one day it was left desolate; and the carcasses were mangled by dogs and wild beasts of the wilderness.

Lot

What the Book of Genesis Teaches Us

Genesis 13:12 Abram dwelled in the land of Canaan, and Lot dwelled in the cities of the plain and pitched his tent toward Sodom.

Based on this scripture, we learn that Lot did not stand in "holy places," as the Lord commanded in the Doctrine and Covenants. The temptations of the cities were too alluring to Lot, and as such, he chose to be in the vicinity of these cities.

Interesting Information

David J. Ridges:

The phrase, "pitched his tent toward Sodom," in verse 12, above, seems to have more meaning than merely saying that he had the door of his tent facing Sodom. We see a similar phrase in the Book of Mormon. In Mosiah 2:6 King Benjamin's people pitched their tents with the doorways facing the temple. The phrase implies that their hearts were toward the temple, desiring God's word and instruction, being loyal to the gospel.

Similarly, Lot's pitching his tent "toward Sodom" implies that Lot's heart was inclined toward the wickedness in Sodom. This unbridled yearning will later lead to the demise of his wife and the undoing of him and his family. (*The Old Testament Made Easier* [2009], 1:242)

Abraham and Isaac

Sacrificing Isaac

What the Book of Genesis Teaches Us

Genesis 22:1–2 And it came to pass after these things, that God did tempt Abraham, and said unto him, Abraham: and he said, Behold, here I am.

And he said, Take now thy son, thine only son Isaac, whom thou lovest, and get thee into the land of Moriah; and offer him there for a burnt offering upon one of the mountains which I will tell thee of.

Interesting Information

Abraham was commanded to sacrifice Isaac on Mt. Moriah. This is the same location as Herod's temple in Jerusalem. Ironically, another sacrifice, the sacrifice of our Savior, took place in the same area (*Scripture Stories*, 14).

What the Book of Genesis Teaches Us

Genesis 22: 3–4, 10–12 And Abraham rose up early in the morning, and saddled his ass, and took two of his young men with him, and Isaac his son, and clave the wood for the burnt offering, and rose up, and went unto the place of which God had told him.

Then on the third day Abraham lifted up his eyes, and saw the place afar off.

And Abraham stretched forth his hand, and took the knife to slay his son.

And the angel of the Lord called unto him out of heaven, and said, Abraham, Abraham: and he said, Here am I.

And he said, Lay not thine hand upon the lad, neither do thou any thing unto him: for now I know that thou fearest God, seeing thou hast not withheld thy son, thine only son from me.

The Teachings of Inspired Church Leaders

President Joseph F. Smith:

If He should require me to give all I possess unto him, I wish to feel that it should be done cheerfully and willingly, as Job, and also Abraham, felt when the Lord called upon them for expressions of their faith. Abraham was called upon to offer up his son—a child of promise—did he stop to reason or argue with the Almighty? No, he went to, without complaint or murmuring, to do what he was commanded. He may have had peculiar feelings, and no doubt he was tried to the very core; his tenderest affections were tested, but for all that he proposed obeying the behest of the Almighty. Abraham did not, however, execute the command, for the Lord, seeing his integrity and willingness, prevented it.

Now, how many of us have the confidence in the Lord that Abraham had? Supposing, He were to ask from you your first born, or any of your loved ones, or your wealth, could you endure it without murmuring? . . . Can we expect to attain a celestial exaltation if we have some corner—something put away—upon which our hearts or dearest affections are set? Ask yourselves, if you are worthy to receive exaltation in the celestial kingdom of God? (In Brian H. Stuy, comp., *Collected Discourses Delivered by Wilford Woodruff, His Two Counselors, the Twelve Apostles, and Others*, 5 vols. [1987–92], 2:279)

What the Scriptures of the Restoration Teach Us

D&C 101:4–5 Therefore, they must needs be chastened and tried, even as Abraham, who was commanded to offer up his only son.

For all those who will not endure chastening, but deny me, cannot be sanctified.

Abraham's obedience

What the Book of Genesis Teaches Us

Genesis 22:17–18 That in blessing I will bless thee, and in multiplying I will multiply thy seed as the stars of the heaven, and as the sand which is upon the sea shore; and thy seed shall possess the gate of his enemies;

And in thy seed shall all the nations of the earth be blessed; because thou hast obeyed my voice.

The Teachings of Inspired Church Leaders

President Joseph F. Smith:

In Abraham we have another example of devotion to the word of God, and faith in ultimately sharing his goodness. . . . In Abraham's willingness to trust in God in the greatest trial that could come to a father—the sacrifice of his son—we observe deep-rooted faith and abiding confidence in the Almighty being able and willing to fulfill his promises, no matter how improbable it might appear under the most trying circumstances. . . . So will he do with all who trust him, for the promise is to all.

Such knowledge, faith, and confidence, supply an important part in revealed religion. . . . Abraham learned the great truth, which we also must impress upon our hearts, that God is just, and will fulfill his promises to the uttermost. And so he was blessed, as we shall be also, in trying circumstances, because he trusted the Lord and obeyed his voice. . . .

The situation is the same today; unless the Saints have an actual knowledge that the course which they are pursuing is in harmony with the will of God, they will grow weary in trial, and will faint under persecution. . . . But, on the contrary, with this trust in God burned into their souls, no matter what comes, they are happy in doing his will, knowing full well that at last the promise shall be theirs. Thus is the world overcome, and the crown of glory obtained which God has laid away for those who love, honor and obey him. . . .

No person can realize the fullness of the blessings of God, unless he can approach, in some degree, at least, the standard of faith in God's justice, exemplified in the examples quoted. He must have founded in his own soul belief and confidence in the justice and mercy of God. It must be individual, no man can act for another. Lessons of this class need be taught and held up before the youth of Zion, to bring forcibly to their minds the truth which alone will make them free and able to stand firm in the faith. Let them, as they are called together in their assemblies, present themselves before God, and be reminded of his gracious benefits, in bringing forth the Book of Mormon, in the scenes of Kirtland, in Zion [Jackson County, Missouri], in Nauvoo, in the trying days of the exodus, and in the wilderness. This that they might count the mercies of God in his promises, and behold how past affliction and sore trial have been turned to the well-being of his people; and so renew their covenants, filled with a deep-rooted, immovable conviction of the goodness and mercy of the Lord. Each individual must learn this lesson, it must be impressed upon his soul, so deep, and be so well-founded that nothing can separate him from a knowledge of the love of God, though death and hell stand in the way. . . .

God is good; his promises never fail; to implicitly trust his goodness and mercy, is a correct principle. Let us, therefore, put our trust in Him. ("Trust in God," *Improvement Era*, Nov. 1903, 53–56)

President Brigham Young:

The heart of man is incapable of fully comprehending the blessings that God has in store for the faithful, unless he has revealed those blessings to them by the revelations of his Spirit. The natural man is contracted in his feelings, in his views, faith and desires, and so are the Saints, unless they live their religion. (In *Journal of Discourses*, 8:188)

Isaac's Sacrifice, a Similitude of the Savior

What the Book of Genesis Teaches Us

Genesis 22:9–12 And they came to the place which God had told him of; and Abraham built an altar there, and laid the wood in order, and bound Isaac his son, and laid him on the altar upon the wood.

And Abraham stretched forth his hand, and took the knife to slay his son.

And the angel of the Lord called unto him out of heaven, and said, Abraham, Abraham: and he said, Here am I.

And he said, Lay not thine hand upon the lad, neither do thou any thing unto him: for now I know that thou fearest God, seeing thou hast not withheld thy son, thine only son from me.

What the Scriptures of the Restoration Teach Us

2 Nephi 25:13 Behold, they will crucify him; and after he is laid in a sepulcher for the space of three days he shall rise from the dead, with healing in his wings; and all those who shall believe on his name shall be saved in the kingdom of God. Wherefore, my soul delighteth to prophesy concerning him, for I have seen his day, and my heart doth magnify his holy name.

The three-day journey Abraham took with his son Isaac represents the three days the Savior was in the tomb.

Where the book of Genesis states that Abraham laid the wood on Isaac to carry, the Joseph Smith Translation reads, "laid it upon his back." This is similar to the cross that Jesus would carry.

D&C 132: 36 Abraham was commanded to offer his son Isaac; nevertheless, it was written: Thou shalt not kill. Abraham, however, did not refuse, and it was accounted unto him for righteousness.

Why did Abraham proceed to sacrifice Isaac and why did Isaac submit? Because of their love to the Lord.

Jacob 4:5 Behold, they believed in Christ and worshiped the Father in his name, and also we worship the Father in his name. And for this intent we keep the law of Moses, it pointing our souls to him; and for this cause it is sanctified unto us for righteousness, even as it was accounted unto Abraham in the wilderness to be obedient unto the commands of God in offering up his son Isaac, which is a similitude of God and his only Begotten Son.

How is the attempted sacrifice of Isaac by Abraham similar to the sacrifice of Jesus Christ? First, the mountain referred to was Mt. Moriah inside the walls of Jerusalem. It was the site of Herod's temple, but today, the Dome of the Rock sits on Moriah's pinnacle (*Scripture Stories*, 14). It was within a stone's throw of this location that Jesus was crucified, just outside the city walls of Jerusalem at Golgotha. And second, Paul, in reference to the events surrounding Abraham and Isaac, refers to Isaac as one of Christ's titles and the same title used by Jacob in Jacob 4:5.

What the New Testament teaches us

Hebrews 11:17 By faith Abraham, when he was tried, offered up Isaac: and he that had received the promises offered up his only begotten son.

Oaths

What the Book of Genesis Teaches Us

This is in relation to Abraham sending his servant to find Isaac a wife. This is also the first recorded instance in the Old Testament where a righteous person takes an oath.

Genesis 24:2–4 And Abraham said unto his eldest servant of his house, that ruled over all that he had, Put, I pray thee, thy hand under my thigh:

And I will make thee swear by the Lord, the God of heaven, and the God of the earth, that thou shalt not take a wife unto my son of the daughters of the Canaanites, among whom I dwell:

But thou shalt go unto my country, and to my kindred, and take a wife unto my son Isaac.

What the Book of Numbers Teaches Us

Numbers 30:2 If a man vow a vow unto the Lord, or swear an oath to bind his soul with a bond; he shall not break his word, he shall do according to all that proceedeth out of his mouth.

What the Scriptures of the Restoration Teach Us

1 Nephi 4:31–37 And now I, Nephi, being a man large in stature, and also having received much strength of the Lord, therefore I did seize upon the servant of Laban, and held him, that he should not flee.

And it came to pass that I spake with him, that if he would hearken unto my words, as the Lord liveth, and as I live, even so that if he would hearken unto our words, we would spare his life.

And I spake unto him, even with an oath, that he need not fear; that he should be a free man like unto us if he would go down in the wilderness with us.

And I also spake unto him, saying: Surely the Lord hath commanded us to do this thing; and shall we not be diligent in keeping the commandments of the Lord? Therefore, if thou wilt go down into the wilderness to my father thou shalt have place with us.

And it came to pass that Zoram did take courage at the words which I spake. Now Zoram was the name of the servant; and he promised that he would go down in the wilderness unto our father. Yea, and he also made an oath unto us that he would tarry with us from that time forth.

Now we were desirous that he should tarry with us for this cause, that the Jews might not know concerning our flight into the wilderness, lest they should pursue us and destroy us.

And it came to pass that when Zoram had made an oath unto us, our fears did cease concerning him.

This was how serious oaths were viewed in ancient times. Zoram's confirmation that he would go into the wilderness with Nephi and his brothers was all it took for complete trust in Zoram.

Ishmael

What the Book of Genesis Teaches Us

Genesis 16:10–12 And the angel of the Lord said unto her [Hagar], I will multiply they seed exceedingly, that it shall not be numbered for multitude.

And the angel of the Lord said unto her, Behold, thou art with child, and shalt bear a son, and shalt call his name Ishmael; because the Lord hath heard thy affliction.

And he will be a wild man; his hand will be against every man, and every man's hand against him; and he shall dwell in the presence of all his brethren.

What is meant by the term *wild man*? Is it possible that it could have reference to someone who dwells in the wilderness, based on the information from **Genesis 21:20**?

And God was with the lad [Ishmael] and he grew, and dwelt in the wilderness, and became an archer.

Like Isaac, Ishmael was promised to be the father of a large nation.

Genesis 21:18 Arise, lift up the lad, and hold him in thine hand; for I will make him a great nation.

Interesting Information

Ishmael would go on to father the Arab nation. One of the most important Islamic festivals in the Muslim world is Eid al-Adha. This festival commemorates Ishmael almost being sacrificed by Abraham. The Muslims do not believe that this was Isaac, but rather Ishmael.

Jacob and Esau

Selling the Birthright

What the Book of Genesis Teaches Us

Genesis 25: 21–34 And Isaac entreated the Lord for his wife, because she was barren: and the Lord was entreated of him, and Rebekah his wife conceived.

And the children struggled together within her; and she said, If it be so, why am I thus? And she went to inquire of the Lord.

And the Lord said unto her, Two nations are in thy womb, and two manner of people shall be separated from thy bowels; and the one people shall be stronger than the other people; and the elder shall serve the younger.

And when her days to be delivered were fulfilled, behold, there were twins in her womb.

And the first came out red, all over like an hairy garment; and they called his name Esau.

And after that came his brother out, and his hand took hold on Esau's heel; and his name was called Jacob: and Isaac was threescore years old when she bare them.

And the boys grew: and Esau was a cunning hunter, a man of the field; and Jacob was a plain man, dwelling in tents.

And Isaac loved Esau, because he did eat of his venison: but Rebekah loved Jacob.

And Jacob sod pottage: and Esau came from the field, and he was faint:

And Esau said to Jacob, Feed me, I pray thee, with that same red pottage; for I am faint: therefore was his name called Edom.

And Jacob said, Sell me this day thy birthright.

And Esau said, Behold, I am at the point to die: and what profit shall this birthright do to me?

And Jacob said, Swear to me this day; and he sware unto him: and he sold his birthright unto Jacob.

Then Jacob gave Esau bread and pottage of lentils; and he did eat and drink, and rose up, and went his way: thus Esau despised his birthright.

The Teachings of Inspired Church Leaders

President Thomas S. Monson:

Some foolish persons turn their backs on the wisdom of God and follow the allurement of fickle fashion, the attraction of false popularity, and the thrill of the moment. Their course of conduct resembles the disastrous experience of Esau, who exchanged his birthright for a mess of pottage.

And what are the results of such action? I testify to you that turning away from God brings broken covenants, shattered dreams, vanished ambitions, evaporated plans, unfulfilled expectations, crushed hopes, misused drives, warped character, and wrecked lives.

Such a quagmire of quicksand must be avoided. We are of a noble birthright. Eternal life in the kingdom of our Father is our goal. ("Crisis at the Crossroads," *New Era*, Nov. 2002, online)

Esau Marries Outside the Covenant

What the Book of Genesis Teaches Us

> **Genesis 26:34–35** And Esau was forty years old when he took to wife Judith the daughter of Beeri the Hittite, and Bashemath the daughter of Elon the Hittite:
> Which were a grief of mind unto Isaac and to Rebekah.

Life is about choices. In fact, many of the choices we make early in life, in large part, determine our future. Esau was a product of his own choices. The birthright could have been his, but rather than pursuing a course of action that would earn him the blessings of the birthright, he chose to "despise his birthright." Part of this neglect was the choice of who he would marry. Esau married Hittite women; women who were raised in a culture whose religious worship was to idolatrous gods. By Esau marrying outside of the covenant people, he separated himself from the blessings of the covenant. Does this mean that all is lost for the future generations of Esau's family? Were Esau's decisions cast in stone so deep that the repercussions would ripple to his posterity? Definitely not! Is a child born in poverty limited to the slums and nothing better? Again, no! Brigham Young sheds more light on this thought and our obligation to save our Father's children.

The Teachings of Inspired Church Leaders

President Brigham Young:

> The Lord has restored the Priesthood in our day for the salvation of Israel. Does he design to save anybody else? Yes; he will save the House of Esau, and I hope to live until I see Mount Zion established, and saviors come up to save those poor, miserable beings who are continually persecuting us—all who have not sinned against the Holy Ghost. Our labor is to save ourselves, to save the house of Israel, to save the house of Esau, and all the Gentile nations—every one that can be saved. (In *Journal of Discourses*, 7:281)

Regrets for the Lost Birthright

What the Book of Genesis Teaches Us

Genesis 27:34 And when Esau heard the words of his father, he cried with a great and exceeding bitter cry, and said unto his father, Bless me, even me also, O my father.

The Teachings of Inspired Church Leaders

Elder Joseph B. Wirthlin:

The problem is that in most cases the search for wealth, pleasure, and power leads to a place that may seem at first glance to be desirable, but the closer you get, the more you see it for what it is. The price for worldly success too often comes at the price of your birthright. Those who make that bargain will one day feel as Esau, who, after realizing what he had lost, "cried with a great and exceeding bitter cry." ("Lessons Learned in the Journey of Life," *Ensign*, Dec. 2000, 9)

Reconciliation

What the Book of Genesis Teaches Us

Genesis 27:41 And Esau hated Jacob because of the blessing wherewith his father blessed him; and Esau said in his heart, The days of mourning for my father are at hand; then will I slay my brother Jacob.

And then many years later:

Genesis 33:1–4 And Jacob lifted up his eyes, and looked, and, behold, Esau came, and with him four hundred men. And he divided the children unto Leah, and unto Rachel, and unto the two handmaids.

And he put the handmaids and their children foremost, and Leah and her children after, and Rachel and Joseph hindermost.

And he passed over before them, and bowed himself to the ground seven times, until he came near to his brother.

And Esau ran to meet him, and embraced him, and fell on his neck, and kissed him: and they wept.

The Teachings of Inspired Church Leaders

Elder Neal A. Maxwell:

> If I were to teach the principle of generosity in human relationships, how marvelous to share with people . . . the relationship of Jacob and Esau. . . .
>
> Just as Jacob and Esau needed time apart, so might we occasionally need time to calm our feelings and reflect on the importance of our family relationships. Yet time and separation alone will not bring resolution. If we are prayerful, the Lord will help us know when the time is right for reconciliation, and we can follow the example of these brothers. How sweet that moment of sincere reconciliation can be! Our Savior will help us. He is the great Mediator, and He is able to soften hearts and heal wounds. He knows how to bring people to a unity of heart and mind. His example of marvelous generosity to us through His Atonement can help inspire forgiveness in our souls. ("Teaching Opportunities from the Old Testament," *Ensign*, Apr. 1981, 59)

Jacob

Angelic Visitations

What the Book of Genesis Teaches Us

Genesis 28:10–13 And Jacob went out from Beer-sheba, and went toward Haran.

And he lighted upon a certain place, and tarried there all night, because the sun was set; and he took of the stones of that place, and put them for his pillows, and lay down in that place to sleep.

And he dreamed, and behold a ladder set up on the earth, and the top of it reached to heaven; and behold the angels of God ascending and descending on it.

And, behold, the Lord stood above it, and said, I am the Lord God of Abraham thy father, and the God of Isaac: the land whereon thou liest, to thee will I give it, and to thy seed.

The Teachings of Inspired Church Leaders

President Joseph Smith taught, "Paul ascended into the third heavens, and he could understand the three principal rounds of Jacob's ladder—the telestial, the terrestrial, and the celestial glories or kingdoms, where Paul saw and heard things which were not lawful for him to utter" (*Teachings of the Prophet Joseph Smith*, 304–5).

President Joseph F. Smith:

We are told by the Prophet Joseph Smith, that "there are no angels who minister to this earth but those who do belong or have belonged to it." Hence, when messengers are sent to minister to the inhabitants of this earth, they are not strangers, but from the ranks of our kindred, friends, and fellow-beings and fellow-servants. The ancient Prophets who died were those who came to visit their fellow-creatures upon the earth. They came to Abraham, to Isaac, and to Jacob; it was such beings—holy beings if you please-that waited upon the Savior and administered to him on the Mount. The angel that visited John when an exile, and unfolded to his vision future events in the history of man upon the earth, was one who had been here, who had toiled and suffered in common with the people of God; for you remember that John, after his eyes had beheld the glories of the great future, was about to fall down and worship him, but was peremptorily forbidden to do so. . . . In like manner our fathers and mothers, brothers, sisters and friends who have passed away from this earth, having been faithful, and worthy to enjoy these rights and privileges, may have a mission given them to visit their relatives and friends upon the earth again, bringing from the divine Presence messages of love, of warning, of reproof and instruction to those whom they had learned to love in the flesh. (In *Journal of Discourses*, 22:351)

Ancient and modern prophets are not the exclusive recipients of angelic communications. I imagine volumes would be filled of heavenly messages to mortals who live average lives, like you and me.

David Whitmer shares the following experience of the angel Moroni appearing to his mother, Mary:

"My father and mother had a large family . . . the addition to it . . . of Joseph, his wife Emma and Oliver very greatly increased the toil and anxiety of my mother," she was met by the Angel Moroni, who said to her, "You have been very faithful and diligent in your labors, but you are tired . . . it is proper therefore that you should receive a witness that your faith may be strengthened." Thereupon, the messenger showed Mary the plates, turning them over leaf by leaf, that she might know that the work was true. He promised her that if she endured in faith to the end, her reward would be sure. (*Millennial Star* 40 [May 2, 1878]: 772–73)

Modern revelation has revealed so much more on the nature and disposition of angels. Because the man that believes the heavens are closed is left to decipher what an angel might look like, has imagined a vision of a personage with wings. On July 2, 1839, the Prophet taught that angels never have wings (in *History of the Church*, 3:392). Joseph Smith would understand this since, on numerous occasions, he was visited by angels.

On June 15, 1842, Joseph Smith wrote the following:

The manifestations of the gift of the Holy Ghost, the ministering of angels, or the development of the power, majesty or glory of God were very seldom manifested publicly, and that generally to the people of God, as to the Israelites; but most generally when angels have come, or God has revealed Himself, it had been to individuals in private, in their chamber; in the wilderness or fields, and that generally without noise or tumult. The angel delivered Peter out of prison in the dead of night; came to Paul unobserved by the rest of the crew; appeared to Mary and Elizabeth without the knowledge of others; spoke to John the Baptist whilst the people around were ignorant of it. (In *History of the Church*, 5:30–31)

What the Scriptures of the Restoration Teach Us

D&C 129:1–9 There are two kinds of beings in heaven, namely: Angels, who are resurrected personages, having bodies of flesh and bones—

For instance, Jesus said: Handle me and see, for a spirit hath not flesh and bones, as ye see me have.

Secondly: the spirits of just men made perfect, they who are not resurrected, but inherit the same glory.

When a messenger comes saying he had a message from God, offer him your hand and request him to shake hands with you.

If he be an angel he will do so, and you will feel his hand.

If he be the spirit of a just man made perfect he will come in his glory; for that is the only way he can appear—

Ask him to shake hands with you, but he will not move, because it is contrary to the order of heaven for a just man to deceive; but he will still deliver his message.

If it be the devil as an angel of light, when you ask him to shake hands he will offer you his hand, and you will not feel anything; you may therefore detect him.

These are three grand keys whereby you may know whether any administration is from God.

Jacob's New Name: Israel

What the Book of Genesis Teaches Us

Genesis 32:24–30 And Jacob was left alone; and there wrestled a man with him until the breaking of the day.

And when he saw that he prevailed not against him, he touched the hollow of his thigh; and the hollow of Jacob's thigh was out of joint, as he wrestled with him.

And he said, Let me go, for the day breaketh. And he said, I will not let thee go, except thou bless me.

And he said unto him, What is thy name? And he said, Jacob.

And he said, Thy name shall be called no more Jacob, but Israel: for as a prince hast thou power with God and with men, and hast prevailed.

And Jacob asked him, and said, Tell me, I pray thee, thy name. And he said, Wherefore is it that thou dost ask after my name? And he blessed him there.

And Jacob called the name of the place Peniel: for I have seen God face to face, and my life is preserved.

The Teachings of Inspired Church Leaders

President Joseph Fielding Smith:

Who wrestled with Jacob on Mount Peniel? The scriptures say it was a man. The Bible interpreters say it was an angel. More than likely it was a messenger sent to Jacob to give him the blessing. To think he wrestled and held an angel who couldn't get away, is out of the question. The term angel as used in the scriptures, at times, refers to messengers who are sent with some important instruction. Later in this chapter when Jacob said he had beheld the Lord, that did not have reference to his wrestling. (*Doctrines of Salvation*, ed. Bruce R. McConkie [1954–56], 1:17)

Bruce R. McConkie:

Literally, the name Israel means *contender with God*, the sense and meaning indicating one who has succeeded in his supplication before the Lord, who has enlisted as a *soldier of God*, who has become a *prince of God*. (*Mormon Doctrine*, 2nd ed. [1966], 389)

Israel the Patriarch

What the Book of Genesis Teaches Us

Genesis 49:1–2 And Jacob called unto his sons, and said, Gather yourselves together, that I may tell you that which shall befall you in the last days.

Gather yourselves together, and hear, ye sons of Jacob; and hearken unto Israel your father.

The Teachings of Inspired Church Leaders

The following quote by Joseph Smith indicates that Jacob gave his sons patriarchal blessings which would lead one to believe that Jacob was also a patriarch. In **Acts 7:8**, "Isaac begat Jacob; and Jacob begat the twelve patriarchs." Again, if Jacob's sons were patriarchs, then this too would indicate that Jacob also held this office.

President Joseph Smith:

An Evangelist is a Patriarch, even the oldest man of the blood of Joseph or of the seed of Abraham. Wherever the Church of Christ is established in the earth, there should be a Patriarch for the benefit of the posterity of the Saints, as it was with Jacob in giving his patriarchal blessing unto his sons, etc. (In *History of the Church*, 3:381)

Interesting Information

September 14, [1835]—In a meeting of a High Council and the Presidency at Kirtland, it was decided that, as the laborer is worthy of his hire, whenever President Joseph Smith, Sen., is called upon to pronounce Patriarchal blessings upon the Church, he be paid for his services at the rate of ten dollars per week and his expenses. It was further decided that President Frederick G. Williams be appointed and hereafter serve as scribe, to attend blessing meetings, and that he receive for his services, at the same ratio, having his expenses borne also. (Joseph Smith, in *History of the Church*, 2:273)

[December 29, 1835]—I [Joseph Smith] remained at home until about ten o'clock. I then attended a blessing meeting at Oliver Olney's, in company with my wife, and father and mother, who had come to live with me. Also my scribe went with us. A large company assembled, when Father Smith made some appropriate remarks. A hymn was sung and father opened the meeting by prayer. About fifteen persons then received patriarchal blessings under his hands. The services were concluded as they commenced. A table was crowned with the bounties of nature; and after invoking the benediction of heaven upon the rich repast, we fared sumptuously; and suffice it to say that we had a glorious meeting throughout, and I was much pleased with the harmony that existed among the brethren and sisters. (Joseph Smith, in *History of the Church*, 2:346–7)

Blessing Ephraim and Manasseh

What the Book of Genesis Teaches Us

The following account is the events surrounding Israel meeting Joseph's sons for the first time, when Israel traveled to Egypt, along with the rest of his family, to sojourn in Egypt with Joseph.

Genesis 48: 8–14, 17–20 And Israel beheld Joseph's sons, and said, Who are these?

And Joseph said unto his father, They are my sons, whom God hath given me in this place. And he said, Bring them I pray thee, unto me, and I will bless them.

Now the eyes of Israel were dim for age, so that he could not see. And he brought them near unto him; and he kissed them, and embraced them.

And Israel said unto Joseph, I had not thought to see they face: and, lo, God hath shewed me also thy seed.

And Joseph brought them out from between his knees, and he bowed himself with his face to the earth.

And Joseph took them both, Ephraim in his right hand toward Israel's left hand, and Manasseh in his left hand toward Israel's right hand, and brought them near unto him.

And Israel stretched out his right hand, and laid it upon Ephraim's head, who was the younger, and his left hand upon Manasseh's head, guiding his hands wittingly; for Manasseh was the firstborn.

And when Joseph saw that his father laid his right hand upon the head of Ephraim, it displeased him: and he held up his father's hand, to remove it from Ephraim's head unto Manasseh's head.

And Joseph said unto his father, Not so, my father: for this is the firstborn; put thy right hand upon his head.

And his father refused, and said, I know it, my son, I know it: he also shall become a people, and he also shall be great: but truly his younger brother shall be greater than he, and his seed shall become a multitude of nations.

And he blessed them that day, saying, In thee shall Israel bless, saying, God make thee as Ephraim and as Manasseh: and he set Ephraim before Manasseh.

What the Scriptures of the Restoration Teach Us

D&C 133:34 Behold, this is the blessing of the everlasting God upon the tribes of Israel, and the richer blessing upon the head of Ephraim and his fellows.

The Teachings of Inspired Church Leaders

President Brigham Young:

We are now gathering the children of Abraham who have come through the loins of Joseph and his sons, more especially through Ephraim, whose children are mixed among all the nations of the earth. The sons of Ephraim are wild and uncultivated, unruly, ungovernable. The spirit in them is turbulent and resolute; they are the Anglo-Saxon race, and they are upon the face of the whole earth, bearing the spirit of rule and dictation, to go forth from conquering to conquer. They search wide creation and scan every nook and corner of his earth to find out what is upon and within it. I see a congregation of them before me today. No hardship will discourage these men; they will penetrate the deepest wilds and overcome almost insurmountable difficulties to develop the treasures of the earth, to further their indomitable spirit of adventure. (In *Journal of Discourses*, 10:188)

President Brigham Young:

It is the House of Israel we are after, and we care not whether they come from the east, the west, the north, or the south, from China, Russia, England, California, North or South America, or some other locality; and it is the very lad on whom Father Jacob laid his hands, that will save the House of Israel. The Book of Mormon came to Ephraim, for Joseph Smith was a pure Ephraimite. (*Discourses of Brigham Young*, 322)

Jacob's Death and Afterlife

What the Book of Genesis Teaches Us

Genesis 49:33 And when Jacob had made an end of commanding his sons, he gathered up his feet into the bed, and yielded up the ghost, and was gathered unto his people.

The Old Testament concludes Jacob's story with his death. Through modern revelation, we learn of his exaltation.

What the Scriptures of the Restoration Teach Us

D&C 132:37 Abraham received concubines, and they bore him children; and it was accounted unto him for righteousness, because they were given unto him, and he abode in my law; as Isaac also and Jacob did none other things than that which they were commanded; and because they did none other things than that which they were commanded, they have entered into their exaltation, according to the promises, and sit upon thrones, and are not angels but are gods.

Embalming

What the Book of Genesis Teaches Us

Genesis 50:2–3, 26 And Joseph commanded his servants the physicians to embalm his father: and the physicians embalmed Israel.

And forty days were fulfilled for him; for so are fulfilled the days of those which are embalmed: and the Egyptians mourned for him threescore and ten days.

So Joseph died, being an hundred and ten years old: and they embalmed him, and he was put in a coffin in Egypt.

The Teachings of Inspired Church Leaders

Is it possible that the ancients embalmed on the American continent?

President Joseph Smith:

A Catacomb of Mummies found in Kentucky

Had Mr. Ash in his researches consulted the Book of Mormon his problem would have been solved, and he would have found no difficulty in accounting for the mummies being found in the above mentioned case. The Book of Mormon gives an account of a number of the descendants of Israel coming to this continent; and it is well known that the art of embalming was known among the Hebrews, as well as among the Egyptians, although, perhaps, not so generally among the former, as among the latter people; and their method of embalming also might be different from that of the Egyptians. Jacob and Joseph were no doubt embalmed in the manner of the Egyptians, as they died in that country. . . .

This art was no doubt transmitted from Jerusalem to this continent, by the before mentioned emigrants, which accounts for the finding of the mummies, and at the same time is another strong evidence of the authenticity of the Book of Mormon. (*Times and Seasons* 3:781–82)

Jacob's Family

Leah's Faith

What the Book of Genesis Teaches Us

Genesis 31:16 For all the riches which God hath taken from our father, that is ours, and our children's: now then, whatsoever God hath said unto thee, do.

The Teachings of Inspired Church Leaders

President Dieter F. Uchtdorf:

Some sins are committed because we do wrong; other sins are committed because we do nothing. Being only sort of committed to the gospel can lead to frustration, unhappiness, and guilt. This should not apply to us because we are a covenant people. . . . Nothing can be more important than keeping a commitment we have made with the Lord.

Let us remember the reply of Rachel and Leah to Jacob in the Old Testament. It was simple and straightforward and showed their commitment: "Whatsoever God hath said unto thee, do" (Genesis 31:16).

Those who are only sort of committed may expect to only sort of receive the blessings of testimony, joy, and peace. The windows of heaven might only be sort of open to them. ("Brother, I'm Committed," *Ensign*, July, 2011, online)

Rachel's Faith

What the Book of Genesis Teaches Us

Genesis 30:1, 22 And when Rachel saw that she bare Jacob no children, Rachel envied her sister; and said unto Jacob, Give me children, or else I die.

And God remembered Rachel, and God hearkened to her, and opened her womb.

The Teachings of Inspired Church Leaders

Elder Wirthlin:

The Lord compensates the faithful for every loss. That which is taken away from those who love the Lord will be added unto them in His own way. While it may not come at the time we desire, the faithful will know that every tear today will eventually be returned a hundredfold with tears of rejoicing and gratitude. ("Come What May, and Love It," *Ensign*, Nov. 2008, 28)

The Twelve Sons of Jacob

What the Book of Genesis Teaches Us

Genesis 35:22–26 Now the sons of Jacob were twelve:

The sons of Leah; Reuben, Jacob's firstborn, and Simeon, and Levi, and Judah, and Isachar, and Zebulun:

The sons of Rachel; Joseph, and Benjamin:

And the sons of Bilhah, Rachel's handmaid; Dan, and Naphtali:

And the sons of Zilpah, Leah's handmaid; Gad, and Asher: these are the sons of Jacob, which were born to him in Padan-aram.

Genesis 49:1–2, 28 And Jacob called unto his sons, and said,

Gather yourselves together, that I may tell you that which shall befall you in the last days.

Gather yourselves together, and hear, ye sons of Jacob; and hearken unto Israel your father.

All these are the twelve tribes of Israel: and this is it that their father spake unto them, and blessed them; every one according to his blessing he blessed them.

What the Scriptures of the Restoration Teach Us

Jacob (Israel) blessing his sons is similar to Lehi's experience providing a blessing to all of his children after they arrived in the promised land, and the case of Alma blessing his sons. At the time Jacob (Israel) provided this blessing to his sons, not all were righteous men. The same can be said of Lehi's sons and Alma's sons when their fathers pled with them to be men of righteousness.

2 Nephi 4:12 And it came to pass after my father, Lehi, had spoken unto all his household, according to the feelings of his heart and the Spirit of the Lord which was in him, he waxed old. And it came to pass that he died, and was buried.

Alma 45:15 And now it came to pass that after Alma had said these things to Helaman, he blessed him, and also his other sons; and he also blessed the earth for the righteous' sake.

The Teachings of Inspired Church Leaders

President Brigham Young:

Who are Israel? They are those who are of the seed of Abraham, who received the promise through their forefathers; and all the rest of the children of men, who receive the truth, are also Israel. My heart is always drawn out for them, whenever I go to the throne of grace. (*Discourses of Brigham Young*, 437)

Many in the Christian world believe that when Israel is spoken of, it is only the Jewish nation. Little do they realize that those who accept the gospel and obey the covenants are also adopted into the house of Israel.

President Joseph Smith:

The Book of Mormon is a record of the forefathers of our western tribes of Indians; having been found through the ministration of an holy angel, and translated into our own language by the gift and power of God, after having been hid up in the earth for the last fourteen hundred years, containing the word of God which was delivered unto them. By it we learn that our western tribes of Indians are descendants from that Joseph who was sold into Egypt, and that the land of America is a promised land unto them, and unto it all the tribes of Israel will come, with as many of the Gentiles as shall comply with the requisitions of the new covenant. But the tribe of Judah will return to old Jerusalem. The city of Zion spoken of by David, in the one hundred and second Psalm, will be built upon the land of America. "And the ransomed of the Lord shall return, and come to Zion with songs and everlasting joy upon their heads." (*Teachings of the Prophet Joseph Smith*, 17)

Interesting Information

Some of the things we do in the Church is in honor to these twelve sons of Jacob (Israel). On August 2, 1831, Joseph Smith records the following event in *History of the Church*:

On the second day of August, I assisted the Colesville branch of the Church to lay the first log, for a house, as a foundation of Zion in Kaw township, twelve miles west of Independence. The log was carried and placed by twelve men, in honor of the twelve tribes of Israel. At the same time, through prayer, the land of Zion was consecrated and dedicated by Elder Sidney Rigdon for the gathering of the Saints. It was a season of joy to those present, and afforded a glimpse of the future, which time will yet unfold to the satisfaction of the faithful. (In *History of the Church*, 1:196)

I listened with interest as a brother spoke in sacrament meeting. He told of a nonmember friend who owned a contracting business and was working in one of our temples. One day, while the two of them were conversing, the contractor asked his LDS friend why we had cattle in our temple. It was a missionary moment where the member could explain the significance of the twelve oxen, and the fact that each one represents one of the twelve sons of Jacob. Incidentally, this carries over from the baptismal font in Solomon's temple, which also was supported on the backs of twelve oxen.

This symbolism carries into the life of Christ with him choosing twelve apostles. That same tradition is mirrored with the Church in this dispensation having twelve apostles.

Joseph

Joseph's Coat

What the Book of Genesis Teaches Us

Genesis 37:28–32 Then there passed by Midianites merchantmen; and they drew and lifted up Joseph out of the pit, and sold Joseph to the Ishmeelites for twenty pieces of silver: and they brought Joseph into Egypt.

And Reuben returned unto the pit; and, behold, Joseph was not in the pit; and he rent his clothes.

And he returned unto his brethren, and said, The child is not; and I, whither shall I go?

And they took Joseph's coat, and killed a kid of the goats, and dipped the coat in the blood;

And they sent the coat of many colours, and they brought it to their father; and said, This have we found: know now whether it be thy son's coat or no.

What the Scriptures of the Restoration Teach Us

Alma 46:24 Yea, let us preserve our liberty as a remnant of Joseph; yea, let us remember the words of Jacob, before his death, for behold, he saw that a part of the remnant of the coat of Joseph was preserved and had not decayed. And he said—Even as this remnant of garment of my son hath been preserved, so shall a remnant of the seed of my son be preserved by the hand of God, and be taken unto himself, which the remainder of the seed of Joseph shall perish, even as the remnant of his garment.

Joseph Sold into Egypt

What the Book of Genesis Teaches Us

Genesis 39:1–2 And Joseph was brought down to Egypt; and Potiphar, an officer of Pharaoh, captain of the guard, an Egyptian, bought him of the hands of the Ishmeelites, which had brought him down thither.

And the Lord was with Joseph, and he was prosperous man; and he was in the house of his master the Egyptian.

The Teachings of Inspired Church Leaders

Elder Hartman Rector Jr.:

This ability to turn everything into something good appears to be a godly characteristic. Our Heavenly Father always seems able to do this. Everything, no matter how dire, becomes a victory to the Lord. Joseph, although a slave and wholly undeserving of this fate, nevertheless remained faithful to the Lord and continued to live the commandments and made something very good of his degrading circumstances. People like this cannot be defeated, because they will not give up. They have the correct, positive attitude, and Dale Carnegie's expression seems to apply: If you feel you have a lemon, you can either complain about how sour it is, or you can make a lemonade. It is all up to you. ("Live above the Law to Be Free," *Ensign*, Jan. 1973, 130)

The Temptation of Joseph

What the Book of Genesis Teaches Us

Genesis 39:7–9 And it came to pass after these things, that his master's wife cast her eyes upon Joseph; and she said, Lie with me.

But he refused, and said unto his master's wife, Behold, my master wotteth not what is with me in the house, and he hath committed all that he hath to my hand;

There is none greater in this house than I; neither hath he kept back any thing from me but thee, because thou art his wife: how then can I do this great wickedness, and sin against God?

The Teachings of Inspired Church Leaders

President Brigham Young said, "The sooner an individual resists temptation to do, say, or think wrong, while he has light to correct his judgment, the quicker he will gain strength and power to overcome every temptation to evil" (*Discourses of Brigham Young*, 266).

Joseph Interprets the Dreams of Pharaoh's officers' and Pharaoh

What the Book of Genesis Teaches Us

Genesis 40: 6–8 And Joseph came in unto them in the morning, and looked upon them, and, behold, they were sad.

And he asked Pharaoh's officers that were with him in the ward of his lord's house, saying, Wherefore look ye so sadly today?

And they said unto him, We have dreamed a dream, and there is no interpreter of it. And Joseph said unto them, Do not interpretations belong to God? Tell me them, I pray you.

Then Pharaoh has a dream which requires interpretation. Of course, we know that Joseph is able to provide the interpretation; however, Joseph is quick to acknowledge God's hand in the interpretation when he states in **Genesis 41: 16**, "It is not in me: God shall give Pharaoh an answer of peace."

What the Scriptures of the Restoration Teach Us

Alma 26: 35 Now have we not reason to rejoice? Yea, I say unto you, there never were men that had so great reason to rejoice as we, since the world began; yea, and my joy is carried away, even unto boasting in my God; for he has all power, all wisdom, and all understanding; he comprehendeth all things, and he is a merciful Being, even unto salvation, to those who will repent and believe on his name.

D&C 6:23 Did I not speak peace to your mind concerning the matter? What greater witness can you have than from God?

I believe Joseph's ability to interpret dreams was a direct relationship with his belief in the power of his God. He humbly accepted his circumstances, even if those circumstances meant the unsanitary conditions of an Egyptian jail, and willingly submitted to his Father and his commandments. By doing that which was right, Joseph gained power and confidence.

Joseph the fruitful bough

What the Book of Genesis Teaches Us

Genesis 49:22–26 Joseph is a fruitful bough, even a fruitful bough by a well; whose branches run over the wall:

The archers have sorely grieved him, and shot at him, and hated him:

But his bow abode in strength, and the arms of his hands were made strong by the hands of the mighty God of Jacob; (from thence is the shepherd, the stone of Israel:)

Even by the God of thy father, who shall help thee; and by the

Almighty, who shall bless thee with blessings of heaven above, blessings of the deep that lieth under, blessings of the breasts, and of the womb:

The blessings of thy father have prevailed above the blessings of my progenitors unto the utmost bound of the everlasting hills: they shall be on the head of Joseph and on the crown of the head of him that was separate from his brethren.

What the Scriptures of the Restoration Teach Us

2 Nephi 3:5–8, 11–16 Wherefore, Joseph truly saw our day. And he obtained a promise of the Lord, that out of the fruit of his loins the Lord God would raise up a righteous branch unto the house of Israel; not the Messiah, but a branch which was to be broken off, nevertheless, to be remembered in the covenants of the Lord that the Messiah should be made manifest unto them in the latter days, in the spirit of power, unto the bringing of them out of darkness unto light—yea, out of hidden darkness and out of captivity unto freedom.

For Joseph truly testified, saying: A seer shall the Lord my God raise; up, who shall be a choice seer unto the fruit of my loins.

Yea, Joseph truly said: Thus saith the Lord unto me: A choice seer will I raise up out of the fruit of thy loins; and he shall be esteemed highly among the fruit of thy loins. And unto him will I give commandment that he shall do a work for the fruit of thy loins, his brethren, which shall be of great worth unto them, even to the bringing of them to the knowledge of the covenants which I have made with thy fathers.

And I will give unto him a commandment that he shall do none other work, save the work which I shall command him. And I will make him great in mine eyes; for he shall do my work.

But a seer will I raise up out of the fruit of thy loins; and unto him will I give power to bring forth my word unto the seed of thy loins— and not to the bringing forth my word only, saith the Lord, but to the convincing them of my word, which shall have already gone forth among them.

Wherefore, the fruit of thy loins shall write; and the fruit of the loins of Judah shall write; and that which shall be written by the fruit of thy loins, and also that which shall be written by the fruit of the loins of Judah, shall grow together, unto the confounding of false doctrines and laying down of contentions, and establishing peace among the fruit of thy loins, and bringing them to the knowledge of their fathers in the latter days, and also to the knowledge of my covenants, said the Lord.

And out of weakness he shall be made strong, in that day when my work shall commence among all my people, unto the restoring thee, O house of Israel, saith the Lord.

And thus prophesied Joseph, saying: Behold that seer will the Lord bless; and they that seek to destroy him shall be confounded; for this promise, which I have obtained of the Lord, of the fruit of my loins, shall be fulfilled. Behold, I am sure of the fulfilling of this promise;

And his name shall be called after me; and it shall be after the name of his father. And he shall be like unto me; for the thing, which the Lord shall bring forth by his hand, by the power of the Lord shall bring my people unto salvation.

Yea, thus prophesied Joseph: I am sure of this thing, even as I am sure of the promise of Moses; for the Lord hath said unto me, I will preserve thy seed forever.

The Teachings of Inspired Church Leaders

Elder Orson Pratt:

There are several things to be understood in the prophecy. First, he should become a multitude of nations. We understand what this means. In the second place, his branches should run over the wall. Now what does this mean? The Lord in ancient times had a meaning for everything. It means that his tribe should become so numerous that they would take up more room than one small inheritance in Canaan, that they would spread out and go to some land at a great distance. . . .

Joseph's peculiar blessing, which I have just read to you, was that he should enjoy possessions above Jacob's progenitors to the utmost bounds of the everlasting hills. This would seem to indicate a very distant land from Palestine. (In *Journal of Discourses*, 14:9)

Interesting Information

On December 9, 1834, Joseph Smith received a blessing from his father, Joseph Smith Sr.

I bless thee with the blessings of thy fathers Abraham, Isaac and Jacob; and even the blessings of thy fathers Joseph, the son of Jacob. Behold, he looked after his posterity in the last days. . . ; he sought diligently to know from whence the son should come who should bring forth the word of the Lord, by which they might be enlightened and brought back to the true fold, and his eyes beheld thee, my son; his heart rejoiced and his soul was satisfied, and he said, . . . "From among my seed, scattered with the Gentiles, shall a choice seer arise. . . , whose heart shall meditate great wisdom, whose intelligence shall circumscribe and comprehend the deep things of God, and whose mouth shall utter the law of the just." . . . Thou shalt hold the keys of this ministry, even the presidency of this church, both in time and in eternity. (Church Archives, Patriarchal Blessings)

Asael Smith, the paternal grandfather of Joseph Smith, Jr., made this statement years before Joseph was born:

"God was going to raise up some branch of his family to be a great benefit to mankind." Many years later when his son Joseph Smith, Sr., gave him a recently published Book of Mormon, he was vitally interested. George A. Smith [the nephew of Joseph Smith, Sr.] recorded, "My grandfather Asael fully believed the Book of Mormon, which he read nearly through." Asael died in the fall of 1830, confident that his grandson Joseph was the long-anticipated prophet and that he had heralded in a new religious age. (*Church History in the Fulness of Times Student Manual*, 2nd ed. [Church Educational System manual, 2003], 17)

Joseph Prophesies

What the Book of Genesis Teaches Us

Genesis 50:24 And Joseph said unto his brethren, I die: and God will surely visit you, and bring you out of this land unto the land which he sware to Abraham, to Isaac, and to Jacob.

What the Scriptures of the Restoration Teach Us

Joseph Smith Translation—Genesis 50:24 And Joseph said unto his brethren, I die, and go unto my fathers; and I go down to my grave with joy. The God of my father Jacob be with you, to deliver you out of affliction in the days of your bondage; for the Lord hath visited me, and I have obtained a promise of the Lord, that out of the fruit of my lions, the Lord God will raise up a righteous branch out of my loins; and unto thee, whom my father Jacob hath named Israel, a prophet; (not the Messiah who is called Shilo;) and this prophet shall deliver my people out of Egypt in the days of thy bondage.

Between verses 24 and 25, Joseph Smith, in his inspired revision of the Bible, added additional verses that help explain the role of the Prophet Joseph Smith:

Joseph Smith Translation—Genesis 50:25–35 And it shall come to pass that they shall be scattered again; and a branch shall be broken off, and shall be carried into a far country; nevertheless they shall be remembered in the covenants of the Lord, when the Messiah cometh; for he shall be made manifest unto them in the latter days, in the Spirit of power; and shall bring them out of darkness into light; out of hidden darkness, and out of captivity unto freedom.

A seer shall the Lord my God raise up, who shall be a choice seer [Joseph Smith] unto the fruit of my loins.

Thus saith the Lord God of my fathers unto me, A choice seer will I raise up out of the fruit of thy loins, and he shall be esteemed highly among the fruit of thy loins; and unto him will I give commandment that he shall do a work for the fruit of thy loins, his brethren.

And he shall bring them to the knowledge of the covenants which I have made with thy fathers; and he shall do whatsoever work I shall command him.

And I will make him great in mine eyes, for he shall do my work; and he shall be great like unto him whom I have said I would raise up unto you, to deliver my people, O house of Israel, out of the land of Egypt; for a seer will I raise up to deliver my people out of the land of Egypt; and he shall be called Moses. And by this name he shall know that he is of thy house; for he shall be nursed by the king's daughter, and shall be called her son.

And again, a seer will I raise up out of the fruit of thy loins, and unto him will I give power to bring forth my word unto the seed of thy loins; and not to the bringing forth of my word only, saith the Lord, but to the convincing them of my word, which shall have already gone forth among them in the last days;

Wherefore the fruit of thy loins shall write, and the fruit of the loins of Judah shall write; and that which shall be written by the fruit of thy loins, and also that which shall be written by the fruit of the loins of Judah, shall grow together unto the confounding of false doctrines, and laying down of contention, and establishing peace among the fruit of thy loins, and bringing them to a knowledge of their fathers in the latter days; and also to the knowledge of my covenants, saith the Lord.

And out of weakness shall he [Joseph Smith] be made strong, in that day when my work shall go forth among all my people, which shall restore them, who are of the house of Israel, in the last days.

And that seer will I bless, and they that seek to destroy him shall be confounded; for this promise I give unto you; for I will remember you from generation to generation; and his name shall be called Joseph, and it shall be after the name of his father [Joseph Smith Sr.]; and he shall be like unto you; for the thing which the Lord shall bring forth by his hand shall bring my people unto salvation.

And the Lord sware unto Joseph that he would preserve his seed for ever, saying, I will raise up Moses, and a rod shall be in his hand, and he shall gather together my people, and he shall lead them as a flock, and he shall smite the waters of the Red Sea with his rod.

And he shall have judgment, and shall write the word of the Lord. And he shall not speak many words, for I will write unto him my law by the finger of mine own hand. And I will make a spokesman for him, and his name shall be called Aaron.

Interesting Information

A blessing pronounced by Joseph Smith on Oliver Cowdery (Dec. 18, 1833) notes that Joseph of Egypt had seen Oliver in a vision and knew of his scribal role in translating the Book of Mormon. Oliver was also told that Joseph of Egypt knew that Oliver would be present when the Aaronic Priesthood, or lesser priesthood, was restored, and again when the Melchizedek Priesthood, or higher priesthood, was restored by messengers who received it from Jesus during his earthly ministry (Joseph F. Smith, "The Restoration of the Melchizedek Priesthood," *Improvement Era*, Oct. 1904, 943).

President Joseph Smith:

If there was anything great or good in the world, it came from God. The construction of the first vessel was given to Noah, by revelation. The design of the ark was given by God, 'a pattern of heavenly things.' The learning of the Egyptians, and their knowledge of astronomy was no doubt taught them by Abraham and Joseph, as their records testify, who received it from the Lord. (*Teachings of the Prophet Joseph Smith*, 251)

On July 6, 1835, Joseph Smith made this note:

Soon after this, some of the Saints at Kirtland purchased the mummies and papyrus, a description of which will appear hereafter, and with W. W. Phelps and Oliver Cowdery as scribes, I commenced the translation of some of the characters or hieroglyphics, and much to our joy found that one of the rolls contained the writings of Abraham, and another the writings of Joseph of Egypt, etc.—a more full account of which will appear in its place, as I proceed to examine or unfold them. Truly we can say, the Lord is beginning to reveal the abundance of peace and truth. (In *History of the Church*, 2:236)

Exodus

Egypt

What the Books of Genesis and Exodus Teach Us

Genesis 46:26–27 All the souls that came with Jacob into Egypt, which came out of his loins, besides Jacob's sons' wives, all the souls were threescore and six [66 individuals];

And the sons of Joseph, which were born him in Egypt, were two souls: all the souls of the house of Jacob, which came into Egypt, were threescore and ten [70 individuals].

Exodus 1:7 And the children of Israel were fruitful, and increased abundantly, and multiplied, and waxed exceeding mighty; and the land was filled with them.

Teachings from inspired Church Leaders

Elder Mark E. Petersen:

The fulfillment of God's promises to Abraham required that Israel should become numerous. To accomplish this, the little family, numbering only 70 persons, needed sufficient time and a peaceful place in which to grow. Egypt was that place. . . .

Palestine was a battleground for warring nations that moved back and forth in their conquests between the Nile and the Euphrates. Israel would have found no peace there. They required stable conditions for their eventual growth and development. . . .

Their bondage certainly was not all on the negative side. It too served a good propose. The cruelty of the taskmasters, the hatred that existed between the Hebrews and the Egyptians, and the length of their trying in servitude fused Jacob's children into a united people. . . .

The hatred they felt toward the Egyptians prevented intermarriage between the Hebrews and their neighbors. To reap the benefits of the Abrahamic promises, Israel had to remain a pure race, and the Lord used this means to achieve it. . . .

Yes, Egypt had her role in the Lord's mighty drama, and she played it well.

At the end of 430 years, the Lord now decreed that the time had arrived for Israel to occupy her own land and there become that "peculiar people" who would await the coming of their Messiah. (*Moses: Man of Miracles* [1978], 27–30)

The New King and the Israelites

What the Book of Exodus Teaches Us

Exodus 1:8 Now there arose up a new king over Egypt, which knew not Joseph.

Interesting Information

Joseph was second in command only to Pharaoh in all of Egypt. **Genesis 41:39–41** states the following:

And Pharaoh said unto Joseph, Forasmuch as God hath shewed thee all this, there is none so discreet and wise as thou art:

Thou shalt be over my house, and according unto thy word shall all my people be ruled: only in the throne will I be greater than thou.

And Pharaoh said unto Joseph, See, I have set thee over all the land of Egypt.

Verse 8 in the first chapter of Exodus makes little sense. If Joseph was that high in power in Egypt, if he actually wielded that much influence, why would there be a Pharaoh "which knew not Joseph"? I'm sure there may have been monuments erected to the Joseph who saved Egypt from seven years of famine. If not monuments, then most definitely his name would be found in at least one scroll of recorded history. To find an answer to this inquiry, we must study the words of scholars who believe that Joseph rose to prominence while the Hyksos people ruled the land of Egypt. These people were not native Egyptian, but rather a Semitic people who came from the north and east of Egypt. Because they were "foreigners," they were hated by the native Egyptians. There were definite similarities between Joseph's ancestry and these Semitic nomads. It becomes clear why Joseph found favor in the eyes of the ruling Pharaoh, and it is also easy to understand why his name, along with any of the other hated Hyksos rulers, was defaced or blotted from past history once the native Egyptians gained control over their own lands (*Old Testament Student Manual: Genesis–2 Samuel*, 3rd ed. [Church Educational System manual, 2003], 103).

Moses

What the Book of Exodus Teaches Us

It is through these next few verses, coupled with the scriptures of the restoration, that we begin to understand how Moses received his priesthood authority. After Moses flees Egypt and the ire of Pharaoh, Moses travels to the land of Midian. Moses helps the priest of Midian's seven daughters save the sheep from intruders. Not only does Moses save the sheep, but he also helps water them.

> **Exodus 2:18** And when they came to Reuel their father, he said, How is it that ye are come so soon to day?

Who is Reuel? If you notice in this scripture, there is a footnote on the name Reuel directing us to read **Exodus 3:1**:

> Now Moses kept the flock of Jethro his father in law, the priest of Midian: and he led the flock to the backside of the desert, and came to the mountain of God, even to Horeb.

What the Scriptures of the Restoration Teach Us

> **D&C 84:6–13** And the sons of Moses, according to the Holy Priesthood which he received [the Melchizedek Priesthood] under the hand of his father-in-law, Jethro;
> > And Jethro received it under the hand of Caleb:
> > And Caleb received it under the hand of Elihu;
> > And Elihu under the hand of Jeremy;
> > And Jeremy under the hand of Gad;
> > And Gad under the hand of Esaias;

And Esaias received it under the hand of God.

Esaias also lived in the days of Abraham, and was blessed of him.

The Teachings of Inspired Church Leaders

President Joseph Smith:

The Priesthood is everlasting. The Savior, Moses, and Elias, gave the keys to Peter, James and John, on the mount when they were transfigured before him. The Priesthood is everlasting—without beginning of days or end of years; without father, mother, etc. If there is no change of ordinances there is no change of Priesthood. Wherever the ordinances of the Gospel are administered, there is the Priesthood. (*Teachings of the Prophet Joseph Smith*, sel. Joseph Fielding Smith [2002], 158)

What the Scriptures of the Restoration Teach Us

Not only did Moses appear to Peter, James, and John at the Mount of Transfiguration, but he also appeared to Joseph Smith and Oliver Cowdery in the Kirtland Temple on April 3, 1836:

D&C 110:11 After this vision closed, the heavens were again opened unto us; and Moses appeared before us, and committed unto us the keys of the gathering of Israel from the four parts of the earth, and the leading of the ten tribes from the land of the north.

The Teachings of Inspired Church Leaders

President John Taylor:

Moses, Elijah, Elias and many of the leading characters mentioned in the Scriptures, who had operated in the various dispensations, came and conferred upon Joseph the various keys, powers, rights, privileges and [permissions] which they enjoyed in their times. . . . Whatever of knowledge, of intelligence, of Priesthood, of powers, of revelation were conferred upon those men in the different ages, were again restored to the earth by the ministration and through the medium of those who held the holy priesthood of God in the different dispensations in which they lived. (*Deseret News: Semi-Weekly*, Apr. 18, 1882, 1)

The Lord's Covenant with the Children of Israel

What the Book of Exodus Teaches Us

Exodus 2:24 And God heard their groaning, and God remembered his covenant with Abraham, with Isaac, and with Jacob.

What the Scriptures of the Restoration Teach Us

Read carefully in the following verse the covenant that the Lord made with Abraham. Part of that blessing was to curse those who cursed the covenant people, just as Pharaoh was doing by holding the children of Israel in bondage.

Abraham 2:11 And I will bless them that bless thee, and curse them that curse thee; and in thee (that is, in thy Priesthood) and in thy seed (that is, thy Priesthood), for I give unto thee a promise that this right shall continue in thee, and in thy seed after thee (that is to say, the literal seed, or the seed of the body) shall all the families of the earth be blessed, even with the blessings of the Gospel, which are the blessings of salvation, even of life eternal.

Moses's Call

What the Book of Exodus Teaches Us

Exodus 3:2, 4–6, 11 And the angel of the Lord appeared unto him [Moses] in a flame of fire out of the midst of a bush: and he looked, and, behold, the bush burned with fire, and the bush was not consumed.

And when the Lord saw that he turned aside to see, God called unto him out of the midst of the bush, and said, Moses, Moses. And he said, Here am I.

And he said, Draw not nigh hither: put off thy shoes from off thy feet, for the place whereon thou standest is holy ground.

Moreover he said, I am the God of thy father, the God of Abraham, the God of Isaac, and the God of Jacob. And Moses hid his face; for he was afraid to look upon God.

And Moses said unto God, Who am I, that I should go unto Pharaoh, and that I should bring forth the children of Israel out of Egypt?

What the Scriptures of the Restoration Teach Us

> **Joseph Smith Translation—Exodus 3:2** And again, the presence of the Lord appeared unto him, in a flame of fire in the midst of a bush; and he looked, and, behold, the bush burned with fire, and the bush was not consumed.

The Teachings of Inspired Church Leaders

President Joseph Smith:

"Now," says God, when He visited Moses in the bush, (Moses was a stammering sort of a boy like me) God said, "Thou shalt be a God unto the children of Israel," God said, "Thou shalt be a God unto Aaron, and he shall be thy spokesman." I believe those Gods that God reveals as Gods to be sons of God, and all can cry, "Abba, Father!" Sons of God who exalt themselves to be Gods, even from before the foundation of the world, and are the only Gods I have a reverence for. (*Teachings of the Prophet Joseph Smith*, 375)

Moses's Tutorial with the Lord

What the Scriptures of the Restoration Teach Us

The Bible is silent on many of those things that Moses was taught by the Lord. We do know that he was taught the plan of salvation, as stated in the book of Moses:

> **Moses 1:37, 39** And the Lord God spake unto Moses, saying: The heavens, they are many, and they cannot be numbered unto man; but they are numbered unto me, for they are mine.
>
> For behold, this is my work and my glory—to bring to pass the immortality and eternal life of man.

I AM

What the Book of Exodus Teaches Us

> **Exodus 3:13–14** And Moses said unto God, Behold, when I come unto the children of Israel, and shall say unto them, The God of your fathers hath sent me unto you; and they say to me, What is his name? What shall I say unto them?

And God said unto Moses, I AM THAT I AM: and he said, Thus shalt thou say unto the children of Israel, I AM hath sent me unto you.

What the Scriptures of the Restoration Teach Us

Not only did the Lord use the name *I AM* in Old Testament times, but he also addressed himself to the Prophet Joseph Smith and six elders of the Church with the same title.

D&C 29:1 Listen to the voice of Jesus Christ, your Redeemer, the Great I AM, whose arm of mercy hath atoned for your sins.

Mouth of God

What the Book of Exodus Teaches Us

Exodus 4:27–31 And the Lord said to Aaron, Go into the wilderness to meet Moses. And he went, and met him in the mount of God, and kissed him.

And Moses told Aaron all the words of the Lord who had sent him, and all the signs which he had commanded him.

And Moses and Aaron went and gathered together all the elders of the children of Israel:

And Aaron spake all the words which the Lord had spoken unto Moses, and did the signs in the sight of the people.

And the people believed: and when they heard that the Lord had visited the children of Israel, and that he had looked upon their affliction, then they bowed their heads and worshipped.

The Teachings of Inspired Church Leaders

President Joseph Smith:

When Egypt was under the superintendence of Joseph it prospered, because he was taught of God; when they oppressed the Israelites, destruction came upon them. When the children of Israel were chosen with Moses at their head, they were to be a peculiar people, among whom God should place His name; their motto was: "The Lord is our lawgiver; the Lord is our Judge; the Lord is our King; and He shall reign over us." While in this state they might truly say, "Happy is that people whose God is the Lord." Their government was a theocracy; they had God to make their laws, and men chosen by Him to administer them;

He was their God, and they were His people. Moses received the word of the Lord from God Himself; he was the mouth of God to Aaron, and Aaron taught the people in both civil and ecclesiastical affairs; they were both one, there was no distinction; so will it be when the purposes of God shall be accomplished: when "the Lord shall be King over the whole earth" and "Jerusalem His throne." "The law shall go forth from Zion, and the word of the Lord from Jerusalem." (*Teachings of the Prophet Joseph Smith*, 252)

What the Book of Exodus Teaches Us

Exodus 7:1 And the Lord said unto Moses, See, I have made thee a god to Pharaoh: and Aaron thy brother shall be thy prophet.

What the Scriptures of the Restoration Teach Us

Joseph Smith Translation—Exodus 7:1 And the Lord said unto Moses, See, I have made thee a prophet to Pharaoh; and Aaron thy brother shall be thy spokesman.

Interesting Information

Elder Bruce R. McConkie makes this statement when speaking of Moses and Christ:

Of all the hosts of our Father's children, these two are singled out a being like each other. . . . But it appears there is a special image, a special similitude, a special likeness where the man Moses and the man Jesus are concerned. It is reasonable to suppose that this similarity, this resemblance, is both physical and spiritual; it is a likeness where both qualities and appearance are concerned. (*The Promised Messiah* [1978], 442)

Aaron

What the Book of Exodus Teaches Us

Exodus 40:12–15 And thou [Moses] shalt bring Aaron and his sons unto the door of the tabernacle of the congregation, and wash them with water.

And thou shalt put upon Aaron the holy garments, and anoint him, and sanctify him; that he may minister unto me in the priest's office.

And thou shalt bring his sons, and clothe them with coats:

And thou shalt anoint them, as thou didst anoint their father, that they may minister unto me in the priest's office: for their anointing shall surely be an everlasting priesthood throughout their generations.

What the Scriptures of the Restoration Teach Us

D&C 84:18, 33–34 And the Lord confirmed a priesthood also upon Aaron and his seed, throughout all their generations, which priesthood also continueth and abideth forever with the priesthood which is after the holiest order of God.

For whoso is faithful unto the obtaining these two priesthoods of which I have spoken, and the magnifying their calling, are sanctified by the Spirit unto the renewing of their bodies.

They become the sons of Moses and of Aaron and the seed of Abraham, and the church and kingdom, and the elect of God.

D&C 132:59 Verily, if a man be called of my Father, as was Aaron, by mine own voice, and by the voice of him that sent me, and I have endowed him with the keys of the power of this priesthood, if he do anything in my name, and according to my law and by my word, he will not commit sin, and I will justify him.

The Teachings of Inspired Church Leaders

"He [Aaron] held the Melchizedek Priesthood, but as chief priest of the lesser priesthood he served in a lesser position equivalent to that of the modern Presiding Bishop" (*Encyclopedia of Mormanism*, 5 vols. [1992], "Aaron, Brother of Moses," 1:5; see also John Taylor, *Items on the Priesthood* [1881], 5).

The Plagues

What the Book of Exodus Teaches Us

Exodus 7: 8–13 And the Lord spake unto Moses and unto Aaron, saying,

When Pharaoh shall speak unto you, saying, Shew a miracle for you: then thou shalt say unto Aaron, Take thy rod, and cast it before Pharaoh, and it shall become a serpent.

And Moses and Aaron went in unto Pharaoh, and they did so as the Lord had commanded: and Aaron cast down his rod before Pharaoh, and before his servants, and it became a serpent.

Then Pharaoh also called the wise men and the sorcerers: now the magicians of Egypt, they also did in like manner with their enchantments.

For they cast down every man his rod, and they became serpents: but Aaron's rod swallowed up their rods.

And he hardened Pharaoh's heart, that he hearkened not unto them; as the Lord had said.

The Teachings of Inspired Church Leaders

President Brigham Young:

As quick as I admit that the history Moses gives of himself is true, I cannot have any question in the world but what in ancient days they understood in a measure how to command the elements. The magicians of Egypt were instructed in things pertaining to true riches, and had obtained keys and powers enough to produce a bogus in opposition to the true coin, as it were, and thus they deceived the king and the people. They could cause frogs to come upon the land, as well as Moses could. They could turn the waters of Egypt into blood, and in many more things compete with Moses. There was one thing, however, they could not do, though they produced a very good bogus, but it was not quite the true coin. When they threw their staffs on the floor before the king, they could not swallow the staff of Moses, but the staff of Moses swallowed the staffs of the magicians. I have no doubt that men can perform many such wonders by the principles of natural philosophy. (In *Journal of Discourses*, 26 vols. [1854–86], 1:270)

What the Book of Exodus Teaches Us

Exodus 10:21–23 And the Lord said unto Moses, Stretch out thine hand toward heaven, that there may be darkness over the land of Egypt, even darkness which may be felt.

And Moses stretched forth his hand toward heaven; and there was a thick darkness in all the land of Egypt three days:

They saw not one another, neither rose any from his place for three days: but all the children of Israel had light in their dwellings.

What the Scriptures of the Restoration Teach Us

How reminiscent this is of the destruction in the new world subsequent to the crucifixion of the Savior and prior to his appearance in the Americas?

3 Nephi 8:20–23 And it came to pass that there was thick darkness upon all the face of the land, insomuch that the inhabitants thereof who had not fallen could feel the vapor of darkness;

And there could be no light, because of the darkness, neither candles, neither torches; neither could there be fire kindled with their fine and exceedingly dry wood, so that there could not be any light at all;

And there was not any light seen, neither fire, nor glimmer, neither the sun, nor the moon, nor the stars, for so great were the mists of darkness which were upon the face of the land.

And it came to pass that it did last for the space of three days that there was no light seen; and there was great mourning and howling and weeping among all the people continually; yea, great were the groanings of the people, because of the darkness and the great destruction which had come upon them.

Zion has been warned that if she does not follow the Lord she too can expect the vengeance of God on her in the form of plagues.

D&C 97:25–26 Nevertheless, Zion shall escape if she observe to do all things whatsoever I have commanded her.

But if she observe not to do whatsoever I have commanded her, I will visit her according to all her works, with sore affliction, with pestilence, with plague, with sword, with vengeance, with devouring fire.

The Passover

What the Book of Exodus Teaches Us

As a way of signifying that the Lord saved the first born in the families of the children of Israel and destroyed the same in the families of the Egyptians, the Lord instituted the Passover.

Exodus 12:14–15, 43, 48 And this day shall be unto you for a memorial; and ye shall keep it a feast to the Lord throughout your generations; ye shall keep it a feast by an ordinance for ever.

Seven days shall ye eat unleavened bread; even the first day ye shall put away leaven out of your houses: for whosoever eateth leavened bread from the first day until the seventh day, that soul shall be cut off from Israel.

And the Lord said unto Moses and Aaron, This is the ordinance of the Passover: There shall no stranger eat thereof:

And when a stranger shall sojourn with thee, and will keep the Passover to the Lord, let all his males be circumcised, and then let him come near and keep it; and he shall be as one that is born in the land: for no uncircumcised person shall eat thereof.

What the Scriptures of the Restoration Teach Us

When Jesus Christ visited the inhabitants in the Americas, he taught the following:

3 Nephi 18:28–32 And now behold, this is the commandment which I give unto you, that ye shall not suffer any one knowingly to partake of my flesh and blood unworthily, when ye shall minister it;

For whoso eateth and drinketh my flesh and blood unworthily eateth and drinketh damnation to his soul; therefore if ye know that a man is unworthy to eat and drink of my flesh and blood ye shall forbid him.

Nevertheless, ye shall not cast him out from among you, but ye shall minister unto him and shall pray for him unto the Father, in my name; and if it so be that he repenteth and is baptized in my name, then shall ye receive him, and shall minister unto him of my flesh and blood.

But if he repent not he shall not be numbered among my people, that he may not destroy my people, for behold I know my sheep, and they are numbered.

Nevertheless, ye shall not cast him out of your synagogues, or your places of worship, for unto such shall ye continue to minister; for ye know not but what they will return and repent, and come unto me with full purpose of heart, and I shall heal them; and ye shall be the means of bringing salvation unto them.

The Teachings of Inspired Church Leaders

Elder Bruce R. McConkie:

As to the eating the flesh of the sacrificial lamb, the divine word was, "No uncircumcised person shall eat thereof," signifying that the blessings of the gospel are reserved for those who come into the fold of Israel, who join the Church, who carry their part of the burden in bearing off the kingdom; signifying also that those who eat his flesh and drink his blood, as he said, shall have eternal life and he will raise them up at the last day. (*The Promised Messiah* [1978], 430)

What the Book of Exodus Teaches Us

Exodus 13:1–2, 11–15 And the Lord spake unto Moses, saying,

Sanctify unto me all the firstborn, whatsoever openeth the womb among the children of Israel, both of man and of beast: it is mine.

And it shall be when the Lord shall bring thee into the land of the Canaanites, as he sware unto thee and to thy fathers, and shall give it thee,

That thou shalt set apart unto the Lord all that openeth the matrix, and every firstling that cometh of a beast which thou hast; the males shall be the Lord's.

And every firstling of an ass thou shalt redeem with a lamb; and if thou wilt not redeem it, then thou shalt break his neck: and all the firstborn of man among thy children shalt thou redeem.

And it shall be when thy son asketh thee in time to come, saying, What is this? That thou shalt say unto him, By strength of hand the Lord brought us out from Egypt, from the house of bondage:

And it came to pass, when Pharaoh would hardly let us go, that the Lord slew all the firstborn in the land of Egypt, both the firstborn of man, and the first born of beast: therefore I sacrifice to the Lord all that openeth the matrix, being males; but all the firstborn of my children I redeem.

The Teachings of Inspired Church Leaders

President John Taylor:

Again, the Lord, through the sprinkling of the blood of a lamb on the door-posts of the Israelites, having saved the lives of all the first-born of Israel, made a claim upon them for their services in His cause. . .

But the first-born of the Egyptians, for whom no lamb as a token of the propitiation was offered, were destroyed. It was through the propitiation and atonement alone that the Israelites were saved, and under the circumstances they must have perished with the Egyptians, who were doomed, had it not been for the contemplated atonement and propitiation of Christ, of which this was a figure.

Hence the Lord claimed those that He saved as righteously belonging to Him, and claiming them as His He demanded their services; but afterwards, as shown in [Numbers 3:12–13]; He accepted the tribe of Levi in lieu of the first-born of Israel; and as there were more of the first-born than there were of the Levites, the balance had to be redeemed with money, which was given to Aaron, as the great High Priest and representative of the Aaronic Priesthood, he being also a Levite. (*The Mediation and Atonement* [1882], 108)

The Exodus

What the Book of Exodus Teaches Us

Exodus 13:3 And Moses said unto the people, Remember this day, in which ye came out from Egypt, out of the house of bondage; for by strength of hand the Lord brought you out from this place: there shall no leavened bread be eaten.

What the Scriptures of the Restoration Teach Us

The exodus of the children of Israel is comparable to the exodus of the Saints. Both were a persecuted people. Both had to leave where they were living to develop a society where they could worship the Lord their God in peace, where they could grow and prosper. Just as the Lord delivered the children of Israel, so too he delivered the Saints.

D&C 84:119 For I, the Lord, have put forth my hand to exert the powers of heaven; ye cannot see it now, yet a little while and ye shall see it, and know that I am, and that I will come and reign with my people.

The Teachings of Inspired Church Leaders

President Joseph F. Smith:

While listening to the brethren this afternoon I was led to reflect upon some of our friends who have passed away. When we look back and think of President Young, Heber C. Kimball, Willard Richards, George A. Smith, Orson Pratt, Parley Pratt, President John Taylor, Erastus Snow, and the thousands of faithful, valiant Saints of God who passed through the persecutions in Ohio, in Missouri, and in Illinois, and were driven from their homes time and time and time again, and finally out into the wilderness, with no knowledge, except the promises of the Holy Spirit in their hearts, that they would ever find a resting place for their weary feet—driven from their homes, their kindred, and their friends with the dimmest prospect in the world, so far as human knowledge or prescience was concerned, of ever reaching a haven of rest, but trudging across the plains with weary step, yet with unshaken confidence in God and unwavering faith in His word—when we look back and think of those scenes we cannot forget the faithful men and women who passed through them. They did not faint by the way; they did not backslide; they did not turn from the truth. The harder the trial, the more difficult the journey, the greater the obstacles, the more firm and determined they were. (*Deseret News: Semi-Weekly*, 9 Aug. 1898, 1.)

What the Book of Exodus Teaches Us

Exodus 14:10, 13, 21–22 And when Pharaoh drew nigh, the children of Israel lifted up their eyes, and, behold, the Egyptians marched after them; and they were sore afraid: and the children of Israel cried out unto the Lord.

And Moses said unto the people, Fear ye not, stand still, and see the salvation of the Lord, which he will shew to you to day: for the Egyptians whom ye have seen to day, ye shall see them again no more for ever.

And Moses stretched out his hand over the sea; and the Lord caused the sea to go back by a strong east wind all that night, and made the sea dry land, and the waters were divided.

And the children of Israel went into the midst of the sea upon the dry ground: and the waters were a wall unto them on their right hand, and on their left.

What the Scriptures of the Restoration Teach Us

It is not uncommon for the less spiritually enlightened to dismiss such miracles as the parting of the Red Sea as a myth or fable. Those with faith are able to comprehend that God is a God of miracles, and as such chooses to bless his believing children with phenomenon that strengthens their faith. Nephi did not have any problem accepting the story of Moses and the Red Sea.

1 Nephi 4:2 Therefore let us go up; let us be strong like unto Moses; for he truly spake unto the waters of the Red Sea and they divided hither and thither, and our fathers came through, out of captivity, on dry ground, and the armies of Pharaoh did follow and were drowned in the waters of the Red Sea.

1 Nephi 17:24–26 Yea, do ye suppose that they would have been led out of bondage, if the Lord had not commanded Moses that he should lead them out of bondage?

Now ye know that the children of Israel were in bondage; and ye know that they were laden with tasks, which were grievous to be borne;

wherefore, ye know that it must needs be a good thing for them, that they should be brought out of bondage.

Now ye know that Moses was commanded of the Lord to do that great work; and ye know that by his word the waters of the Red Sea were divided hither and thither, and they passed through on dry ground.

What the Book of Exodus Teaches Us

Exodus 16:11–15 And the Lord spake unto Moses, saying,

I have heard the murmurings of the children of Israel: speak unto them, saying, At even ye shall eat flesh, and in the morning ye shall be filled with bread; and ye shall know that I am the Lord your God.

And it came to pass, that at even the quails came up, and covered the camp: and in the morning the dew lay round about the host.

And when the dew that lay was gone up, behold, upon the face of the wilderness there lay a small round thing, as small as the hoar frost on the ground.

And when the children of Israel saw it, they said one to another, It is manna: for they wist not what it was. And Moses said unto them, This is the bread which the Lord hath given you to eat.

The Teachings of Inspired Church Leaders

President Brigham Young:

Exactly thirty years today myself, with others, came out of what we named Emigration Canyon; we crossed the Big and Little mountains, and came down the valley about three quarters of a mile south of this. We located, and we looked about, and finally we came and camped between the two forks of City Creek, one of which ran southwest and the other west. Here we planted our standard on this temple block and the one above it; here we pitched our camps and determined that here we would settle and stop. Still our brethren who tarried by the way were toiling through poverty and distress. At one time, I was told, they would have perished from starvation, had not the Lord sent quails among them. These birds flew against their wagons, and they either killed or stunned themselves, and the brethren and sisters gathered them up, which furnished them with food for days, until they made their way in the wilderness. (In *Journal of Discourses*, 19:60)

Interesting Information

[July 14, 1841:] The following is translated from the Arabic, in the *Malta Times*—"Aleppo, 3rd May. A great famine has happened in Aleppo, Malitia, and Karbat, insomuch that many people died with hunger, and others sold their sons and daughters to get bread to eat. But the Almighty God rained upon them seed (manna), and fed them withal." "Of the veracity of these words," adds the *Malta Times*, "extracted from an Arabic letter, we are perfectly satisfied. The seed alluded to is known in Malta, being nearly like 'hab' or 'dazz,' and which being kept a little while becomes white, like 'semola' (very fine wheaten flour)." (In *History of the Church*, ed. B. H. Roberts [1932–51], 4:383)

[September 1, 1841:] The *New York Sun* contains an account of some singular phenomena; viz., a shower of flesh and blood, a pillar of smoke, and a shower of manna. (In *History of the Church*, 4:414)

What the Book of Exodus Teaches Us

Exodus 17:5–6 And the Lord said unto Moses, Go on before the people, and take with thee of the elders of Israel; and thy rod, wherewith thou smotest the river, take in thine hand, and go.

Behold, I will stand before thee there upon the rock in Horeb; and thou shalt smith the rock, and there shall come water out if it, that the people may drink. And Moses did so in the sight of the elders of Israel.

What the Scriptures of the Restoration Teach Us

Just as the water that the Lord provided for the Children of Israel in the wilderness gave and sustained life, so too, these waters are a representation of the water of life that is spoken of in latter-day scripture.

1 Nephi 11:25 And it came to pass that I beheld that the rod of iron, which my father had seen, was the word of God, which led to the fountain of living waters, or to the tree of life; which waters are a representation of the love of God; and I also beheld that the tree of life was a representation of the love of God.

D&C 63:23 But unto him that keepeth my commandments I will give the mysteries of my kingdom, and the same shall be in him a well of living water, springing up unto everlasting life.

What the Book of Exodus Teaches Us

Exodus 17:8–13 Then came Amalek, and fought with Israel in Rephidim.

And Moses said unto Joshua, Choose us out men, and go out, fight with Amalek: to morrow I will stand on the top of the hill with the rod of God in mine hand.

So Joshua did as Moses had said to him, and fought with Amalek: and Moses, Aaron, and Hur went up to the top of the hill.

And it came to pass, when Moses held up his hand, that Israel prevailed: and when he let down his hand, Amalek prevailed.

But Moses' hands were heavy; and they took a stone, and put it under him, and he sat thereon; and Aaron and Hur stayed up his hands, the one on the one side, and the other on the other side; and his hands were steady until the going down of the sun.

And Joshua discomfited Amalek and his people with the edge of the sword.

The Teachings of Inspired Church Leaders

President George Albert Smith:

When Moses led Israel from Egypt through the wilderness and into the promised land; Amalek attacked Israel at Rephidim. Moses directed Joshua to choose fighting men to protect Israel. Moses, Aaron, and Hur went to the top of a hill overlooking the battlefield. While Moses held the rod of God above his head, Israel prevailed, but when he let his hands down because of weakness, Amalek prevailed. A stone seat was provided and Aaron and [Hur] held up his hands in order that the blessings of God could flow to Israel that their warriors might prevail and the battle was won (EX. 17:8–13). The power of God was upon Moses and remained with him until he had finished his work. When he had the support of his people they too were blessed, and so it has been with every servant of the Lord who has presided over Israel. . . .

Just as long as [the president] presides over this Church, it matters not how many years it will be, our Heavenly Father will give him strength, power, wisdom, judgment, and inspiration to talk to Israel as they need to be talked to. We, in following his leadership, must be like Aaron and Hur of ancient times; we must uphold his hands, that through him the Lord will let the blessings of heaven descend on us and this people. (In Conference Report, Apr. 1942, 14)

What the Book of Exodus Teaches Us

Exodus 32:1 And when the people saw that Moses delayed to come down out of the mount, the people gathered themselves together unto Aaron, and said unto him, Up, make us gods, which shall go before us; for as for this Moses, the man that brought us up out of the land of Egypt, we wot not what is become of him.

The Teachings of Inspired Church Leaders

President Brigham Young said, "If they had been sanctified and holy, the children of Israel would not have traveled one year with Moses before they would have received their endowments and the Melchizedek Priesthood" (*Discourses of Brigham Young*, comp. John A. Widtsoe [1954], 106).

The Ten Commandments

What the Book of Exodus Teaches Us

Exodus 20:1–6 And God spake all these words, saying,
I am the Lord thy God, which have brought thee out of the land of Egypt, out of the house of bondage.
Thou shalt have no other gods before me.
Thou shalt not make unto thee any graven image, or any likeness of any thing that is in heaven above, or that is in the earth beneath, or that is in the water under the earth:
Thou shalt not bow down thyself to them, nor serve them: for I the Lord thy God am a jealous God, visiting the iniquity of the fathers upon the children unto the third and fourth generation of them that hate me;
And shewing mercy unto thousands of them that love me, and keep my commandments.

What the Scriptures of the Restoration Teach Us

D&C 1:14–16 And the arm of the Lord shall be revealed; and the day cometh that they who will not hear the voice of the Lord, neither the voice of his servants, neither give heed of his servants, neither give heed to the words of the prophets and apostles, shall be cut off from among the people;
For they have strayed from mine ordinances, and have broken mine everlasting covenant;

They seek not the Lord to establish his righteousness, but every man walketh in his own way, and after the image of his own god, whose image is in the likeness of the world, and whose substance is that of an idol, which waxeth old and shall perish in Babylon, even Babylon the great, which shall fall.

Ether 7:23–26 And also in the reign of Shule there came prophets among the people, who were sent from the Lord, prophesying that the wickedness and idolatry of the people was bringing a curse upon the land, and they should be destroyed if they did not repent.

And it came to pass that the people did revile against the prophets, and did mock them. And it came to pass that king Shule did execute judgment against all those who did revile against the prophets.

And he did execute a law throughout all the land, which gave power unto the prophets that they should go whithersoever they would; and by this cause the people were brought unto repentance.

And because the people did repent of their iniquities and idolatries the Lord did spare them, and they began to prosper again in the land. And it came to pass that Shule begat sons and daughters in his old age.

2 Nephi 9:36–37 Wo unto them who commit whoredoms, for they shall be thrust down to hell.

Yea, wo unto those that worship idols, for the devil of all devils delighteth in them.

The Teachings of Inspired Church Leaders

President Brigham Young:

Every son and daughter of God is expected to obey with a willing heart every word which the Lord has spoken, and which He will in the future speak to us. It is expected that we hearken to the revelations of His will, and adhere to them, cleave to them with all our might; for this is salvation, and anything short of this clips the salvation and the glory of the Saints. (In *Journal of Discourses*, 2:2)

What the Book of Exodus Teaches Us

Exodus 20:12 Honour thy father and thy mother: that thy days may be long upon the land which the Lord thy God giveth thee.

What the Scriptures of the Restoration Teach Us

1 Nephi 17:55 And now, they said: We know of a surety that the Lord is with thee, for we know that it is the power of the Lord that has shaken us. And they fell down before me, and were about to worship me, but I would not suffer them, saying: I am thy brother, yea, even thy younger brother; wherefore, worship the Lord thy God, and honor thy father and thy mother, that thy days may be long in the land which the Lord thy God shall give thee.

The Teachings of Inspired Church Leaders

President Brigham Young said, "Obedience is one of the plainest, most everyday and home principles that you ever thought or knew anything about. In the first place, learn that you have a father, and then learn strict obedience to that parent. Is not that a plain, domestic, home principle?" (In *Journal of Discourses*, 6:173).

What the Book of Exodus Teaches Us

Exodus 20:8–11 Remember the sabbath day, to keep it holy.
Six days shalt thou labour, and do all thy work:
But the seventh day is the sabbath of the Lord thy God: in it thou shalt not do any work, thou, nor thy son, nor thy daughter, thy manservant, nor thy maidservant, nor thy cattle, nor thy stranger that is within thy gates:
For in six days the Lord made heaven and earth, the sea, and all that in them is, and rested the seventh day: wherefore the Lord blessed the sabbath day, and hallowed it.

What the Scriptures of the Restoration Teach Us

Moses 3:3 And I, God, blessed the seventh day, and sanctified it; because that in it I had rested from all my work which I, God, had created and made.

D&C 77:12 Q. What are we to understand by the sounding of the trumpets, mentioned in the 8th chapter of Revelation?
A. We are to understand that as God made the world in six days, and on the seventh day he finished his work, and sanctified it.

The Teachings of Inspired Church Leaders

President Brigham Young:

You take this Book [the book of Doctrine and Covenants] and you will read here that the Saints are to meet together on the Sabbath day. It is what we call the first day of the week. No matter whether it is the Jewish Sabbath or not. I do not think there is anybody who can bring facts to prove which is the seventh day, or when Adam was put in the garden, or the day about which the Lord spoke to Moses. This matter is not very well known, so we call the day on which we rest and worship God, the first day of the week. This people called Latter-day Saints, are required by the revelations that the Lord has given, to assemble themselves together on this day. . . . In this commandment we are required to come together and repent of our sins and confess our sins and partake of the bread and of the wine; or water, in commemoration of the death and sufferings of our Lord and Savior. (In *Journal of Discourses*, 16:168)

Interesting Information

Since its beginning, the LDS Church has observed the Sabbath on the first, rather than the seventh, day of the week ([apart] for some exceptions in the Middle East). . . .

For many years, following the organization of the Sunday School in 1849, Sabbath services consisted of Sunday school in the morning and sacrament meeting in the afternoon or early evening. Weekly ward Priesthood meetings were held on Monday evenings, and fast and testimony meeting on the first Thursday of each month. In 1896, fast day was changed to the first Sunday to make attendance more convenient and not disruptive to members in their employment; in the 1930s, priesthood meeting was changed to Sunday mornings. (*Encyclopedia of Mormanism*, 5 vols. [1992], "Sabbath Day," 1241–42)

What the Book of Exodus Teaches Us

Exodus 20:17 Thou shalt not covet thy neighbour's house, thou shalt not covet thy neighbour's wife, nor his manservant, nor his maidservant, nor his ox, nor his ass, nor any thing that is thy neighbour's.

The Teachings of Inspired Church Leaders

President Brigham Young:

There is too much covetousness in the church, and too much disposition amongst the brethren to seek after power and has been from the beginning, but this feeling is diminishing and the brethren begin to know better. In consequence of such feelings Joseph [Smith] left the people in the dark on many subjects of importance and they still remain in the dark. We have got to rid such principles from our hearts. (In *History of the Church*, 7:545)

President Brigham Young also stated the following:

Some of you may ask, "Is there a single ordinance to be dispensed with? Is there one of the commandments that God has enjoined upon the people, that he will excuse them from obeying?" Not one, no matter how trifling or small in our own estimation. No matter if we esteem them non-essential, or least or last of all the commandments of the house of God, we are under obligation to observe them. (In *Journal of Discourses*, 8:339)

President Joseph Smith:

From what has already been introduced as testimony to prove that no man can be saved without baptism, it will be seen and acknowledged that if there was sin among men, repentance was as necessary at one time or age of the world as another—and that other foundation can no man lay than that is laid, which is Jesus Christ. If, then, Abel was a righteous man he had to become so by keeping the commandments; if Enoch was righteous enough to come into the presence of God and walk with him, he must have become so by keeping his commandments, and so of every righteous person, whether it was Noah, a preacher of righteousness; Abraham, the father of the faithful; Jacob, the prevailer with God; Moses, the man who wrote of Christ, and brought forth the law by commandment, as a schoolmaster to bring men to Christ, or whether it was Jesus Christ himself, who had no need of repentance, having no sin, according to his solemn declaration to John:—now let me be baptized: for no man can enter the kingdom without obeying this ordinance: for thus it becometh us to fulfill ALL RIGHTEOUSNESS. Surely, then, if it became John and Jesus Christ, the Savior, to fulfil all righteousness to be baptized—so surely, then, it will become every other person that seeks the kingdom of heaven to go and do likewise: for he the door, and if any person climbs up any other way, the same is a thief and a robber!" (*Teachings of the Prophet Joseph Smith*, 265–66).

The Mosaic Law

What the Book of Exodus Teaches Us

Exodus 24:3 And Moses came and told the people all the words of the Lord, and all the judgments: and all the people answered with one voice, and said, All the words which the Lord hath said will we do.

What the Scriptures of the Restoration Teach Us

Jacob 4:5 Behold, they believed in Christ and worshiped the Father in his name, and also we worship the Father in his name. And for this intent we keep the law of Moses, it pointing our souls to him; and for this cause it is sanctified unto us for righteousness, even as it was accounted unto Abraham in the wilderness to be obedient unto the commands of God in offering up his son Isaac, which is a similitude of God and his Only Begotten Son.

D&C 84:26–27 And the lesser priesthood continued, which priesthood holdeth the key of the ministering of angels and the preparatory gospel;

Which gospel is the gospel of repentance and of baptism, and the remission of sins, and the law of carnal commandments, which the Lord in his wrath caused to continue with the house of Aaron among the children of Israel until John, whom God raised up, being filled with the Holy Ghost from his mother's womb.

The Teachings of Inspired Church Leaders

President Brigham Young:

The Gospel was among the children of men from the days of Adam until the coming of the Messiah; this Gospel of Christ is from the beginning to the end. Then why was the law of Moses given? In consequence of the disobedience of the Children of Israel, the elect of God; the very seed that he had selected to be his people, and upon whom he said he would place his name. This seed of Abraham so rebelled against him and his commands that the Lord said to Moses, "I will give you a law which shall be a schoolmaster to bring them to Christ." But this law is grievous; it is a law of carnal commandments. (*Discourses of Brigham Young*, 104)

President Joseph Smith:

We find also, that when the Israelites came out of Egypt they had the Gospel preached to them, according to Paul in his letter to the Hebrews, which says: "For unto us was the Gospel preached, as well as unto them: but the word preached did not profit them, not being mixed with faith in them that heard it" (see Hebrews 4:2). It is said again, in Gal. 3:19, that the law (of Moses, or the Levitical law) was "added" because of transgression. What, we ask, was this law added to, if it was not added to the Gospel? It must be plain that it was added to the Gospel, since we learn that they had the Gospel preached to them. From these few facts, we conclude that whenever the Lord revealed Himself to men in ancient days, and commanded them to offer sacrifice to Him, that it was done that they might look forward in faith to the time of His coming, and rely upon the power of that atonement for a remission of their sins. And this they have done, thousands who have gone before us, whose garments are spotless, and who are, like Job, waiting with an assurance like his, that they will see Him in the *latter day* upon the earth, even in their flesh.

We may conclude, that though there were different dispensations, yet all things which God communicated to His people were calculated to draw their minds to the great object, and to teach them to rely upon God alone as the author of their salvation, as contained in His law. (In *History of the Church*, 2:17)

President Joseph Smith also said, "When God offers a blessing or knowledge to a man, and he refuses to receive it, he will be damned. The Israelites prayed that God would speak to Moses and not to them; in consequence of which he cursed them with a carnal law" (In *History of the Church*, 5:555).

Interesting Information

Rabbi Simlai stated, "613 commandments were revealed to Moses at Sinai, 365 being prohibitions equal in number to the solar days, and 248 being mandates corresponding in number to the limbs of the human body" (Abraham Hirsch Rabinowitz, "Commandments, the 613," *Encyclopedia Judaica* 5:73).

The Desert Tabernacle

What the Book of Exodus Teaches Us

Exodus 25:1–2 And the Lord spake unto Moses, saying,

Speak unto the children of Israel, that they bring me an offering [toward the construction of a tabernacle]: of every man that giveth it willingly with his heart ye shall take my offering.

What the Scriptures of the Restoration Teach Us

D&C 59:15–16 And inasmuch as ye do these things with thanksgiving, with cheerful hearts and countenances, not with much laughter, for this is sin, but with a glad heart and a cheerful countenance—

Verily I say, that inasmuch as ye do this, the fulness of the earth is yours, the beasts of the field and the fowls of the air, and that which climbeth upon the trees and walketh upon the earth.

D&C 97:8–16 Verily I say unto you, all among them who know their hearts are honest, and are broken, and their spirits contrite, and are willing to observe their covenants by sacrifice—yea, every sacrifice which I, the Lord, shall command—they are accepted of me.

For I, the Lord, will cause them to bring forth as a very fruitful tree which is planted in a goodly land, by a pure stream, that yieldeth much precious fruit.

Verily I say unto you, that it is my will that a house should be built unto me in the land of Zion, like unto the pattern which I have given you.

Yea, let it be built speedily, by the tithing of my people.

Behold, this is the tithing and the sacrifice which I, the Lord, require at their hands, that there may be a house built unto me for the salvation of Zion—

For a place of thanksgiving for all saints, and for a place of instruction for all those who are called to the work of the ministry in all their several callings and offices;

That they may be perfected in the understanding of their ministry, in theory, in principle, and in doctrine, in all things pertaining to the kingdom of God on the earth, the keys of which kingdom have been conferred upon you.

And inasmuch as my people build a house unto me in the name of the Lord, and do not suffer any unclean thing to come into it, that it be not defiled, my glory shall rest upon it;

Yea, and my presence shall be there, for I will come into it, and all the pure in heart that shall come into it shall see God.

The Teachings of Inspired Church Leaders

President Brigham Young said, "Some say, 'I do not like to do it, for we never began to build a temple without the bells of hell beginning to ring.' I want to hear them ring again" (*Discourses of Brigham Young*, 410).

What the Book of Exodus Teaches Us

Exodus 25:8–9 And let them make me a sanctuary; that I may dwell among them.

According to all that I shew thee, after the pattern of the tabernacle, and the pattern of all the instruments thereof, even so shall ye make it.

What the Scriptures of the Restoration Teach Us

D&C 124:38–44 For, for this cause I commanded Moses that he should build a tabernacle, that they should bear it with them in the wilderness, and to build a house in the land of promise, that those ordinances might be revealed which had been hid from before the word was.

Therefore, verily I say unto you, that your anointing, and your washings, and your baptisms for the dead, and your solemn assemblies, and your memorials for your sacrifices by the sons of Levi, and for your oracles in your most holy places wherein you receive conversations, and your statutes and judgments, for the beginning of the revelations and foundation of Zion, and for the glory, honor, and endowment of all her municipals, are ordained by the ordinance of my holy house, which my people are always commanded to build unto my holy name.

And verily I say unto you, let this house be built unto my name, that I may reveal mine ordinances therein unto my people;

For I deign to reveal unto my church things which have been kept hid from before the foundation of the world, things that pertain to the dispensation of the fulness of times.

And I will show unto my servant Joseph all things pertaining to this house, and the priesthood thereof, and the place whereon it shall be built.

And ye shall build it on the place where you have contemplated building it, for that is the spot which I have chosen for you to build it.

If ye labor with all your might, I will consecrate that spot that it shall be made holy.

What the Book of Exodus teaches Us

Exodus 29:42–44 This shall be a continual burnt offering through-out your generations at the door of the tabernacle of the congregation before the Lord: where I will meet you, to speak there unto thee.

And there I will meet with the children of Israel, and the tabernacle shall be sanctified by my glory.

And I will sanctify the tabernacle of the congregation, and the altar: I will sanctify also both Aaron and his sons, to minister to me in the priest's office.

The Teachings of Inspired Church Leaders

President Brigham Young:

The earth, the Lord says, abides its creation; it has been baptized with water, and will, in the future, be baptized with fire and the Holy Ghost, to be prepared to go back into the celestial presence of God, with all things that dwell upon it which have, like the earth, abided the law of their creation. Taking this view of the matter, it may be asked why we build temples. We build temples because there is not a house on the face of the whole earth that has been reared to God's name, which will in anywise compare with his character, and that he can consistently call his house. There are places on the earth where the Lord can come and dwell, if he pleases. They may be found on the tops of high mountains, or in some cavern or places where sinful man has never marked the soil with his polluted feet.

He requires his servants to build Him a house that He can come to, and where He can make known His will. (In *Journal of Discourses*, 10:252)

President Brigham Young:

It is for us to do those things which the Lord requires at our hands, and leave the result with him. It is for us to labor with a cheerful good will; and if we build a temple that is worth a million of money, and it requires all our time and means, we should leave it with cheerful hearts, if the Lord in his providence tells us so to do. If the Lord permits our enemies to drive us from it, why, we should abandon it with as much cheerfulness of heart as we ever enjoy a blessing. It is no matter to us what the Lord does, or how he disposes of the labor of his servant. But when he commands, it is for his people to obey. We should be as cheerful in building this temple, if we knew beforehand that we should never enter into it when it was finished, as we would though we knew we were to live here a thousand years to enjoy it. (*Discourses of Brigham Young*, 411)

Interesting Information

It is interesting that the sons of Levi began their ministry in the portable tabernacle at the age of thirty, the same age that the Savior began his earthly mission (Numbers 4:3, 23, 30; Luke 3: 22–23).

The Golden Calf

What the Book of Exodus Teaches Us

Exodus 32:1–4 And when the people saw that Moses delayed to come down out of the mount, the people gathered themselves together unto Aaron, and said unto him, Up, make us gods, which shall go before us; for as for this Moses, the man that brought us up out of the land of Egypt, we wot not what is become of him.

And Aaron said unto them, Brake off the golden earrings, which are in the ears of your wives, of your sons, and of your daughters, and bring them unto me.

And all the people brake off the golden earrings which were in their ears, and brought them unto Aaron.

And he received them at their hand, and fashioned it with a graving tool, after he had made it a molten calf: and they said, These by thy gods, O Israel, which brought thee up out of the land of Egypt.

What the Scriptures of the Restoration Teach Us

D&C 124:84 And with my servant Almon Babbitt, there are many things with which I am not pleased; behold, he aspireth to establish his counsel instead of the counsel which I have ordained, even that of the Presidency of my Church; and he setteth up a golden calf for the worship of my people.

The Teachings of Inspired Church Leaders

President Spencer W. Kimball:

Idolatry is among the most serious of sins. . . .

Modern idols or false gods can take such forms as clothes, homes, businesses, machines, automobiles, pleasure boats, and numerous other material deflectors from the path to godhood. . . .

Intangible things make just as ready gods. Degrees and letters and titles can become idols. . . .

Many people build and furnish a home and buy the automobile first—and then find they "cannot afford" to pay tithing. Whom do they worship? Certainly not the Lord of heaven and earth. . . .

Many worship the hunt, the fishing trip, the vacation, the weekend picnics and outings. Others have as their idols the games of sport, baseball, football, the bullfight, or golf. . . .

Still another image men worship is that of power and prestige. . . . These gods of power, wealth, and influence are most demanding and are quite as real as the golden calves of the children of Israel in the wilderness. (*Miracle of Forgiveness* [1969], 40–42)

What the Scriptures of the Restoration Teach Us

Mormon 8:39 Ye adorn yourselves with that which hath no life, and yet suffer the hungry, and the needy, and the naked, and the sick and the afflicted to pass by you, and notice them not.

Leviticus

Sacrifices

What the Book of Leviticus Teaches Us

Leviticus 2:2–3 And he shall bring it to Aaron's sons the priests: and he shall take thereout his handful of the flour thereof, and of the oil thereof, with all the frankincense thereof; and the priest shall burn the memorial of it upon the altar, to be an offering made by fire, of a sweet savour unto the Lord:

And the remnant of the meat offering shall be Aaron's and his sons': it is a thing most holy of the offerings of the Lord made by fire.

The Teachings of Inspired Church Leaders

Elder Bruce R. McConkie:

Of all the elements of the ordinance of sacrifice, nothing played a more prominent part than the administration of the blood of the offering. The manner of this offering was minutely specified by the Lord. . . The Lord chose blood to dramatize the consequences of sin and what was involved in the process of forgiveness and reconciliation. Therefore, blood symbolized both life and the giving of one's life. Death is the consequence of sin and so the animal was slain to show what happens when man sins. Also, the animal was a type of Christ. Through the giving of His life for man, by the shedding of His blood, one who is spiritually dead because of sin can find new life." (*The Promised Messiah* [1978], 258)

143

President Joseph Smith:

It is a very prevalent opinion that the sacrifices which were offered were entirely consumed. This was not the case; if you read Leviticus, second chap., second and third verses, you will observe that the priests took a part as a memorial and offered it up before the Lord, while the remainder was kept for the maintenance of the priests; so that the offerings and sacrifices are not all consumed upon the altar—but the blood is sprinkled, and the fat and certain other portions are consumed.

These sacrifices, as well as every ordinance belonging to the Priesthood, will, when the Temple of the Lord shall be built, and the sons of Levi be purified, be fully restored and attended to in all their powers, ramifications and blessings. This ever did and ever will exist when the powers of the Melchisedic Priesthood are sufficiently manifest; else how can the restitution of all things spoken of by the holy Prophets be brought to pass? . . . But those things which existed prior to Moses' day, namely, sacrifice, will be continued.

It may be asked by some, what necessity for sacrifice, since the Great Sacrifice was offered? In answer to which, if repentance, baptism, and faith existed prior to the days of Christ, what necessity for them since that time? The Priesthood has descended in a regular line from father to son, through their succeeding generations. (In *History of the Church*, ed. B. H. Roberts [1932–51], 4:211–12)

The Sin Offering

What the Book of Leviticus Teaches Us

Leviticus 4:1–3 And the Lord spake unto Moses, saying,

Speak unto the children of Israel, saying, if a soul shall sin through ignorance against any of the commandments of the Lord concerning things which ought not to be done, and shall do against any of them:

If the priest that is anointed do sin according to the sin of the people; then let him bring for his sin, which he hath sinned, a young bullock without blemish unto the Lord for a sin offering.

What the Scriptures of the Restoration Teach Us

D&C 45:3–5 Listen to him who is the advocate with the Father, who is pleading your cause before him—

Saying: Father, behold the sufferings and death of him who did no sin, in whom thou wast well pleased; behold the blood of thy Son which was shed, the blood of him whom thou gavest that thyself might be glorified;

Wherefore, Father, spare these my brethren that believe on my name, that they may come unto me and have everlasting life.

The Teachings of Inspired Church Leaders

Elder James E. Talmage:

Christ's agony in the garden is unfathomable by the finite mind, both as to intensity and cause. . . . He struggled and groaned under a burden such as no other being who has lived on earth might even conceive as possible. It was not physical pain, nor mental anguish alone, that caused Him to suffer such torture as to produce an extrusion of blood from every pore; but a spiritual agony of soul such as only God was capable of experiencing. . . .

In some manner, actual and terribly real though to man incomprehensible, the Savior took upon Himself the burden of the sins of mankind from Adam to the end of the world. (*Jesus the Christ* [1916], 613)

Aaron and the "Strange Fire"

What the Book of Leviticus Teaches Us

Leviticus 10:1–2 And Nadab and Abihu, the sons of Aaron, took either of them his censer, and put fire therein, and put incense thereon, and offered strange fire before the Lord, which he commanded them not.

And there went out fire from the Lord, and devoured them, and they died before the Lord.

What the Scriptures of the Restoration Teach Us

D&C 132:59 Verily, if a man be called of my Father, as was Aaron, by mine own voice, and by the voice of him that sent me, and I have endowed him with the keys of the power of this priesthood, if he do anything in my name, and according to my law and by my word, he will not commit sin, and I will justify him.

Chastisement

What the Book of Leviticus Teaches Us

Leviticus 10:3 Then Moses said unto Aaron, This is it that the Lord spake, saying, I will be sanctified in them that come nigh me, and before all the people I will be glorified. And Aaron held his peace.

What the Scriptures of the Restoration Teach Us

D&C 101:5 For all those who will not endure chastening, but deny me, cannot be sanctified.

The Teachings of Inspired Church Leaders

President Joseph Smith:

"Some people say I am a fallen Prophet, because I do not bring forth more of the word of the Lord, Why do I not do it? Are we able to receive it? No! Not one in this room." He then chastened the congregation for their wickedness and unbelief, " 'for whom the Lord loveth he chasteneth, and scourgeth every son and daughter whom he receiveth,' and if we do not receive chastisements then we are bastards and not sons." (*Teachings of the Prophet Joseph Smith*, sel. Joseph Fielding Smith [2002], 194)

President Joseph Smith:

We have been chastened by the hand of God heretofore for not obeying His commands, although we never violated any human law, or transgressed any human precept; yet we have treated lightly His commands, and departed from His ordinances, and the Lord has chastened us sore, and we have felt His arm and kissed the rod; let us be wise in time to come and ever remember that "to obey is better than sacrifice, and to hearken than the fat of rams." The Lord has told us to build the Temple and the Nauvoo House; and that command is as binding upon us as any other; and that man who engages not in these things is as much a transgressor as though he broke any other commandment; he is not a doer of God's will, not a fulfiller of His laws. (*Teachings of the Prophet Joseph Smith*, 253–54)

The Lord's Law of Health

What the Book of Leviticus Teaches Us

Leviticus 11:2, 44–47 Speak unto the children of Israel, saying, These are the beasts which ye shall eat among all the beasts that are on the earth.

For I am the Lord your God: ye shall therefore sanctify yourselves, and ye shall be holy; for I am holy: neither shall ye defile yourselves with any manner of creeping thing that creepeth upon the earth.

For I am the Lord that bringeth you up out of the land of Egypt, to be your God: ye shall therefore be holy, for I am holy.

This is the law of the beasts, and of the fowl, and of every living creature that moveth in the waters, and of every creature that creepeth upon the earth:

To make a difference between the unclean and the clean, and between the beast that may be eaten and the best that may not be eaten.

What the Scriptures of the Restoration Teach Us

D&C 89:12–13, 18–19 Yea, flesh also of beasts and of the fowls of the air, I, the Lord, have ordained for the use of man with thanksgiving; nevertheless they are to be used sparingly;

And it is pleasing unto me that they should not be used, only in times of winter, or of cold, or famine.

And all saints who remember to keep and do these sayings, walking in obedience to the commandments, shall receive health in their navel and marrow to their bones;

And shall find wisdom and great treasures of knowledge, even hidden treasures.

Interesting Information

If the dietary code is seen both symbolically and as part of a system of laws that covered all the customary acts of life, it becomes apparent how it served. God was using the diet as a teaching tool. People may forget or neglect prayer, play, work, or worship, but hey seldom forget a meal. By voluntarily abstaining from certain foods or by cooking them in a special way, one made a daily, personal commitment to act in one's faith. At every meal a formal choice was made, generating quiet self-discipline. (*Old Testament Student Manual: Genesis–2 Samuel*, 3rd ed. [Church Educational System manual, 2003], 173)

The Teachings of Inspired Church Leaders

President Joseph F. Smith:

I simply want to say to you my brethren and sisters, that there is no other course that we can take in the world, in relation to our temporal welfare and health, better than that which the Lord God has pointed out to us. Why can we not realize this? Why will we not come to a perfect understanding of it? Why will we not deny ourselves that which our craven appetites desire? Why can we not observe more closely the will of the Lord as made known to us in this revelation? . . . If this commandment were observed by the whole people, the vast amount of money that now goes out to the world for strong drink and these other things forbidden in the word of wisdom, would be saved at home, and the health, prosperity and temporal salvation of the people would correspondingly increased. No man can violate the laws of God with reference to health and temporal salvation, and enjoy those blessings in the same degree that he could do and would do if he would obey the commands of God. . . .

Perhaps those who are accustomed to these habits think this is a very trivial or very unimportant thing to talk about to a vast congregation like this, but I never see a boy or a man, young or old, addicted to this habit and practicing it openly but I am forced to the conclusion to the conviction in my mind that he is either ignorant of God's will concerning man or he is defiant of God's will and does not care anything about the word of the Lord, and that alone is sufficient to bring sorrow to the heart of any man who has any regard or respect of the word or will of the Lord and would like to see it obeyed. . . .

We pray God to heal us when we are sick, and then we turn round from our prayers and partake of the very things that He has told us are not good for us! How inconsistent it is for men to ask God to bless them, when they themselves are taking a course to injure and to bring evil upon themselves. No wonder we don't get our prayers answered more than we do, and no wonder our health is no better than it is, when we are addicted to practices that God has said are not good for us, and thereby entail evils upon our life and physical being; and then to turn to the Lord and ask Him to heal us from the consequence of our own folly, and pernicious practices; from the effects of the evil that we have brought upon ourselves and that we knew better than to do. How foolish it is! (Clark, Messages of the First Presidency, 4:179–80, 182–85)

The Canaanites

What the Book of Leviticus Teaches Us

Leviticus 18:1–5 And the Lord spake unto Moses, saying,

Speak unto the children of Israel, and say unto them, I am the Lord your God.

After the doings of the land of Egypt, wherein ye dwelt, shall ye not do: and after the doings of the land of Canaan, whither I bring you, shall ye not do: neither shall ye walk in their ordinances.

Ye shall do my judgments, and keep mine ordinances, to walk therein: I am the Lord your God.

Ye shall therefore keep my statutes, and my judgments: which if a man do, he shall live in them: I am the Lord.

What the Scriptures of the Restoration Teach Us

3 Nephi 15:9–10 Behold, I am the law, and the light. Look unto me, and endure to the end, and ye shall live; for unto him that endureth to the end will I give eternal life.

Behold, I have given unto you the commandments; therefore keep my commandments. And this is the law and the prophets, for they truly testified of me.

The Lord warned his people from the gods of those nations that bordered ancient Israel, and today, in our dispensation, he warns us against ourselves. In a sense, this was what the Lord was doing when he instructed ancient Israel against the "doings of Egypt and Canaan." He knew the children of Israel better than they knew themselves and he was providing a warning to them against themselves:

D&C 84:43–44 And I now give unto you a commandment to beware concerning yourselves, to give diligent heed to the words of eternal life.

For you shall live by every word that proceedeth forth from the mouth of God.

Blasphemy

What the Book of Leviticus Teaches Us

Leviticus 24:16 And he that blasphemeth the name of the Lord, he shall surely be put to death, and all the congregation shall certainly stone him: as well the stranger, as he that is born in the land, when he blasphemeth the name of the Lord, shall be put to death.

Interesting Information

Blasphemy is defined in the Bible Dictionary as "Generally denotes contemptuous speech concerning God or concerning something that stands in a sacred relation toward God, such as His temple, His law, or His prophet."

I find it interesting that not only was blasphemy one of the accusations directed at Jesus Christ, but it was also an accusation used in this dispensation. Joseph Smith records the following in *History of the Church*, June 22, 1841:

> Elder Theodore Curtis, having previously been arraigned before a magistrate, and bound over in the sum of forty pounds, for "blasphemy," i.e., preaching the Gospel, appeared at the Court of Sessions, at Gloucester, England, and after remaining five days [in prison], was informed on inquiry, that no bill was found against him, and he was suffered to go at large again after paying one pound and one shilling cost. Thus we see that the same opposition to truth prevails in other countries, as well as in this. (In *History of the Church*, 4:380)

Numbers

A House of Order

What the Book of Numbers Teaches Us

Numbers 2:1–3, 5 And the Lord spake unto Moses and unto Aaron, saying,

Every man of the children of Israel shall pitch by his own standard, with the ensign of their father's house: far off about the tabernacle of the congregation shall they pitch.

And on the east side toward the rising of the sun shall they of the standard of the camp of Judah pitch throughout their armies: and Nahshon the son of Amminadab shall be captain of the children of Judah.

And those that do pitch next unto him shall be the tribe of Issachar: and Nethaneel the son of Zuar shall be captain of the children of Issachar.

What the Scriptures of the Restoration Teach Us

D&C 132:8 Behold, mine house is a house of order, saith the Lord God, and not a house of confusion.

The Levites

What the Book of Numbers Teaches Us

Numbers 3:9–10 And thou shalt give the Levites unto Aaron and to his sons: they are wholly given unto him out of the children of Israel.

And thou shalt appoint Aaron and his sons, and they shall wait on their priest's office: and the stranger that cometh nigh shall be put to death.

What the Scriptures of the Restoration Teach Us

D&C 107:1, 6, 10 There are, in the church, two priesthoods, namely, the Melchizedek and Aaronic, including the Levitical Priesthood.

But there are two divisions or grand heads—one is the Melchizedek Priesthood and the other is the Aaronic or Levitical Priesthood.

High priests after the order of the Melchizedek Priesthood have a right to officiate in their own standing, under the direction of the presidency, in administering spiritual things, and also in the office of an elder, priest (of the Levitical order), teacher, deacon, and member.

D&C 68:14–16 There remain hereafter, in the due time of the Lord, other bishops to be set apart unto the church, to minister even according to the first;

Wherefore they shall be high priests who are worthy, and they shall be appointed by the First Presidency of the Melchizedek Priesthood, except they be literal descendants of Aaron.

And if they be literal descendants of Aaron they have a legal right to the bishopric, if they are the firstborn among the sons of Aaron.

The Sons of Levi and Temple Service

What the Book of Numbers Teaches Us

Numbers 4:1–4 And the Lord spake unto Moses and unto Aaron, saying,

Take the sum of the sons of Kohath from among the sons of Levi, after their families, by the house of their fathers,

From thirty years old and upward even until fifty years old, all that enter into the host, to do the work in the tabernacle of the congregation.

This shall be the service of the sons of Kohath in the tabernacle of the congregation, about the most holy things.

Interesting Information

It may seem odd that men during Moses's time were not called to the Aaronic Priesthood unless they were at least thirty years of age.

Surprisingly, prior to 1854, boys were not usually ordained to the Aaronic Priesthood. However, in 1854 Wilford Woodruff recorded, "We are now beginning to ordain our young sons to the lesser priesthood here in Zion" (in *History of the Church*, ed. B. H. Roberts [1932–51], 4:540–41). Not everything is standardized in the Church. We experienced this in the October 2012 general conference when President Thomas S. Monson announced that young men can now serve missions at the age of eighteen and young women at the age of nineteen. Brigham Young provides this interesting perspective:

> Now will it cause some of you to marvel that I was not ordained a High Priest before I was ordained an Apostle? Brother Kimball and myself were never ordained High Priests. How wonderful! I was going to say how little some of the brethren understood the Priesthood, after the Twelve were called. In our early career in this Church, on one occasion, in one of our Councils, we were telling about some of the Twelve wanting to ordain us High Priests, and what I said to Brother Patten when he wanted to ordain me in York State: said I, Brother Patten, wait until I can lift my hand to heaven and say I have magnified the office of an Elder. After our conversation was over in the Council, some of the brethren began to query, and said we ought to be ordained High Priests; at the same time I did not consider that an Apostle needed to be ordained a High Priest and Elder, or a Teacher. I did not express my views on the subject, at that time, but thought I would hear what brother Joseph would say about it. It was William E. McLellin who told Joseph that I and Heber were not ordained High Priests, and wanted to know if it should not be done. Said Joseph, "Will you insult the Priesthood? Is that all the knowledge you have of the office of an Apostle? Do you not know that the man who received the Apostleship receives all the keys that ever were, or that can be, conferred upon mortal man? What are you talking about? I am astonished!" Nothing more was said about it. (*Discourses of Brigham Young*, comp. John A. Widtsoe [1954], 141)

"By the Voice of My Prophet"

What the Book of Numbers Teaches Us

Numbers 12:1–3, 6–9 And Miriam and Aaron spake against Moses because of the Ethiopian woman whom he had married: for he had married an Ethiopian woman.

And they said, Hath the Lord indeed spoken only by Moses? Hath he not spoken also by us? And the Lord heard it.

(Now the man Moses was very meek, above all the men which were upon the face of the earth.)

And he said, Hear now my words; If there be a prophet among you, I the Lord will make myself known unto him in a vision, and will speak unto him in a dream.

My servant Moses is not so, who is faithful in all mine house.

With him will I speak mouth to mouth, even apparently, and no in dark speeches; and the similitude of the Lord shall he behold: wherefore then were ye not to afraid to speak against my servant Moses?

And the anger of the Lord was kindled against them; and he departed.

What the Scriptures of the Restoration Teach Us

D&C 28:2–3, 6–7, 11–13 But, behold, verily, verily, I say unto thee, no one shall be appointed to receive commandments and revelations in this church excepting my servant Joseph Smith, Jun., for he receiveth them even as Moses.

And thou shalt be obedient unto the things which I shall give unto him, even as Aaron, to declare faithfully the commandments and the revelations, with power and authority unto the church.

And thou shalt not command him who is at thy head, and at the head of the church;

For I have given him the keys of the mysteries, and the revelations which are sealed, until I shall appoint unto them another in his stead.

And again, thou shalt take thy brother, Hiram Page, between him and thee alone, and tell him that those things which he hath written from that stone are not of me and that Satan decieveth him;

For, behold, these things have not been appointed unto him, neither shall anything be appointed unto any of this church contrary to the church covenants.

For all things must be done in order, and by common consent in the church, by the prayer of faith.

D&C 43:5–7 And this shall be a law unto you, that ye receive not the teachings of any that shall come before you as revelations or commandments;

And this I give unto you that you may not be deceived, that you may know they are not of me.

For verily I say unto you, that he that is ordained of me shall come in at the gate and be ordained as I have told you before, to teach those revelations which you have received and shall receive through him whom I have appointed.

The Teachings of Inspired Church Leaders

President Joseph Smith:

I will give you one of the *Keys* of the mysteries of the Kingdom. It is an eternal principle, that has existed with God from all eternity: That man who rises up to condemn others, finding fault with the Church, saying that they are out of the way, while he himself is righteous, then know assuredly, that that man is in the high road to apostasy; and if he does not repent, will apostatize, as God lives. The principle is as correct as the one that Jesus put forth in saying that he who seeketh a sign is an adulterous person; and that principle is eternal, undeviating, and firm as the pillars of heaven; for whenever you see a man seeking after a sigh, you may set it down that he is an adulterous man. (In *History of the Church*, 3:385)

Interesting Information

When the Church was organized on April 6, 1830, the Lord declared through his prophet that the members of the Church are to "give heed unto all his words and commandments. . . . For his word ye shall receive, as if from mine own mouth, in all patience and faith" (D&C 21:4–5). In just a few short months, it was necessary for the Prophet to repeat this lesson again during the Hiram Page seer stone incident. Joseph received revelation in the form of section 28, in which the Lord states in verse 2, "no one shall be appointed to receive commandments and revelations in this church excepting my servant Joseph Smith, Jun." One and a half years later, it became imperative for the Lord to repeat a third time to the young Church the role of revelation from the Lord for the Church through his prophet. This time, the Lord not only stated that Joseph was the only one that could receive revelations for the Church, but he also added, "Ye receive not the teachings of any that shall come before you as revelation or commandments; And this I give unto you that you may not be deceived, that you may know they are not of me" (D&C 43:5–6).

This third situation surfaced when a Mrs. Hubble claimed to have received revelations for the Church. John Whitmer wrote the following:

She professed to be a prophetess of the Lord, and professed to have many revelations, and knew the Book of Mormon was true, and that she should become a teacher in the church of Christ. She appeared to be very sanctimonious and deceived some who were not able to detect her in her hypocrisy; others, however, had the spirit of discernment and her follies and abominations were manifest. (As quoted in *History of the Church*, 1:154, 12n)

Elder George A. Smith stated that in the early Church, some elders had the notion that the Prophet was wrong on certain matters and took it into their own hands to spread deceiving reports, which only served to confuse some of the members. It was because of these types of actions the Prophet went to the Lord and was given revelation recorded as Doctrine and Covenants 43 (In *Journal of Discourses*, 26 vols. [1854–86], 11:7–9).

The Reward for Unbelief

What the Book of Numbers Teaches Us

Numbers 20:12 And the Lord spake unto Moses and Aaron, Because ye believed me not, to sanctify me in the eyes of the children of Israel, therefore ye shall not bring this congregation into the land which I have given them.

What the Scriptures of the Restoration Teach Us

D&C 84:23–25 Now this Moses plainly taught to the children of Israel in the wilderness, and sought diligently to sanctify his people that they might behold the face of God;

But they hardened their hearts and could not endure his presence; therefore, the Lord in his wrath, for this anger was kindled against them, swore that they should not enter into his rest while in the wilderness, which rest is the fulness of his glory.

Therefore, he took Moses out of their midst, and the Holy Priesthood also;

Bitten by the Serpents

What the Book of Numbers Teaches Us

Numbers 21:7–9 Therefore the people came to Moses, and said, We have sinned, for we have spoken against the Lord, and against thee; pray unto the Lord, that he take away the serpents from us. And Moses prayed for the people.

And the Lord said unto Moses, Make thee a fiery serpent, and set it upon a pole: and it shall come to pass, that every one that is bitten, when he looketh upon it, shall live.

And Moses made a serpent of brass, and put it upon a pole, and it came to pass, that if a serpent had bitten any man, when he beheld the serpent of brass, he lived.

What the Scriptures of the Restoration Teach Us

1 Nephi 17:41 And he did straiten them in the wilderness with his rod; for they hardened their hearts, even as ye have; and the Lord straitened them because of their iniquity. He sent fiery flying serpents among them; and after they were bitten he prepared a way that they might be healed; and the labor which they had to perform was to look; and because of the simpleness of the way, or the easiness of it, there were many who perished.

Alma 33:19–21 Behold, he was spoken of by Moses; yea, and behold a type was raised up in the wilderness, that whosoever would look upon it might live. And many did look and live.

But few understood the meaning of those things, and this because of the hardness of their hearts. But there were many who were so hardened that they would not look, therefore they perished. Now the reason they would not look is because they did not believe that it would heal them.

O my brethren, if ye could be healed by merely casting about your eyes that ye might be healed, would ye not behold quickly, or would ye rather harden your hearts in unbelief, and be slothful, that ye would not cast about your eyes, that ye might perish?

Helaman 8:14–15 Yea, did he not bear record that the Son of God should come? And as he lifted up the brazen serpent in the wilderness, even so shall he be lifted up who should come.

And as many as should look upon that serpent should live, even so as many as should look upon the Son of God with faith, having a contrite spirit, might live, even unto that life which is eternal.

Inheritances

What the Book of Numbers Teaches Us

Numbers 33: 54 And ye shall divide the land by lot for an inheritance among your families: and to the more ye shall give the more inheritance, and to the fewer ye shall give the less inheritance: every man's inheritance shall be in the place where his lot falleth; according to the tribes of your fathers ye shall inherit.

What the Scriptures of the Restoration Teach Us

D&C 85:1–7 It is the duty of the Lord's clerk, whom he has appointed, to keep a history, and a general church record of all things that transpire in Zion, and of all those who consecrate properties, and receive inheritances legally from the bishop;

And also their manner of life, their faith, and works; and also of the apostates who apostatize after receiving their inheritances.

It is contrary to the will and commandment of God that those who receive not their inheritance by consecration, agreeable to his law, which he has given, that he may tithe his people, to prepare them against the day of vengeance and burning, should have their names enrolled with the people of God.

Neither is their genealogy to be kept, or to be had where it may be found on any of the records or history of the church.

Their names shall not be found, neither the names of the fathers, nor the names of the children written in the book of the law of God, saith the Lord of Hosts.

Yea, thus saith the still small voice, which whispereth through and pierceth all things, and often times it maketh my bones to quake while it maketh manifest, saying:

And it shall come to pass that I, the Lord God, will send one mighty and strong, holding the scepter of power in his hand, clothed with light for a covering, whose mouth shall utter words, eternal words; while his bowels shall be a fountain of truth, to set in order the house of God, and to arrange by lot the inheritances of the saints whose names are found, and the names of their fathers, and of their children, enrolled in the book of the law of God.

Deuteronomy

Moses's Final Instructions

What the Book of Deuteronomy Teaches Us

Deuteronomy 7:22–26 And the Lord thy God will put out those nations before thee by little and little: thou mayest not consume them at once, lest the beasts of the field increase upon thee.

But the Lord thy God shall deliver them unto thee, and shall destroy them with a mighty destruction, until they be destroyed.

And he shall deliver their kings into thine hand, and thou shalt destroy their name from under heaven: there shall no man be able to stand before thee, until thou have destroyed them.

The graven images of their gods shall ye burn with fire: thou shalt not desire the silver or gold that is on them, nor take it unto thee, lest thou be snared therein: for it is an abomination to the Lord thy God.

Neither shalt thou bring an abomination into thine house, lest thou be a cursed thing like it: but thou shalt utterly detest it, and thou shalt utterly abhor it; for it is a cursed thing.

What the Scriptures of the Restoration Teach Us

Alma 5:57 And now I say unto you, all you that are desirous to follow the voice of the good shepherd, come ye out from the wicked, and be ye separate, and touch not their unclean things; and behold, their names shall be blotted out, that the names of the wicked shall not be numbered among the names of the righteous, that the word of God may be fulfilled, which saith: The names of the wicked shall not be mingled with the names of my people.

D&C 133:5, 14 Go ye out from Babylon. Be ye clean that bear the vessels of the Lord.

Go ye out from among the nations, even from Babylon, from the midst of wickedness, which is spiritual Babylon.

Manna and the Word of the Lord

What the Book of Deuteronomy Teaches Us

Deuteronomy 8:3; 6:13, 16 And he humbled thee, and suffered thee to hunger, and fed thee with manna, which thou knewest not, neither did thy fathers know; that he might make thee know that man doth not live by bread only, but by every word that proceedeth out of the mouth of the Lord doth man live.

Thou shalt fear the Lord thy God, and serve him, and shalt swear by his name.

Ye shall not tempt the Lord your God, as ye tempted him in Massah.

What the Scriptures of the Restoration Teach Us

D&C 84:43–44 And I now give unto you a commandment to beware concerning yourselves, to give diligent heed to the words of eternal life.

For you shall live by every word that proceedeth forth from the mouth of God.

The Teachings of Inspired Church Leaders

Elder Marion G. Romney:

Thorough knowledge of the scriptures is evidenced by the fact that He [Jesus] repeatedly cited them. When the devil tempted Him to turn the stones into bread, He countered by quoting from Deuteronomy: ". . . It is written, Man shall not live by bread alone, but by every word that proceedeth out of the mouth of God." When the tempter challenged Him to cast Himself down from the pinnacle of the temple, He responded by quoting from the same book: "It is written again, Thou shalt not tempt the Lord thy God." For the third time He quoted from Deuteronomy when Satan offered Him the kingdoms of the world, saying: "Get thee hence, Satan: for it is written, Thou shalt worship the Lord thy God, and him only shalt thou serve." (*Jesus Christ, Man's Greatest Exemplar*, Brigham Young University Speeches of the Year [May 9, 1967], 9)

Driving the Inhabitants from the Land

What the Book of Deuteronomy Teaches Us

Deuteronomy 9:4 Speak not thou in thine heart, after that the Lord thy God hath cast them out from before thee, saying, For my righteousness the Lord hath brought me in to possess this land: but for the wickedness of these nations the Lord doth drive them out from before thee.

What the Scriptures of the Restoration Teach Us

1 Nephi 17:32–38 And after they had crossed the river Jordan he did make them mighty unto the driving out of the children of the land, yea, unto the scattering them to destruction.

And now, do ye suppose that the children of this land, who were in the land of promise, who were driven out by our fathers, do ye suppose that they were righteous? Behold, I say unto you, Nay.

Do ye suppose that our fathers would have been more choice than they if they had been righteous? I say unto you, Nay.

Behold, the Lord esteemed all flesh in one; he that is righteous is favored of God. But behold, this people had rejected every word of God, and they were ripe in iniquity; and the fulness of the wrath of God was upon them; and the Lord did curse the land against them, and bless it unto our fathers; yea, he did curse it against them unto their destruction, and he did bless it unto our fathers unto their obtaining power over it.

Behold, the Lord hath created the earth that it should be inhabited; and he hath create his children that they should possess it.

And he raiseth up a righteous nation, and destroyeth the nations of the wicked.

And he leadeth away the righteous into precious lands, and the wicked he destroyeth, and curseth the land unto them for their sakes.

The Teachings of Inspired Church Leaders

The Lord attempted on a number of occasions to send his people away that they could grow and thrive. We know of the Jaredites, the children of Israel, the Nephites, and the pilgrims who all were directed by the hand of the Lord with his blessings and prospered for a time. The same is true of the Saints in this dispensation. It was during a meeting held in the schoolhouse just above the Isaac Morley farm that Wilford Woodruff heard and recorded the following prophecy of Joseph Smith:

On Sunday night the Prophet called on all who held the Priesthood to gather into the little log school house they had there. It was a small house, perhaps 14 feet square. But it held the whole of the Priesthood of the Church of Jesus Christ of Latter-day Saints who were then in the town of Kirtland. . . . When we got together the Prophet called upon the Elders of Israel with him to bear testimony of this work. . . . When they got through the Prophet said, "Brethren, I have been very much edified and instructed in your testimonies here tonight. but I want to say to you before the Lord, that you know no more concerning the destinies of this Church and kingdom than a babe upon its mother's lap. You don't comprehend it." I was rather surprised. He said "it is only a little handful of Priesthood you see here tonight, but this Church will fill North and South America—it will fill the world. . . . This people will go into the Rocky Mountains; they will there build temples to the Most High. They will raise up a posterity there." (In Conference Report, Apr. 1898, 57)

The Tribe of Levi

What the Book of Deuteronomy Teaches Us

Deuteronomy 10:8 At that time the Lord separated the tribe of Levi, to bear the ark of the covenant of the Lord, to stand before the Lord to minister unto him, and to bless in his name, unto this day.

What the Scriptures of the Restoration Teach Us

3 Nephi 24:3 And he shall sit as a refiner and purifier of silver; and he shall purify the sons of Levi, and purge them as gold and silver, that they may offer unto the Lord an offering in righteousness.

D&C 128:24 Behold, the great day of the Lord is at hand; and who can abide the day of his coming, and who can stand when he appeareth? For he is like a refiner's fire, and like fuller's soap; and he shall sit as a refiner and purifier of silver, and he shall purify the sons of Levi, and purge them as gold and silver, that they may offer unto the Lord an offering in righteousness. Let us, therefore, as a church and a people, and as Latter-day Saints, offer unto the Lord an offering in righteousness; and let us present in his holy temple, when it is finished, a book containing the records of our dead, which shall be worthy of all acceptation.

Interesting Information

A number of years ago I was told the following story from a friend:

There was a group of women in a Bible study of the book of Malachi. As they were studying chapter three, they came across verse three that says, "He will sit as a refiner and purifier of silver." This verse puzzled the women and they wondered what this statement meant about the character and nature of God. One of the women offered to find out about the process of refining silver and get back to the group at their next Bible study.

That week this woman called up a silver smith and made an appointment to watch him at work. She didn't mention anything about the reason for her interest in silver beyond her curiosity about the process of refining silver. As she watched the silver smith, he held a piece of silver over the fire and let it heat up.

He explained that in refining silver, one needed to hold the silver in the middle of the fire where the flames were hottest so as to burn away all the impurities. The woman thought about God holding us in such a hot spot—then she thought again about the verse, that He sits as a refiner and purifier of silver.

She asked the silver smith if it was true that he had to sit there in front of the fire the whole time the silver was being refined. The man answered that, yes, he not only had to sit there holding the silver, but he had to keep his eyes on the silver the entire time it was in the fire. For if the silver was left even a moment too long in the flames, it would be destroyed.

The woman was silent for a moment. Then she asked the silver smith, "How do you know when the silver is fully refined?" He smiled at her and answered, "Oh, that's the easy part—when I see my image reflected in it."

Love the Lord

What the Book of Deuteronomy Teaches Us

Deuteronomy 10:12–13 And now, Israel, what doth the Lord thy God require of thee, but to fear the Lord thy God, to walk in all his ways, and to love him, and to serve the Lord thy God with all they heart and with all thy soul,

To keep the commandments of the Lord, and his statutes, which I command thee this day for thy good?

What the Scriptures of the Restoration Teach Us

D&C 21:6 For by doing these things the gates of hell shall not prevail against you; yea, and the Lord God will disperse the powers of darkness from before you, and cause the heavens to shake for your good, and his name's glory.

Judging the Children of Israel

What the Book of Deuteronomy Teaches Us

Deuteronomy 17:8–9 If there arise a matter too hard for thee in judgment, between blood and blood, between plea and plea, and between stroke and stroke, being matters of controversy within thy gates: then shalt thou arise, and get thee up into the place which the Lord thy God shall choose;

And thou shalt come unto the priests the Levites, and unto the judge that shall be in those days, and inquire; and they shall shew thee the sentence of judgment.

What the Scriptures of the Restoration Teach Us

D&C 58: 14–18 Yea, for this cause I have sent you hither, and have selected my servant Edward Partridge, and have appointed unto him his mission in this land.

But if he repent not of his sins, which are unbelief and blindness of heart, let him take heed lest he fall

Behold his mission is given unto him, and it shall not be given again.

And whoso standeth in this mission is appointed to be a judge in Israel, like as it was in ancient days, to divide the lands of the heritage of God unto his children;

And to judge his people by the testimony of the just, and by the assistance of his counselors, according to the laws of the kingdom which are given by the prophets of God.

Raising Up Another Prophet

What the Book of Deuteronomy Teaches Us

Deuteronomy 18:15–19 The Lord thy God will raise up unto thee a

Prophet from the midst of thee, of thy brethren, like unto me; unto him ye shall hearken;

According to all that thou desiredst of the Lord thy God in Horeb in the day of the assembly, saying, Let me not hear again the voice of the Lord my God, neither let me see this great fire anymore, that I die not.

And the Lord said unto me, They have well spoken that which they have spoken.

I will raise them up a Prophet from among their brethren, like unto thee, and will put my words in his mouth; and he shall speak unto them all that I shall command him.

And it shall come to pass, that whosoever will not hearken unto my words which he shall speak in my name, I will require it of him.

What the Scriptures of the Restoration Teach Us

Who is the Prophet that will be like unto Moses?

1 Nephi 22:20–21 And the Lord will surely prepare a way for his people, unto the fulfilling of the words of Moses, which he spake, saying: A prophet shall the Lord your God raise up unto you, like unto me; him shall ye hear in all things whatsoever he shall say unto you. And it shall come to pass that all those who will not hear that prophet shall be cut off from among the people.

And now I, Nephi, declare unto you, that this prophet of whom Moses spake was the Holy One of Israel [Jesus Christ]; wherefore, he shall execute judgment in righteousness.

3 Nephi 20:23 Behold, I am he [Jesus Christ] of whom Moses spake, saying: A prophet shall the Lord your God raise up unto you of our brethren, like unto me; him shall ye hear in all things whatsoever he shall say unto you. And it shall come to pass that every soul who will not hear that prophet shall be cut off from among the people.

The Land Divided to the Nations

What the Book of Deuteronomy Teaches Us

Deuteronomy 32:8–9 When the most High divided to the nations their inheritance, when he separated the sons of Adam, he set the bounds of the people according to the number of the children of Israel.

For the Lord's portion is his people; Jacob is the lot of his inheritance.

The Teachings of Inspired Church Leaders

Elder James E. Talmage:

From this we learn that the earth was allotted to the nations, according to the number of the children of Israel; it is evident therefore that the number was known prior to the existence of the Israelitish nation in the flesh; this is most easily explained on the basis of a previous existence in which the spirits of the future nation were known. (*Articles of Faith* [1981], 193)

The Lord Takes Moses

What the Book of Deuteronomy Teaches Us

Deuteronomy 34:1, 4–5 And Moses went up from the plains of Moab unto the mountain of Nebo, to the top of Pisgah, that is over against Jericho. And the Lord shewed him all the land of Gilead, unto Dan,

And the Lord said unto him, This is the land which I sware unto Abraham, unto Isaac, and unto Jacob, saying, I will give it unto thy seed: I have caused thee to see it with thine eyes, but thou shalt not go over thither.

So Moses the servant of the Lord died there in the land of Moab, according to the word of the Lord.

What the Scriptures of the Restoration Teach Us

D&C 84:25 Therefore, he took Moses out of their midst, and the Holy Priesthood also.

Alma 45:19 Behold, this we know, that he was a righteous man; and the saying went abroad in the church that he was taken up by the Spirit, or buried by the hand of the Lord, even as Moses. But behold, the scriptures saith the Lord took Moses unto himself; and we suppose that he has also received Alma in the spirit, unto himself; therefore, for this cause we know nothing concerning his death and burial.

Interesting Information

Rebellion among the children of Israel was not at all uncommon in their desert wanderings. The rebellion described in these verses, however, was especially serious because it apparently led Moses, the prophet of God, to momentarily forget what the Lord had commanded him to do. The Lord had told Moses to provide water for murmuring Israel in a special way. Pointing out a certain rock, the Lord told Moses, "Speak ye unto the rock before their [Israel's] eyes; and it shall give forth his water" (v. 8). But Moses was weary and angry with Israel. "Hear now, ye rebels," he said. "Must *we* fetch you water out of this rock?" (v. 10; emphasis added). Then, instead of speaking to the rock as God commanded, Moses "smote the rock twice" and water gushed forth (v. 11). The Lord then chided Moses and Aaron for their failure to sanctify Him in the eyes of the people and told both men that neither of them would be allowed to bring Israel into the promised land (see v. 12). Not only did they not follow the Lord's instructions carefully but they also suggested by the use of *we* that they were the ones who provided the water.

This incident, taken together with other scripture, creates a number of questions. Did Moses really sin against the Lord? Was that the reason Moses was not permitted to enter the promised land? Did Moses really assume glory to himself, or was he simply angry with the lack of faith exhibited by the children of Israel? Was this one error enough to cancel out years of great faith, obedience, and devotion?

At least two other Old Testament passages indicate that Moses did sin in striking the rock at Meribah (see Numbers 27:12–14; Deuteronomy 32:51–52). Other passages, however, help to clarify the matter. Deuteronomy 3:26 and 4:21 indicate that the Lord told Moses that the reason he could not enter the promised land was that the Lord was angry with him "*for your sakes*" (emphasis added). This statement could imply that there were reasons other than the error of Moses for the prohibition. Two other facts strengthen this supposition. First, both Moses and the higher priesthood were taken from Israel because of the people's unworthiness, not Moses' (see D&C 84:23–25). Second, Moses was translated when his mortal ministry was finished (see Alma 45:19). In other words, Moses was privileged to enter a land of promise far greater than the land of Canaan. He had finished his calling in mortality, and a new leader was to take Israel into the promised land. And, Moses was translated—hardly a punishment for sinning against God. (*Old Testament Student Manual: Genesis–2 Samuel*, 3rd ed. [Church Educational System manual, 2003], 208)

Joshua

The Promised Land

What the Book of Joshua Teaches Us

Joshua 1:1–4 Now after the death of Moses the servant of the Lord it came to pass, that the Lord spake unto Joshua the son of Nun, Moses' minister, saying,

Moses my servant is dead; now therefore arise, go over this Jordan, thou, and all this people, unto the land which I do give to them, even to the children of Israel.

Every place that the sole of your foot shall tread upon, that have I given unto you, as I said unto Moses.

From the wilderness and this Lebanon even unto the great river, the river Euphrates, all the land of the Hittites, and unto the great sea toward the going down of the sun, shall be your coast.

What the Scriptures of the Restoration Teach Us

The scriptures of the restoration also make mention of the promised land. The Doctrine and Covenants refers to when the Savior will come a second time, and the Book of Mormon scriptures indicate America as the promised land sought for. To clarify, there are two promised lands: the Holy Land that the children of Israel possessed and America.

D&C 38:18–20 And I hold forth and deign to give unto you greater riches, even a land of promise, a land flowing with milk and honey, upon which there shall be no curse when the Lord cometh;

And I will give it unto you for the land of your inheritance, if you seek it with all your hearts.

this shall be my covenant with you, ye shall have it for the ... of your inheritance, and for the inheritance of your children forever, while the earth shall stand and ye shall possess it again in eternity, no more to pass away.

1 Nephi 2:19–20 And it came to pass that the Lord spake unto me, saying: Blessed art thou, Nephi, because of thy faith, for thou hast sought me diligently, with lowliness of heart.

And inasmuch as ye shall keep my commandments, ye shall prosper, and shall be led to a land of promise; yea even a land which I have prepared for you; yea, a land which is choice above all other lands.

Ether 2:7–9 And the Lord would not suffer that they should stop beyond the sea in the wilderness, but he would that they should come forth even unto the land of promise, which was choice above all other lands, which the Lord God had preserved for a righteous people.

And he had sworn in his wrath unto the brother of Jared, that whoso should possess this land of promise, from that time henceforth and forever, should serve him, the true and only God, or they should be swept off when the fulness of his wrath should come upon them.

And now, we can behold the decrees of God concerning this land, that it is a land of promise; and whatsoever nation shall possess it shall serve God, or they shall be swept off when the fulness of his wrath shall come upon them. And the fulness of his wrath cometh upon them when they are ripened in iniquity.

Interesting Information

Early Church pioneer Philo Dibble records in his journal a vision of what possibly may be the future New Jerusalem:

On my return home, when I got to Liberty, midway between Lexington and Far West, I concluded I would travel from there home by night, as it was very warm during the day. The road led through a strip of timber for four miles, and after that across a prairie for twenty miles.

When I had traveled about two-thirds of the way across the prairie, riding on horseback, I heard the cooing of the prairie hens. I looked northward and saw, apparently with my natural vision, a beautiful city, the streets of which ran north and south. I also knew there were streets running east and west, but could not trace them with my eye for the buildings. The walks on each side of the streets were as white as marble, and the trees on the outer side of the marble walks had the appearance of locust trees in autumn. This city was in view for about one hour-and-a-half, as near as I could judge, as I traveled along. When I began to descend towards the Crooked River the timber through which I passed hid the city from my view. Every block in this mighty city had sixteen spires, four on each corner, each block being built in the form of a hollow square, within which I seemed to know that the gardens of the inhabitants were situated. The corner buildings on which the spires rested were larger and higher than the others, and the several blocks were uniformly alike. The beauty and grandeur of the scene I cannot describe. While viewing the city the buildings appeared to be transparent. I could not discern the inmates, but I appeared to understand that they could discern whatever passed outside.

Whether this was a city that has been or is to be I cannot tell. It extended as far north as Adam-ondi-Ahman, a distance of about twenty-eight miles. Whatever is revealed to us by the Holy Ghost will never be forgotten. ("Early Scenes in Church History," in *Four Faith Promoting Classics* [1968], 74–96)

Joshua's Authority

What the Book of Joshua Teaches Us

Joshua 1:5–9 There shall not any man be able to stand before thee all the days of thy life: as I was with Moses, so I will be with thee: I will not fail thee, nor forsake thee.

Be strong and of a good courage: for unto this people shalt thou divide for an inheritance the land, which I sware unto their fathers to give them.

Only be thou strong and very courageous, that thou mayest observe to do according to all the law, which Moses my servant commanded thee: turn not from it to the right hand or to the left, that thou mayest prosper whithersoever thou goest.

This book of the law shall not depart out of thy mouth; but thou shalt meditate therein day and night, that thou mayest observe to do according to all that is written therein: for then thou shalt make thy way prosperous, and then thou shalt have good success.

Have not I commanded thee? Be strong and of a good courage; be not afraid, neither be thou dismayed: for the Lord thy God is with thee whithersoever thou goest.

What the Scriptures of the Restoration Teach Us

> **D&C 28:2** But, behold, verily, verily, I say unto thee, no one shall be appointed to receive commandments and revelations in this church excepting my servant Joseph Smith, Jun., for he receiveth them even as Moses.

> **D&C 107:91–92** And again, the duty of the President of the office of the High Priesthood is to preside over the whole church, and to be like unto Moses—
>
> Behold, here is wisdom; yea, to be a seer, a revelator, a translator, and a prophet, having all the gifts of God which he bestows upon the head of the church.

The Lord promises Joshua in verse 5 that he would not fail or forsake him. The Doctrine and Covenants sheds more light on the Lord's promise:

> **D&C 88:83** He that seeketh me early shall find me, and shall not be forsaken.

The Lord commanded Joshua to "be courageous." Again in the latter days, the Lord adds clarity to the meaning:

> **D&C 52:17** And again, he that trembleth under my power shall be made strong, and shall bring forth fruits of praise and wisdom, according to the revelations and truths which I have given you.

> **D&C 66:7–8** Go unto the eastern lands, bear testimony in every place, unto every people and in their synagogues, reasoning with the people.
>
> Let my servant Samuel H. Smith go with you, and forsake him not, and give him thine instructions; and he that is faithful shall be made strong in every place; and I, the Lord, will go with you.

Just how much power and confidence will he give to those who believe and follow him? This next verse gives us an indication what the Lord would have done for the children of Israel had they held true to their covenants and not followed after other gods.

> **D&C 133:58** To prepare the weak for those things which are coming on the earth, and for the Lord's errand in the day when the weak shall confound the wise, and the little one become a strong nation, and two shall put their tens of thousands to flight.

The Invasion of Jericho

What the Book of Joshua Teaches Us

Joshua 6:1–2, 20 Now Jericho was straitly shut up because of the children of Israel: none went out, and none came in.

And the Lord said unto Joshua, See, I have given into thine hand Jericho, and the king thereof, and the mighty men of valour.

So the people shouted when the priests blew with the trumpets: and it came to pass, when the people heard the sound of the trumpet, and the people shouted with a great shout, that the wall fell down flat, so that the people went up into the city, every man straight before him, and they took the city.

The Teachings of Inspired Church Leaders

Elder James E. Talmage:

May we not believe that when Israel encompassed Jericho, the captain of the Lord's host and his heavenly train were there, and that before their supermortal agency, sustained by the faith and obedience of the human army, the walls were leveled?

Some of the latest and highest achievements of man in the utilization of natural forces approach the conditions of spiritual operations. To count the ticking of a watch thousands of miles away; to speak in but an ordinary tone and be heard across the continent; to signal from one hemisphere and be understood on the other though oceans roll and roar between; to bring the lightning into our homes and make it serve as fire and torch; to navigate the air and to travel beneath the ocean surface; to make chemical and atomic energies obey our will—are not these miracles? The possibility of such would not have been received with credence before their actual accomplishment. Nevertheless, these and all other miracles are accomplished through the operation of the laws of nature, which are the laws of God. (*Articles of Faith* [1981], 222–23)

Joshua's Reaction to the Loss at the Battle of Ai

What the Book of Joshua Teaches Us

The Lord promised the children of Israel that he would make them mighty in clearing out the land of its inhabitants so that they could occupy what was rightfully theirs. Some may misunderstand the Lord's purpose in removing the inhabitants of the land to make room for the children of Israel. As stated, the promised land was the land promised by the Lord to Abraham. It was the land the Lord wanted to bestow on his covenant people. Those currently occupying the land were not the covenant people; in fact, far from it, they were idol worshippers. In order for the Lord to raise up a covenant people, he knew it would be essential to remove all distractions around the children of Israel. However, the Israelites may not have understood that in order for this to be achieved, they had to follow the Lord and keep his commandments. They allowed transgression to enter their camp and as a consequence lost the Battle of Ai. As a result of the loss in battle we find Joshua in the tabernacle.

> **Joshua 7:6** And Joshua rent his clothes, and fell to the earth upon his face before the ark of the Lord until the eventide, he and the elders of Israel, and put dust upon their heads.

What the Scriptures of the Restoration Teach Us

Why would Joshua and the elders of the people place dust on their heads? Mosiah helps to shed a little light on this:

> **Mosiah 4:2** And they had viewed themselves in their own carnal state, even less than the dust of the earth. And they all cried aloud with one voice, saying: O have mercy, and apply the atoning blood of Christ that we may receive forgiveness of our sins, and our hearts may be purified; for we believe in Jesus Christ, the Son of God, who created heaven and earth, and all things; who shall come down among the children of men.

Heavenly Wonders

What the Book of Joshua Teaches Us

> **Joshua 10:12–14** Then spake Joshua to the Lord in the day when the Lord delivered up the Amorites before the children of Israel, and he said in the sight of Israel, Sun, stand thou still upon Gibeon; and thou, Moon, in the valley of Ajalon.
>
> And the sun stood still, and the moon stayed, until the people had avenged themselves upon their enemies. Is not this written in the book of Jasher? So the sun stood still in the midst of heaven, and hasten not to go down about a whole day.

And there was no day like that before it or after it, that the Lord hearkened unto the voice of a man: for the Lord fought for Israel.

What the Scriptures of the Restoration Teach Us

Helaman 12:13–17 Yea, and if he say unto the earth—Move—it is moved.

Yea, if he say unto the earth—Thou shalt go back, that it lengthen out the day for many hours—it is done;

And thus, according to his word the earth goeth back, and it appeareth unto man that the sun standeth still; yea, and behold, this is so; for surely it is the earth that moveth and not the sun.

And behold, also, if he say unto the waters of the great deep—Be thou dried up—it is done.

Behold, if he say unto this mountain—Be thou raised up, and come over and fall upon that city, that it be buried up—behold it is done.

D&C 29:14 But, behold, I say unto you that before this great day shall come the sun shall be darkened, and the moon shall be turned into blood, and the stars shall fall from heaven, and there shall be greater signs in heaven above and in the earth beneath.

Interesting Information

The evening that Joseph Smith received the plates from the angel Moroni on September 22, 1827, the heavens were alive with a panorama that caused many to take note. The Knights and Kimballs, who had never heard of Joseph Smith, took note of the night sky. Heber C. Kimball records the following in his journal:

I had retired to bed, when John P. Greene who was living within a hundred steps of my house, came and waked me up, calling upon me to come out and behold the scenery in the heavens. I woke up and called my wife and Sister Fanny Young . . . who was living with us, and we went out-of-doors.

It was one of the most beautiful starlight nights, so clear that we could see to pick up a pin. We looked to the eastern horizon, and beheld a white smoke arise toward the heavens; as it ascended, it formed itself into a belt, and made a noise like the sound of a mighty wind, and continued southwest, forming a regular bow dipping in the western horizon. After the bow had formed, it began to widen out and grow clear and transparent, . . . it grew wide enough to contain twelve men abreast.

In this bow an army moved, commencing from the east and marching to the west; they continued marching until they reached the western horizon. They moved in platoons, and walked so close that the rear ranks trod in the steps of their file leaders, until the whole bow was literally crowded with soldiers. We could distinctly see the muskets, bayonets and knapsacks of the men, who wore caps and feathers like those used by the American soldiers in the last war with Britain; and also saw their officers with their swords and equipage, and the clashing and jingling of their implements of war, and could discover the forms and features of the men. The most profound order existed through out the entire army; when the foremost man stepped every man stepped at the same time; I could hear the steps. When the front rank reached the western horizon a battle ensued, as we could distinctly hear the report of arms and the rush.

No man could judge of my feelings when I beheld that army of men, as plainly as ever I saw armies of men in the flesh; it seemed as though every hair of my head was alive. This scenery we gazed upon for hours, until it began to disappear.

After I became acquainted with Mormonism, I learned that this took place the same evening that Joseph Smith received the records of the Book of Mormon from the angel Moroni who had held those records in his possession.

John Young, Sen., and John P. Greene's wife, Rhoda, were also witnesses.

My wife, being frightened at what she saw, said, "Father Young, what does all this mean?"

"Why it's one of the signs of the coming of the Son of Man," he replied, in a lively, pleased manner. (Orson F. Whitney, *Life of Heber C. Kimball* [1992], 15–17)

Early Church member Philo Dibble shares the following experience:

I will here observe that about the time of which I write, there were many signs and wonders seen in the heavens above and in the earth beneath in the region of Kirtland, both by Saints and strangers. A pillar of light was seen every evening for more than a month hovering over the place where we did our baptizing. One evening also, as Brother William Blakesley and I were returning home from meeting, we observed that it was unusually light, even for moonlight; but, on reflection, we found the moon was not to be seen that night. Although it was cloudy, it was as light as noonday, and we could seemingly see a tree farther that night than we could in the day time. ("Early Scenes in Church History," *Four Faith Promoting Classics* [1968], 74–96)

After reading a letter written by Elizabeth Haven Barlow dated February 25, 1839, I realized that there have been amazing sights in the day sky also:

P.S. #14 About two weeks after we left Far West three suns were seen to rise one morning which were seen by the people there. The sun, the great orb of the day was in the center, the other two were not quite so bright but produced shadows only dim. Light projected into the heavens from all three. They were seen several hours, but as the sun traveled towards the meridian of the day the others disappeared. (Ora H. Barlow, *The Israel Barlow Story and Mormon Mores* [1968], 115)

Choosing to Serve the Lord

What the Book of Joshua Teaches Us

Joshua 24:1, 15 And Joshua gathered all the tribes of Israel to Shechem, and called for the elders of Israel, and for their heads, and for their judges, and for their officers; and they presented themselves before God.

And if it seem evil unto you to serve the Lord, choose you this day whom ye will serve; whether the gods which your fathers served that were on the other side of the flood, or the gods of the Amorites, in whose land ye dwell: but as for me and my house, we will serve the Lord.

Joshua 24:22 And Joshua said unto the people, Ye are witnesses against yourselves that ye have chosen you the Lord, to serve him. And they said, We are witnesses.

What the Scriptures of the Restoration Teach Us

D&C 4:2 Therefore, O ye that embark in the service of God, see that ye serve him with all your heart, might, mind and strength, that ye may stand blameless before God at the last day.

The Teachings of Inspired Church Leaders

Elder Erastus Snow:

If good and evil is placed before us, does not the person who chooses the good and refuses the evil exhibit his agency and manhood as much as the man who chooses the evil and refuses the good? Or is the independence of manhood all on the side of the evil-doer? I leave you to answer this question in your own mind. To me, I think the angels and saints and all good people have exercised their agency by choosing the good and refusing the evil; and in doing so they not only exhibit their independence and manhood as much, but show a much higher and greater nobility of character and disposition; and I leave the future to determine who are wise in the choice of their freedom and independence.

Joshua said to ancient Israel: "Choose ye this day whom ye will serve; if the Lord be God, serve him; if Baal, serve him. But as for me and my house, we will serve the Lord." I think what we need to learn are the true principles that shall lead us to peace, to wealth and happiness in this world, and glory and exaltation in the world to come. And that if we can learn these principles, and receive them in good and honest hearts, and teach them as our faith, and practice them in our lives, we shall show our manhood, our independence and our agency as creditably before the angels and the Gods, as any wicked man can, in refusing the good and cleaving to the evil, exhibit his before the devil and his angels. (In *Journal of Discourses*, 26 vols. [1854–86], 19:180–81)

Warning on Following after Other Gods

What the Book of Joshua Teaches Us

Joshua 24:20 If ye forsake the Lord, and serve strange gods, then he will turn and do you hurt, and consume you, after that he hath done you good.

What the Scriptures of the Restoration Teach Us

Mosiah 7:29 For behold, the Lord hath said: I will not succor my people in the day of their transgression; but I will hedge up their ways that they prosper not; and their doings shall be as a stumbling block before them.

Helaman 12:3 And thus we see that except the Lord doth chasten his people with many afflictions, yea, except he doth visit them with death and with terror, and with famine and with all manner of pestilence, they will not remember him.

Judges

An Angel's Rebuke

What the Book of Judges Teaches Us

Judges 2:1–2 And an angel of the Lord came up from Gilgal to Bochim, and said, I made you to go up out of Egypt, and have brought you unto the land which I sware unto your fathers; and I said, I will never break my covenant with you.

And ye shall make no league with the inhabitants of this land; ye shall throw down their altars: but ye have not obeyed my voice: why have ye done this?

What the Scriptures of the Restoration Teach Us

D&C 82:10 I, the Lord, am bound when ye do what I say; but when ye do not what I say, ye have no promise.

A Generation Knowing Not the Lord

What the Book of Judges Teaches Us

Judges 2:10 And also all that generation were gathered unto their fathers: and there arose another generation after them which knew not the Lord, nor yet the works which he had done for Israel.

What the Scriptures of the Restoration Teach Us

Mosiah 26:1–3 Now it came to pass that there were many of the rising generation that could not understand the words of king Benjamin, being little children at the time he spake unto his people; and they did not believe the tradition of their fathers.

They did not believe what had been said concerning the resurrection of the dead, neither did they believe concerning the coming of Christ.

And now because of their unbelief they could not understand the word of God; and their hearts were hardened.

The Teachings of Inspired Church Leaders

President Brigham Young:

If we do not take the pains to train our children, to teach and instruct them concerning these revealed truths, the condemnation will be upon us, as parents, or at least in a measure.

Teach your children from their youth, never to set their hearts immoderately upon an object of this world.

Bring up your children in the love and fear of the Lord. . . .

Parents, teach your children by precept and example, the importance of addressing the Throne of grace; teach them how to live, how to draw from the elements the necessaries of life, and teach them the laws of life that they may know how to preserve themselves in health and be able to minister to others. . . .

Teach our children honesty and uprightness, and teach them also never to injure others. . . .

If parents will continually set before their children examples worthy of their imitation and the approval of our Father in Heaven, they will turn the current, and the tide of feelings of their children, and they, eventually, will desire righteousness more than evil. (*Discourses of Brigham Young*, comp. John A. Widtsoe [1954], 207–8)

Deborah

What the Book of Judges Teaches Us

Judges 4:4 And Deborah, a prophetess, the wife of Lapidoth, she judged Israel at that time.

Interesting Information

Whatever the reason for her leadership calling, Deborah certainly followed the pattern of earlier Old Testament women in recognizing a need, heeding the word of the Lord, and acting accordingly. Rebekah ensured that the appropriate birthright blessing would be given to her son Jacob. Shiprah and Pual, the Hebrew midwives, defied Pharaoh and refused to slay infant male Israelites. And Miriam the prophetess, sister of Moses, helped her mother save her baby brother. Stories of these women may in fact have influenced Deborah.

Acting with honesty, integrity, courage, unwavering faith, and unquestioning obedience, Deborah was honored with great responsibilities both by her own people and by the Lord. She judged her people righteously; she heard and acted upon the word of the Lord when it came to her; she accompanied the Israelite army; and she gave glory to the Lord for her people's deliverance. (Kristin E. Litchman, "Deborah and the Book of Judges," *Ensign*, Jan. 1990, online)

The Teachings of Inspired Church Leaders

Elder James E. Talmage:

No special ordination in the Priesthood is essential to man's receiving the gift of prophecy; bearers of the Melchizedek Priesthood, Adam, Noah, Moses, and a multitude of others were prophets, but not more truly so than others who were specifically called to the Aaronic order, as exemplified in the instance of John the Baptist. The ministrations of Miriam and Deborah show that this gift may be possessed by women also. (*Articles of Faith* [1981], 228–29)

Gideon and Sign Seeking

What the Book of Judges Teaches Us

Judges 6:11–17 And there came an angel of the Lord, and sat under an oak which was in Ophrah, that pertained unto Joash the Abi-ezrite: and his son Gideon threshed wheat by the winepress, to hide it from the Midianites.

And the angel of the Lord appeared unto him, and said unto him, The Lord is with thee, thou mighty man of valour.

And Gideon said unto him, Oh my Lord, if the Lord be with us, why then is all this befallen us? And where be all his miracles which our fathers told us of, saying, Did not the Lord bring us up from Egypt? But now the Lord hath forsaken us, and delivered us into the hands of the Midianites.

And the Lord looked upon him, and said, Go in this thy might, and thou shalt save Israel from the hand of the Midianites: have not I sent thee?

And he said unto him, Oh my Lord, wherewith shall I save Israel? behold, my family is poor in Manasseh, and I am the least in my father's house.

And the Lord said unto him, Surely I will be with thee, and thou shalt smite the Midianites as one man.

And he said unto him, If now I have found grace in thy sight, then shew me a sign that thou talkest with me.

What the Scriptures of the Restoration Teach Us

The Lord has condemned man on various occasions for seeking after a sign. He has said, "It's an adulterous generation that seeketh for a sign" (Matt 12:39, etc.). Understanding this, why was Gideon seeking the Lord for a sign? The Doctrine and Covenants provides insight for those who want proof from the Lord.

> D&C 63:10–12 Yea, signs come by faith, not by the will of men, nor as they please, but by the will of God.
>
> Yea, signs come by faith, unto mighty works, for without faith no man pleaseth God; and with whom God is angry he is not well pleased; wherefore, unto such he showeth no signs, only in wrath unto their condemnation.
>
> Wherefore, I, the Lord, am not pleased with those among you who have sought after signs and wonders for faith, and not for the good of men unto my glory.

Walking in Their Own Paths

What the Book of Judges Teaches Us

> Judges 21:25 In those days there was no king in Israel: every man did that which was right in his own eyes.

What the Scriptures of the Restoration Teach Us

Men have never really taken the lessons of history and tried to correct what is wrong when it comes to spiritual matters. Man, for the most part, is channeled along by the grooves and ruts created by the past. Many of the warnings and scoldings the Lord has given to the ancients are the same given to men in this dispensation.

D&C 1:16 They seek not the Lord to establish his righteousness, but every man walketh in his own way, and after the image of his own god, whose image is in the likeness of the world, and whose substance is that of an idol, which waxeth old and shall perish in Babylon, even Babylon the great, which shall fall.

Samson and Strength from the Lord

What the Book of Judges Teaches Us

Judges 15:11–16 Then three thousand men of Judah went to the top of the rock Etam, and said to Samson, Knowest thou not that the Philistines are rulers over us? What is this that thou hast done unto us? And he said unto them, As they did unto me, so have I done unto them.

And they said unto him, we are come down to bind thee, that we may deliver thee into the hand of the Philistines. And Samson said unto them, Swear unto me, that ye will not fall upon me yourselves.

And they spake unto him, saying, No; but we will bind thee fast, and deliver thee into their hand: but surely we will not kill thee. And they bound him with two new cords, and brought him up from the rock.

And when he came unto Lehi, the Philistines shouted against him: and the Spirit of the Lord came mightily upon him, and the cords that were upon his arms became as flax that was burnt with fire, and his bands loosed from off his hands.

And he found a new jawbone of an ass, and put forth his hand, and took it, and slew a thousand men therewith.

And Samson said, With the jawbone of an ass, heaps upon heaps, with the jaw of an ass have I slain a thousand men.

What the Scriptures of the Restoration Teach Us

1 Nephi 7:16–18 And it came to pass that when I, Nephi, had spoken these words unto my brethren, they were angry with me. And it came to pass that they did lay their hands upon me, for behold, they were exceedingly wroth, and they did bind me with cords, for they sought to take away my life, that they might leave me in the wilderness to be devoured by wild beasts.

But it came to pass that I prayed unto the Lord, saying: O Lord, according to my faith which is in thee, wilt thou deliver me from the hands of my brethren; yea, even give me strength that I may burst these bands with which I am bound.

And it came to pass that when I had said these words, behold, the bands were loosed from off my hands and feet, and I stood before my brethren, and I spake unto them again.

Alma 2:26–30 And it came to pass that the people of Nephi took their tents, and departed out of the valley of Gideon towards their city, which was the city of Zarahemla

And behold, as they were crossing the river Sidon, the Lamanites and the Amlicites, being as numerous almost, as it were, as the sands of the sea, came upon them to destroy them.

Nevertheless, the Nephites being strengthened by the hand of the Lord, having prayed mightily to him that he would deliver them out of the hands of their enemies, therefore the Lord did hear their cries, and did strengthen them, and the Lamanites and the Amlicites did fall before them.

And it came to pass that Alma fought with Amlici with the sword, face to face; and they did contend mightily, one with another.

And it came to pass that Alma, being a man of God, being exercised with much faith, cried, saying: O Lord, have mercy and spare my life, that I may be an instrument in thy hands to save and preserve this people.

D&C 3:4 For although a man may have many revelations, and have power to do many mighty works, yet if he boasts of his own strength, and sets at naught the counsels of God, and follows after the dictates of his own will and carnal desires, he must fall and incur the vengeance of a just God upon him.

Samson and Delilah

What the Book of Judges Teaches Us

Judges 16:4–6 And it came to pass afterward, that he [Samson] loved a woman in the valley of Sorek, whose name was Delilah.

And the lords of the Philistines came up unto her, and said unto her, Entice him, and see wherein his great strength lieth, and by what means we may prevail against him, that we may bind him to afflict him: and we will give thee every one of us eleven hundred pieces of silver.

And Delilah said to Samson, Tell me, I pray thee, wherein thy great strength lieth, and wherewith thou mightiest be bound to afflict thee.

The Teachings of Inspired Church Leaders

President Wilford Woodruff:

I have seen Oliver Cowdery when it seemed as though the earth trembled under his feet. I never heard a man bear a stronger testimony than he did when under the influence of the Spirit. But the moment he left the kingdom of God, that moment his power fell like lightning from Heaven. He was shorn of his strength like Samson in the lap of Delilah. He lost the power and the testimony which he had enjoyed, and he never recovered it again in its fulness while in the flesh, although he died in the Church. (Stanley R. Gunn, *Oliver Cowdery—Second Elder and Scribe* [1962], 73)

Israel's Downfall

What the Book of Judges Teaches Us

Judges 21:21 And see, and, behold, if the daughters of Shiloh come out to dance in dances, then come ye out of the vineyards, and catch you every man his wife of the daughters of Shiloh, and go to the land of Benjamin.

The leaders of the children of Israel (elders) had degenerated to the point that they gave carnal commandments such as the above to the people.

What the Scriptures of the Restoration Teach Us

This situation is similar to the Book of Mormon setting when the daughters of the Lamanites gathered to dance. It was here that the wicked priests of king Noah stole the daughters of the Lamanites and made them their wives.

Mosiah 20:1–5 Now there was a place in Shemlon where the daughters of the Lamanites did gather themselves together to sing, and to dance, and to make themselves merry.

And it came to pass that there was one day a small number of them gathered together to sing and to dance.

And now the priests of king Noah, being ashamed to return to the city of Nephi, yea, and also fearing that the people would slay them, therefore they durst not return to their wives and their children.

And having tarried in the wilderness, and having discovered the daughters of the Lamanites, they laid and watched them;

And when there were but few of them gathered together to dance, they came forth out of their secret places and took them and carried them into the wilderness; yea, twenty and four of the daughters of the Lamanites they carried into the wilderness.

Ruth

Lessons in Obedience

What the Book of Ruth Teaches Us

Ruth 1:16 And Ruth said, Entreat me not to leave thee, or to return from following after thee: for whither thou goest, I will go; and where thou lodgest, I will lodge: thy people shall be my people, and thy God my God.

The Teachings of Inspired Church Leaders

President John Taylor:

"Thanks be to the God of Israel who has counted us worthy to receive the principles of truth." These were the feelings you had and enjoyed in your far distant homes [Nauvoo]. And your obedience to those principles tore you from your homes, firesides and associations and brought you here [Salt Lake Valley], for you felt like one of old, when she said, "Whither thou goest I will go; thy God shall be my God, thy people shall be my people, and where thou diest there will I be buried." And you have gathered to Zion that you might be taught and instructed in the laws of life and listen to the words which emanate from God, become one people and one nation, partake of one spirit, and prepare yourselves, your progenitors and posterity for an everlasting inheritance in the celestial kingdom of God. (In *Journal of Discourses*, 26 vols. [1854–86], 14:189)

Ruth Bares a Son

What the Book of Ruth Teaches Us

Ruth 4:13 So Boaz took Ruth, and she was his wife: and when he went in unto her, the Lord gave her conception, and she bare a son.

The Teachings of Inspired Church Leaders

President Thomas S. Monson:

How very important was Ruth's obedience to Naomi and the resulting marriage to Boaz by which Ruth—the foreigner and a Moabite convert—became a great-grandmother of David and therefore an ancestress of Jesus Christ. The book of the Holy Bible that bears her name contains language poetic in style, reflective of her spirit of determination and courage. ("They Showed the Way," *Ensign*, May 1997, 50)

Interesting Information

"From 1928 to 1972, Ruth and her gleaning were official models for Church women eighteen years and older in Gleaner classes of the Young Women's Mutual Improvement Association and its successor, the Young Women organization" (*Encyclopedia of Mormanism*, 5 vols. [1992], "Ruth," 1240).

1 Samuel

Hannah

What the Book of 1 Samuel Teaches Us

It is through this scripture and other latter-day scripture that we begin to understand the earnestness with which we must pray if we desire an answer to our supplications.

> **1 Samuel 1:12–16** And it came to pass, as she continued praying before the Lord, that Eli marked her mouth.
>
> Now Hannah, she spake in her heart; only her lips moved, but her voice was not heard: therefore Eli thought she had been drunken.
>
> And Eli said unto her, How long wilt thou be drunken? Put away thy wine from thee.
>
> And Hannah answered and said, No, my lord, I am a woman of a sorrowful spirit: I have drunk neither wine nor strong drink, but have poured out my soul before the Lord.
>
> Count not thine handmaid for a daughter of Belial: for out of the abundance of my complaint and grief have I spoken hitherto.

What the Scriptures of the Restoration Teach Us

> **Alma 34:26–27** But this is not all; ye must pour out your souls in your closets, and your secret places, and in your wilderness.
>
> Yea, and when you do not cry unto the Lord, let your hearts be full, drawn out in prayer unto him continually for your welfare, and also for the welfare of those who are around you.

The Teachings of Inspired Church Leaders

President Wilford Woodruff:

There is one admonition of our Savior that all the Saints of God should observe, but which, I fear, we do not as we should, and that is, to pray always and faint not. I fear, as a people, we do not pray enough in faith. We should call upon the Lord in mighty prayer, and make all our wants known unto him. For if he does not protect and deliver us and save us, no other power will. Therefore our trust is entirely in him. Therefore our prayers should ascend into the ears of our Heavenly Father day and night. (*Discourses of Wilford Woodruff*, sel. G. Homer Durham [1995], 221)

Hannah's Song

What the Book of 1 Samuel Teaches Us

1 Samuel 2:3 Talk no more so exceeding proudly; let not arrogancy come out of your mouth: for the Lord is a God of knowledge, and by him actions are weighed.

As Hannah sings praises to the Lord, she makes an interesting statement. What did she mean when she stated, "and by him actions are weighed"?

What the Scriptures of the Restoration Teach Us

3 Nephi 27:14–15 And my Father sent me that I might be lifted up upon the cross; and after that I had been lifted up upon the cross, that I might draw all men unto me, that as I have been lifted up by men even so should men be lifted up by the Father, to stand before me, to be judged of their works, whether they be good or whether they be evil—
And for this cause have I been lifted up; therefore, according to the power of the Father I will draw all man unto me, that they may be judged according to their works.

Eli and His Sons

What the Book of 1 Samuel Teaches Us

Since Eli made little attempt at controlling his sons' behavior, the Lord reminded Eli that he could replace his sons as priests at any time with someone that was righteous. Interestingly, this same warning was given by the Lord in this dispensation.

1 Samuel 2:24, 35 Nay, my sons; for it is no good report that I hear: ye make the Lord's people to transgress.

And I will raise me up a faithful priest, that shall do according to that which is in mine heart and in my mind: and I will build him a sure house; and he shall walk before mine anointed for ever.

What the Scriptures of the Restoration Teach Us

D&C 114:2 For verily thus saith the Lord, that inasmuch as there are those among you who deny my name, others shall be planted in their stead and receive their bishopric. Amen.

Samuel

What the Book of 1 Samuel Teaches Us

1 Samuel 3:1 And the child Samuel ministered unto the Lord before Eli. And the word of the Lord was precious in those days; there was no open vision.

What the Scriptures of the Restoration Teach Us

Mormon 1:13–14 But wickedness did prevail upon the face of the whole land, insomuch that the Lord did take away his beloved disciples, and the work of miracles and of healing did cease because of the iniquity of the people.

And there were no gifts from the Lord, and the Holy Ghost did not come upon any, because of their wickedness and unbelief.

Joseph Smith—History 1:21 Some few days after I had this vision, I happened to be in company with one of the Methodist preachers, who was very active in the before mentioned religious excitement; and, conversing with him on the subject of religion, I took occasion to give him an account of the vision which I had had. I was greatly surprised at his behavior; he treated my communication not only lightly, but with great contempt, saying it was all of the devil, that there were no such things as visions or revelations in these days; that all such things had ceased with the apostles, and that there would never be any more of them.

The Teachings of Inspired Church Leaders

President Harold B. Lee:

"And the child Samuel ministered unto the Lord before Eli. And the word of the Lord was precious in those days; there was no open vision. . . .'"

That means that there was no prophet upon the earth through whom the Lord could reveal his will, either by personal experience, or by revelation. (*"But Arise and Stand upon Thy Feet"—and I Will Speak with Thee*, Brigham Young University Speeches of the Year [Feb. 7, 1956], 2)

Inspired Prophecy

What the Book of 1 Samuel Teaches Us

1 Samuel 3:19 And Samuel grew, and the Lord was with him, and did let none of his words fall to the ground.

The Teachings of Inspired Church Leaders

President Heber J. Grant:

You need have no fear that when one of the apostles of the Lord Jesus Christ delivers a prophecy in the name of Jesus Christ, because he is inspired to do that, that it will fall by the wayside. I know of more than one prophecy, which, looking at it naturally, seemed as though it would fall to the ground as year after year passed. But lo and behold, in the providences of the Lord, that prophecy was fulfilled. (*Gospel Standards*, comp. G. Homer Durham [1976], 68)

The Dangers of a King

What the Book of 1 Samuel Teaches Us

It is in these verses that Samuel discusses the dangers of having a king to rule over the people.

1 Samuel 8:11–19 And he said, This will be the manner of the king that shall reign over you: He will take your sons, and appoint them for himself, for his chariots, and to be his horsemen; and some shall run before his chariots.

And he will appoint him captains over thousands, and captains over fifties; and will set them to ear his ground, and to reap his harvest, and to make his instruments of war, and instruments of his chariots.

And he will take your daughters to be confectionaries, and to be cooks, and to be bakers.

And he will take your fields, and your vineyards, and your olive-yards, even the best of them, and give them to his servants.

And he will take the tenth of your seed, and of your vineyards, and give to his officers, and to his servants.

And he will take your menservants, and your maidservants, and your goodliest young men, and your asses, and put them to his work.

He will take the tenth of your sheep: and ye shall be his servants.

And ye shall cry out in that day because of your king which ye shall have chosen you; and the Lord will not hear you in that day.

Nevertheless the people refused to obey the voice of Samuel; and they said, Nay; but we will have a king over us.

What the Scriptures of the Restoration Teach Us

Mosiah 29:16–18, 21–25 Now I say unto you, that because all men are not just it is not expedient that ye should have a king or kings to rule over you.

For behold, how much iniquity doth one wicked king cause to be committed, yea, and what great destruction!

Yea, remember king Noah, his wickedness and his abominations, and also the wickedness and abominations of his people. Behold what great destruction did come upon them; and also because of their iniquities they were brought into bondage.

And behold, now I say unto you, ye cannot dethrone an iniquitous king save it be through much contention, and the shedding of much blood.

For behold, he has his friends in iniquity, and he keepeth his guards about him; and he teareth up the laws of those who have reigned in righteousness before him; and he trampleth under his feet the commandments of God;

And he enacteth laws, and sendeth them forth among his people, yea, laws after the manner of his own wickedness; and whosoever doth not obey his laws he causeth to be destroyed; and whosoever doth rebel against him he will send his armies against them to war, and if he can he will destroy them; and thus an unrighteous king doth pervert the ways of all righteousness.

And now behold I say unto you, it is not expedient that such abominations should come upon you.

Therefore, choose you by the voice of this people, judges, that ye may be judged according to the laws which have been given you by our fathers, which are correct, and which were given by the hand of the Lord.

Prophets and Seers

What the Book of 1 Samuel Teaches Us

1 Samuel 9:9 (Beforetime in Israel, when a man went to inquire of God, thus he spake, Come, and let us go to the seer: for he that is now called a Prophet was beforetime called a Seer.)

What the Scriptures of the Restoration Teach Us

Mosiah 8:13–17 Now Ammon said unto him: I can assuredly tell thee, O king, of a man that can translate the records; for he has wherewith that he can look, and translate all records that are of ancient date; and it is a gift from God. And the things are called interpreters, and no man can look in them except he be commanded, lest he should look for that he ought not and he should perish. And whosoever is commanded to look in them, the same is called seer.

And behold, the king of the people who are in the land of Zarahemla is the man that is commanded to do these things, and who has this high gift from God.

And the king said that a seer is greater than a prophet.

And Ammon said that a seer is a revelator and a prophet also; and a gift which is greater can no man have, except he should possess the power of God, which no man can; yet a man may have great power given him from God.

But a seer can know of things which are past, and also of things which are to come, and by them shall all things be revealed, or, rather, shall secret things be made manifest, and hidden things shall come to light, and things which are not known shall be made known by them, and also things shall be made known by them which otherwise could not be known.

Interesting Information

Elder Orson F. Whitney:

About the first of February, 1831, a sleigh containing four persons, drove through the streets of Kirtland and drew up at the door of Gilbert and Whitney's mercantile establishment. . . . One of the men, a young and stalwart personage, alighted, and springing up the steps, walked into the store and to where the junior partner was standing.

"Newel K. Whitney! Thou art the man!" he exclaimed, extending his hand cordially, as if to an old and familiar acquaintance.

"You have the advantage of me," replied the [storekeeper], as he mechanically took the proffered hand—a half-amused, half-mystified look overspreading his countenance—"I could not call you by name, as you have me."

"I am Joseph, the Prophet," said the stranger, smiling. "You've prayed me here; now what do you want of me?"

Mr. Whitney, astonished, but no less delighted, as soon as his surprise would permit, conducted the party . . . across the street to his house on the corner, and introduced them to his wife [Elizabeth Ann]. She shared fully his surprise and ecstasy. Joseph said of this episode: "We were kindly received and welcomed into the house of Brother N. K. Whitney. I and my wife lived in the family of Brother Whiney several weeks, and received every kindness and attention that could be expected." [See *History of the Church*, 1:145–46.] . . . .

"By what power did this remarkable man, Joseph Smith, recognize one whom he had never before seen in the flesh? Why did not Newel K. Whitney recognize him? It was because Joseph Smith was a seer, a choice seer; he had actually seen Newel K. Whitney upon his knees, hundreds of miles away, praying for his coming to Kirtland. Marvelous—but true!" (*Teachings of Presidents of the Church: Joseph Smith* [2011], 159–60)

King Saul

What the Book of 1 Samuel Teaches Us

1 Samuel 13:9–10, 13–14 And Saul said, Bring hither a burnt offering to me, and peace offerings. And he offered the burnt offering.

And it came to pass, that as soon as he had made an end of offering the burnt offering, behold, Samuel came; and Saul went out to meet him, that he might salute him.

And Samuel said to Saul, Thou hast done foolishly: thou hast not kept the commandment of the Lord thy God, which he commanded thee: for now would the Lord have established thy kingdom upon Israel for ever.

But now thy kingdom shall not continue: the Lord hath sought him a man after his own heart, and the Lord hath commanded him to be captain over his people, because thou hast not kept that which the Lord commanded thee.

What the Scriptures of the Restoration Teach Us

D&C 121:39 We have learned by sad experience that it is the nature and disposition of almost all men, as soon as they get a little authority, as they suppose, they will immediately begin to exercise unrighteous dominion.

The Teachings of Inspired Church Leaders

Elder James Talmage:

Think also of Saul who had been called from the field to be made king of the nation. When the Philistines were marshaled against Israel in Michmash, Saul waited for Samuel, under whose hand he had received his kingly anointing and to whom he had looked in the days of this humility for guidance; he asked that the prophet come and offer sacrifices to the Lord in behalf of the people. But, growing impatient at Samuel's delay, Saul prepared the burnt offering himself, forgetting that though he occupied the throne, wore the crown, and bore the scepter, these insignia of kingly power gave him no right to officiate even as a deacon in the Priesthood of God; and for this and other instances of his unrighteous presumption he was rejected of God and another was made king in his place. (*Articles of Faith* [1981], 184–85)

What the Book of 1 Samuel Teaches Us

1 Samuel 15:35 And Samuel came no more to see Saul until the day of his death: nevertheless Samuel mourned for Saul: and the Lord repented that he had made Saul king over Israel.

Joseph Smith Translation—1 Samuel 15:35 And Samuel came no more to see Saul until the day of his death; nevertheless Samuel mourned for Saul; and the Lord rent the kingdom from Saul whom he had made king over Israel.

David and Goliath

What the Book of 1 Samuel Teaches Us

1 Samuel 17:45 Then said David to the Philistine, Thou comest to me with a sword, and with a spear, and with a shield: but I come to thee in the name of the Lord of hosts, the God of the armies of Israel, whom thou hast defied.

The Teachings of Inspired Church Leaders

President Gordon B. Hinckley:

There are Goliaths all around you, hulking giants with evil intent to destroy you. These are not nine-foot-tall men, but they are men and institutions that control attractive but evil things that may challenge and weaken and destroy you. . . .

Victory will be yours. . . . You have His power within you to sustain you. You have the right to ministering angels about you to protect you. Do not let Goliath frighten you. Stand your ground and hold your place, and you will be triumphant. ("Overpowering the Goliaths in Our Lives," *Ensign*, May 1983, online)

Is There Not a Cause?

What the Book of 1 Samuel Teaches Us

1 Samuel 17:29 And David said, What have I now done? Is there not a cause?

The Teachings of Inspired Church Leaders

Elder Victor L. Brown:

A youth asking his wavering adult leaders, "Is there not a cause?" There are thousands of young men and women today who are asking the same question: "Is there not a cause?" Some hear no reply; others hear replies of little substance. And still others are led astray by causes which are counterfeit. . . .

I declare with all my soul—there is a cause! It is a cause worth giving one's life for. It is the cause of righteousness. It is a cause that every youth in this Church should rally to as he declares war on Satan and his legions. As David said to Goliath, so each youth should declare to Satan, "Thou comes to me with a sword, and with a spear, and with a shield; but I come to thee in the name of the Lord of hosts, the God of the armies of Israel, whom thou hast defied." (1 Samuel 17:45) ("Is There Not a Cause?," *Ensign*, Nov. 1974, 104)

David and Jonathan

What the Book of 1 Samuel Teaches Us

1 Samuel 18:1–4 And it came to pass, when he had made an end of speaking unto Saul, that the soul of Jonathan was knit with the soul of David, and Jonathan loved him as his own soul.

And Saul took him that day, and would let him go no more home to his father's house.

Then Jonathan and David made a covenant, because he loved him as his own soul.

And Jonathan stripped himself of the robe that was upon him, and gave it to David, and his garments, even to his sword, and to his bow, and to his girdle.

What the Scriptures of the Restoration Teach Us

It is incredible to think that Jonathan and David could be such good friends in spite of the less than stellar example set by Saul, Jonathan's father. Saul was blinded by jealousy, and couldn't get over the fact that David was more of a hero to Israel then Saul could ever hope to be. It was Saul that should have set the example of oneness to his son, yet it was Jonathan who exhibited true Christian love.

Mosiah 18:21 And he commanded them that there should be no contention one with another, but that they should look forward with one eye, having one faith and one baptism, having their hearts knit together in unity and in love one towards another.

D&C 88:123 See that ye love one another; cease to be covetous; learn to impart one to another as the gospel requires.

King Saul and David

What the Book of 1 Samuel Teaches Us

1 Samuel 19:18–24 So David fled, and escaped, and came to Samuel to Ramah, and told him all that Saul had done to him. And he and Samuel went and dwelt in Naioth.

And it was told Saul, saying, Behold, David is at Naioth in Ramah.

And Saul sent messengers to take David: and when they saw the company of the prophets prophesying, and Samuel standing as appointed over them, the Spirit of God was upon the messengers of Saul, and they also prophesied.

And when it was told Saul, he sent other messengers, and they prophesied likewise. And Saul sent messengers again the third time, and they prophesied also.

Then went he also to Ramah, and came to a great well that is in Sechu: and he asked and said, Where are Samuel and David? And one said, Behold, they be at Naioth in Ramah.

And he went thither to Naioth in Ramah: and the Spirit of God was upon him also, and he went on, and prophesied, until he came to Naioth in Ramah.

And he stripped off his clothes also, and prophesied before Samuel in like manner, and lay down naked all that day and all that night. Wherefore they say, Is Saul also among the prophets?

The Teachings of Inspired Church Leaders

As incredible as it may seem, the above story in the book of 1 Samuel has repeated itself in this dispensation in a situation that involved President Wilford Woodruff while serving a mission to England.

President Wilford Woodruff:

When I arose to speak at Brother Benbow's house, a man entered the door and informed me that he was a constable, and had been sent by the rector of the parish with a warrant to arrest me. I asked him, "For what crime?" He said, "For preaching to the people." I told him that I, as well as the rector, had a license for preaching the gospel to the people, and that if he would take a chair I would wait upon him after meeting. He took my chair and sat beside me. For an hour and a quarter I preached the first principles of the everlasting gospel. The power of God rested upon me, the spirit filled the house, and the people were convinced. At the close of the meeting I opened the door for baptism, and seven offered themselves. Among the number were four preachers and the constable. The latter arose and said, "Mr. Woodruff, I would like to be baptized." I told him I would like to baptize him. I went down into the pool and baptized the seven. We then came together. I confirmed thirteen, administered the Sacrament, and we all rejoiced together.

The constable went to the rector and told him that if he wanted Mr. Woodruff taken for preaching the gospel, he must go himself and serve the writ; for he had heard him preach the only true gospel sermon he had ever listened to in his life. The rector did not know what to make of it, so he sent two clerks of the Church of England as spies, to attend our meeting, and find out what we did preach. They both were pricked in their hearts, received the word of the Lord gladly, and were baptized and confirmed members of the Church of Jesus Christ of Latter-day Saints. The rector became alarmed, and did not venture to send anybody else. (Matthias Cowley, *Wilford Woodruff* [1970], 118)

Not One Left Standing by the Wall

What the Book of 1 Samuel Teaches Us

1 Samuel 25:22 So and more also do God unto the enemies of David, if I leave of all that pertain to him by the morning light any that pisseth against the wall.

What the Scriptures of the Restoration Teach Us

A less crude way of saying the same thing is found in the following:

D&C 121:15 And not many years hence, that they and their posterity shall be swept from under heaven, saith God, that not one of them is left to stand by the wall.

The Witch of En-dor

What the Book of 1 Samuel Teaches Us

1 Samuel 28:6–15 And when Saul enquired of the Lord, the Lord answered him not, neither by dreams, nor by Urim, nor by prophets.

Then said Saul unto his servants, Seek me a woman that hath a familiar spirit, that I may go to her, and enquire of her. And his servants said to him, Behold, there is a woman that hath a familiar spirit at En-dor.

And Saul disguised himself, and put on other raiment, and he went, and two men with him, and they came to the woman by night: and he said, I pray thee, divine unto me by the familiar spirit, and bring me him up, whom I shall name unto thee.

And the woman said unto him, Behold, thou knowest what Saul hath done, how he hath cut off those that have familiar spirits, and the wizards, out of the land: wherefore then layest thou a snare for my life, to cause me to die?

And Saul sware to her by the Lord, saying, As the Lord liveth, there shall no punishment happen to thee for this thing.

Then said the woman, Whom shall I bring up unto thee? And he said, Bring me up Samuel.

And when the woman saw Samuel, she cried with a loud voice: and the woman spake to Saul, saying, Why hast thou deceived me? For thou are Saul.

And the king said unto her, Be not afraid: for what sawest thou? And the woman said unto Saul, I saw gods ascending out of the earth.

And he said unto her, What form is he of? And she said, An old man cometh up; and he is covered with a mantle, And Saul perceived that it was Samuel, and he stooped with his face to the ground, and bowed himself.

And Samuel said to Saul, Why hast thou disquieted me, to bring me up? And Saul answered, I am sore distressed; for the Philistines make war against me, and God is departed from me, and answereth me no more, neither by prophets, nor by dreams: therefore I have called thee, that thou mayest make known unto me what I shall do.

The Teachings of Inspired Church Leaders

President Joseph Smith:

The witch of Endor is a no less singular personage; clothed with a powerful agency she raised the Prophet Samuel from his grave, and he appeared before the astonished king, and revealed unto him his future destiny. Who is to tell whether this woman is of God, and a righteous woman—or whether the power she possessed was of the devil, and she a witch as represented by the Bible? It is easy for us to say now, but if we had lived in her day, which of us could have unraveled the mystery? (In *History of the Church*, 4:571)

2 Samuel

Nathan and King David

What the Book of 2 Samuel Teaches Us

> **2 Samuel 12:13** And David said unto Nathan, I have sinned against the Lord. And Nathan said unto David, The Lord also hath put away thy sin; thou shalt not die.

What the Scriptures of the Restoration Teach Us

> **Joseph Smith Translation—2 Samuel 12:13** And David said unto Nathan, I have sinned against the Lord. And Nathan said unto David, The Lord also hath not put away thy sin that thou shalt not die.

> **D&C 132:39** David's wives and concubines were given unto him of me, by the hand of Nathan, my servant, and others of the prophets who had the keys of this power; and in none of these things did he sin against me save in the case of Uriah and his wife; and, therefore he hath fallen from his exaltation, and received his portion; and he shall not inherit them out of the world, for I gave them unto another, saith the Lord.

The Teachings of Inspired Church Leaders

The Prophet Joseph Smith taught that "the throne and kingdom of David is to be taken from him and given to another by the name of David in the last days, raised up out of his lineage" (*Teachings of the Prophet Joseph Smith*, sel. Joseph Fielding Smith [2002], 339). Elder Orson Hyde, in his dedicatory prayer on the Mount of Olives, October 24, 1841, prophesied that the Jews would return to Jerusalem and that in time a leader called David, "even a descendant from the loins of ancient David, [would] be their king" (in *History of the Church*, ed. B. H. Roberts [1932–51], 4:457).

1 Kings

King Solomon

What the Book of 1 Kings Teaches Us

1 Kings 5:1–5 And Hiram king of Tyre sent his servants unto Solomon; for he had heard that they had anointed him king in the room of his father: for Hiram was ever a lover of David.

And Solomon sent to Hiram, saying,

Thou knowest how that David my father could not build an house unto the name of the Lord his God for the wars which were about him on every side, until the Lord put them under the soles of his feet.

But now the Lord my God hath given me rest on every side, so that there is neither adversary nor evil occurrent.

And behold, I purpose to build an house unto the name of the Lord my God, as the Lord spake unto David my father, saying, Thy son, whom I will set upon thy throne in thy room, he shall build an house unto my name.

The inspired teachings of Church Leaders

Elder James E. Talmage:

Soon after Solomon's accession to the throne he set about the labor, which, as heritage and honor, had come to him with his crown. He laid the foundation in the fourth year of his reign, and the building was completed within seven years and a half. With the great wealth accumulated by his kingly father and specifically reserved for the building of the Temple, Solomon was able to put the [surrounding lands] under tribute, and to enlist the co-operation of nations in his great undertaking. The temple workmen numbered scores of thousands, and every department was in charge of master craftsmen. To serve on the great structure in any capacity was an honor; and labor acquired a dignity never before recognized. . . . The erection of the Temple of Solomon was an epoch-making event, not alone in the history of Israel, but in that of the world. (*House of the Lord* [1968], 5–6)

Solomon's Temple

What the Book of 1 Kings Teaches Us

1 Kings 6:1–4 And it came to pass in the four hundred and eightieth year after the children of Israel were come out of the land of Egypt, in the fourth year of Solomon's reign over Israel, in the month Zif, which is the second month, that he began to build the house of the Lord.

And the house which king Solomon built for the Lord, the length thereof was threescore cubits, and the breadth thereof twenty cubits, and the height thereof thirty cubits.

And the porch before the temple of the house, twenty cubits was the length thereof, according to the breadth of the house; and ten cubits was the breadth thereof before the house.

And for the house he made windows of narrow lights.

The Teachings of Inspired Church Leaders

President Brigham Young:

The pattern of this temple, the length and breadth, and height of the inner and outer courts, with all the fixtures thereunto appertaining, were given to Solomon by revelation, through the proper source. And why was this revelation-pattern necessary? Because Solomon had never built a temple, and did not know what was necessary in the arrangement of the different apartments, any better than Moses did what was needed in the tabernacle. (*Discourses of Brigham Young*, comp. John A. Widtsoe [1954], 414).

Elder James E. Talmage:

A comparison of the plan of Solomon's Temple with that of the earlier Tabernacle shows that in all essentials of arrangement and proportion the two were so nearly alike as to be practically identical. True, the Tabernacle had but one enclosure, while the Temple was surrounded by courts, but the inner structure itself, the Temple proper, closely followed the earlier design. The dimensions of the Holy of Holies, the Holy Place, and the Porch, were in the Temple exactly double those of the corresponding parts in the Tabernacle. (*House of the Lord* [1968], 6)

What the Scriptures of the Restoration Teach Us

2 Nephi 5:16 And I, Nephi, did build a temple; and I did construct it after the manner of the temple of Solomon save it were not built of so many precious things; for they were not to be found upon the land, wherefore, it could not be built like unto Solomon's temple. But the manner of the construction was like unto the temple of Solomon; and the workmanship thereof was exceedingly fine.

The Lord makes reference to the temple that is to be built on the temple lot in Jackson County, Missouri:

D&C 84:31 Therefore, as I said concerning the sons of Moses—for the sons of Moses and also the sons of Aaron shall offer an acceptable offering and sacrifice in the house of the Lord, which house shall be built unto the Lord in this generation, upon the consecrated spot as I have appointed.

D&C 97:10–17 Verily I say unto you, that it is my will that a house should be built unto me in the land of Zion [Jackson County, Missouri], like unto the pattern which I have given you.

Yea, let it be built speedily, by the tithing of my people.

Behold, this is the tithing and the sacrifice which I, the Lord, require at their hands, that there may be a house built unto me for the salvation of Zion—

For a place of thanksgiving for all saints, and for a place of instruction for all those who are called to the work of the ministry in all their several callings and offices;

That they may be perfected in the understanding of their ministry, in theory, in principle, and in doctrine, in all things pertaining to the kingdom of God on the earth, the keys of which kingdom have been conferred upon you.

And inasmuch as my people build a house unto me in the name of the Lord, and do not suffer any unclean thing to come into it, that it be not defiled, my glory shall rest upon it;

Yea, and my presence shall be there, for I will come into it, and all the pure in heart that shall come into it shall see God.

But if it be defiled I will not come into it, and my glory shall not be there; for I will not come into unholy temples.

The Teachings of Inspired Church Leaders

President Joseph Smith:

The Lord commanded us, in Kirtland, to build a house of God . . . this is the word of the Lord to us, and we must, yea, the Lord helping us, we will obey: as on conditions of our obedience He has promised us great things; yea, even a visit from the heavens to honor us with His own presence. We greatly fear before the Lord lest we should fail of this great honor, which our Master proposes to confer on us; we are seeking for humility and great faith lest we be ashamed in His presence. (In *History of the Church*, ed. B. H. Roberts [1932–51], 1:316–17)

The following are the words of the Prophet Joseph Smith in reference to the Nauvoo Temple:

Believing the time has now come, when it is necessary to erect a house of prayer, a house of order, a house for the worship of our God, where the ordinances can be attended to agreeably to His divine will, in this region of country—to accomplish which, considerable exertion must be made, and means will be required—and as the work must be hastened in righteousness, it behooves the Saints to weigh the importance of these things, in their minds, in all their bearings, and then take such steps as are necessary to carry them into operation; and arming themselves with courage, resolve to do all they can, and feel themselves as much interested as though the whole labor depended on themselves alone. By so doing they will emulate the glorious deeds of the fathers and secure the blessings of heaven upon themselves and their posterity to the latest generation. (In *History of the Church*, 4:186)

President Joseph Smith also said, "The Church is not fully organized, in its proper order, and cannot be, until the Temple is completed, where places will be provided for the administration of the ordinances of the Priesthood" (in *History of the Church*, 4:603).

A Cloud Filling the House of the Lord

What the Book of 1 Kings Teaches Us

1 Kings 8:10–11 And it came to pass, when the priests were come out of the holy place, that the cloud filled the house of the Lord.

So that the priests could not stand to minister because of the cloud: for the glory of the Lord had filled the house of the Lord.

What the Scriptures of the Restoration Teach Us

D&C 84:5 For verily this generation shall not all pass away until an house shall be built unto the Lord, and a cloud shall rest upon it, which cloud shall be even the glory of the Lord, which shall fill the house.

D&C 94:8–9 And ye shall not suffer any unclean thing to come in unto it; and my glory shall be there, and my presence shall be there.

But if there shall come into it any unclean thing, my glory shall not be there; and my presence shall not come into it.

D&C 109:12 That thy glory may rest down upon thy people, and upon this thy house, which we now dedicate to thee, that it may be sanctified and consecrated to be holy, and that thy holy presence may be continually in this house.

The Teachings of Inspired Church Leaders

Elder James E. Talmage:

Then Solomon addressed the assembled multitude, reciting the circumstances under which the building of the Temple had been conceived by his father David and executed by himself, and proclaiming the mercy and goodness of Israel's God. Standing before the altar of the Lord, in the court of the Temple, the king spread froth his hands toward heaven, and offered the dedicatory prayer. (*House of the Lord* [1968], 34–35)

The Destruction of the Temple

In chapter 9, the Lord promises blessings if Israel is obedient but promises its destruction along with the temple if Israel chooses to turn from him.

What the Book of 1 Kings Teaches Us

1 Kings 9:7 Then will I cut off Israel out of the land which I have given them; and this house, which I have hallowed for my name, will I cast out of my sight; and Israel shall be a proverb and a byword among all people.

The Teachings of Inspired Church Leaders

Elder James E. Talmage:

The glorious pre-eminence of this splendid structure was of brief duration. Thirty-four years after its dedication, and but five years subsequent to the death of Solomon, its decline began; and this decline was soon to develop into general spoliation, and finally to become an actual desecration. Solomon the king, the man of wisdom, the master-builder, had been led astray by the wiles of idolatrous women, and his wayward ways had fostered iniquity in Israel. The nation was no longer a unit; there factions and sects, parties and creeds, some worshipping on the hill-tops, others under green trees, each party claiming excellence for its own particular shrine. The Temple soon lost its sanctity. The gift became depreciated by the perfidy of the giver, and Jehovah withdrew His protecting presence from the place no longer holy. (*House of the Lord* [1968], 6–7)

King Solomon's Decline

What the Book of 1 Kings Teaches Us

1 Kings 11:1–3 But king Solomon loved many strange women, together with the daughter of Pharaoh, women of the Moabites, Ammonites, Edomites, Zidonians, and Hittites;

Of the nations concerning which the Lord said unto the children of Israel, Ye shall not go in to them, neither shall they come in unto you: for surely they will turn away your heart after their gods: Solomon clave unto these in love.

And he had seven hundred wives, princesses, and three hundred concubines: and his wives turned away his heart.

What the Scriptures of the Restoration Teach Us

Jacob 2:23–24 But the word of God burdens me because of your grosser crimes. For behold, thus saith the Lord: This people begin to wax in iniquity; they understand not the scriptures, for they seek to excuse themselves in committing whoredoms, because of the things which were written concerning David, and Solomon his son.

Behold, David and Solomon truly had many wives and concubines, which thing was abominable before me, saith the Lord.

Elijah and the Holy Ghost

What the Book of 1 Kings Teaches Us

1 Kings 19:9–13 And he [Elijah] came thither unto a cave, and lodged there; and, behold, the word of the Lord came to him, and he said unto him, What doest thou here, Elijah?

And he said, I have been very jealous for the Lord God of hosts: for the children of Israel have forsaken thy covenant, thrown down thine altars, and slain thy prophets with the sword; and I, even I only, am left; and they seek my life, to take it away.

And he said, Go forth, and stand upon the mount before the Lord. And, behold, the Lord passed by, and a great and strong wind rent the mountains, and brake in pieces the rocks before the Lord; but the Lord was not in the wind: and after the wind an earthquake; but the Lord was not in the earthquake:

And after the earthquake a fire; but the Lord was not in the fire: and after the fire a still small voice.

And it was so, when Elijah heard it, that he wrapped his face in his mantle, and went out, and stood in the entering in of the cave. And, behold, there came a voice unto him, and said, What doest thou here, Elijah?

What the Scriptures of the Restoration Teach Us

Helaman 5:30 And it came to pass when they heard this voice, and beheld that it was not a voice of thunder, neither was it a voice of a great tumultuous noise, but behold, it was a still voice of perfect mildness, as if it had been a whisper, and it did pierce even to the very soul—

3 Nephi 11:3 And it came to pass that while they were thus conversing one with another, they heard a voice as if it came out of heaven; and they cast their eyes round about, for they understood not the voice which they heard; and it was not a harsh voice, neither was it a loud voice; nevertheless, and notwithstanding it being a small voice it did pierce them that did hear to the center, insomuch that there was no part of their frame that it did not cause to quake; yea, it did pierce them to the very soul, and did cause their hearts to burn.

2 Kings

Elijah and the Fire from Heaven

What the Book of 2 Kings Teaches Us

2 Kings 1:10 And Elijah answered and said to the captain of fifty, If I be a man of God, then let fire come down from heaven, and consume thee and thy fifty. And there came down fire from heaven, and consumed him and his fifty.

What the Scriptures of the Restoration Teach Us

Helaman 13:13 But blessed are they who will repent, for them will I spare. But behold, if it were not for the righteous who are in this great city, behold, I would cause that fire should come down out of heaven and destroy it.

3 Nephi 9:11 And because they did cast them all out, that there were none righteous among them, I did send down fire and destroy them, that their wickedness and abominations might be hid from before my face, that the blood of the prophets and the saints whom I sent among them might not cry unto me from the ground against them.

The Taking Up of Elijah

What the Book of 2 Kings Teaches Us

2 Kings 2:16 And they said unto him, Behold now, there be with thy servants fifty strong men; let them go, we pray thee, and seek thy master [Elijah]: lest peradventure the Spirit of the Lord hath taken him up, and cast him upon some mountain, or into some valley. And he said, Ye shall not send.

What the Scriptures of the Restoration Teach Us

Alma 45:17–19 And now, when Alma had said these words he blessed the church, yea, all those who should stand fast in the faith from that time henceforth.

And when Alma had done this he departed out of the land of Zarahemla, as if to go into the land of Melek. And it came to pass that he was never heard of more; as to his death or burial we know not of.

Behold, this we know, that he was a righteous man; and the saying went abroad in the church that he was taken up by the Spirit, or buried by the hand of the Lord, even as Moses. But behold, the scriptures saith the Lord took Moses unto himself; and we suppose that he has also received Alma in the spirit, unto himself; therefore, for this cause we know nothing concerning his death and burial.

Elisha

What the Book of 2 Kings Teaches Us

2 Kings 2:15 And when the sons of the prophets which were to view at Jericho saw him, they said, The spirit of Elijah doth rest on Elisha. And they came to meet him, and bowed themselves to the ground before him.

What the Scriptures of the Restoration Teach Us

What was the spirit that rested on Elisha?

D&C 2:2 And he shall plant in the hearts of the children the promises made to the fathers, and the hearts of the children shall turn to their fathers.

By Small and Simple Things: Elisha and Naaman

What the Book of 2 Kings Teaches Us

2 Kings 5:9–14 So Naaman came with his horses and with his chariot, and stood at the door of the house of Elisha.

And Elisha sent a messenger unto him, saying, Go and wash in Jordan seven times, and thy flesh shall come again to thee, and thou shalt be clean.

But Naaman was wroth, and went away, and said, Behold, I thought, He will surely come out to me, and stand, and call on the name of the Lord his God, and strike his hand over the place, and recover the leper.

Are not Abana and Pharpar, rivers in Damascus, better than all the waters of Israel? May I not wash in them, and be clean? So he turned and went away in a rage.

And his servants came near, and spake unto him, and said, My father, if the prophet had bid thee do some great thing, wouldest thou not have done it? How much rather then, when he saith to thee, Wash, and be clean?

Then went he down, and dipped himself seven times in Jordan, according to the saying of the man of God: and his flesh came again like unto the flesh of a little child, and he was clean.

What the Scriptures of the Restoration Teach Us

When the children of Israel were bitten by the serpents, Moses, by the Lord's direction, provided a way for them to be healed. However, the way was too easy and all that failed to look perished from the bite inflicted by the snakes. The same is true of Naaman. A prophet provided the healing measure, but the way was too easy for Naaman. It didn't make any sense to him that Elisha would specify the Jordan River when there were rivers in Damascus that would do. Too many feel that the way must be nothing short of miraculous, a parting-of-the-Red-Sea-type of miracle, for the prophetic instruction to be heaven sanctioned.

> **Alma 37:6–7, 41** Now ye may suppose that this is foolishness in me; but behold I say unto you, that by small and simple things are great things brought to pass; and small means in many instances doth confound the wise.
>
> And the Lord God doth work by means to bring about his great and eternal purposes; and by very small means the Lord doth confound the wise and bringeth about the salvation of many souls.
>
> Nevertheless, because those miracles were worked by small means it did show unto them marvelous works. They were slothful, and forgot to exercise their faith and diligence and then those marvelous works ceased, and they did not progress in their journey.

D&C 64:33 Wherefore, be not weary in well-doing, for ye are laying the foundation of a great work. And out of small things proceedeth that which is great.

The Teaching of the Priest of Samaria

What the Book of 2 Kings Teaches Us

2 Kings 17:39 But the Lord your God ye shall fear; and he shall deliver you out of the hand of all your enemies.

What the Scriptures of the Restoration Teach Us

2 Nephi 6:17 But thus saith the Lord: Even the captives of the mighty shall be taken away, and the prey of the terrible shall be delivered; for the Mighty God shall deliver his covenant people. For thus saith the Lord: I will contend with them that contendeth with thee.

Alma 58:37 But, behold, it mattereth not—we trust God will deliver us, notwithstanding the weakness of our armies, yea, and deliver us out of the hands of our enemies.

D&C 108:8 And behold, and lo, I am with you to bless you and deliver you forever. Amen.

Carried Away to Babylon

What the Book of 2 Kings Teaches Us

2 Kings 20:17 Behold, the days come, that all that is in thine house, and that which thy fathers have laid up in store unto this day, shall be carried into Babylon: nothing shall be left, saith the Lord.

What the Scriptures of the Restoration Teach Us

1 Nephi 1:13 And he read, saying: Wo, wo, unto Jerusalem, for I have seen thine abominations! Yea, and many things did my father read concerning Jerusalem—that it should be destroyed, and the inhabitants thereof; many should perish by the sword, and many should be carried away captive into Babylon.

Huldah's Prophecy

What the Book of 2 Kings Teaches Us

2 Kings 22:20 Behold therefore, I will gather thee unto thy fathers, and thou shalt be gathered into thy grave in peace; and thine eyes shall not see all the evil which I will bring upon this place. And they brought the king word again.

What the Scriptures of the Restoration Teach Us

Alma 40:12 And then shall it come to pass, that the spirits of those who are righteous are received into a state of happiness, which is called paradise, a state of rest, a state of peace, where they shall rest from all their troubles and from all care, and sorrow.

D&C 45:46 Wherefore, if ye have slept in peace blessed are you; for as you now behold me and know that I am, even so shall ye come unto me and your souls shall live, and your redemption shall be perfected; and the saints shall come forth from the four quarters of the earth.

1 Chronicles

Temple Service

What the Book of 1 Chronicles Teaches Us

1 Chronicles 6:32 And they ministered before the dwelling place of the tabernacle of the congregation with singing, until Solomon had built the house of the Lord in Jerusalem: and then they waited on their office according to their order.

What the Scriptures of the Restoration Teach Us

D&C 94:6 And it shall be dedicated unto the Lord from the foundation thereof, according to the order of the priesthood, according to the pattern which shall be given unto you hereafter.

The Teachings of Inspired Church Leaders

President Wilford Woodruff:

I do not wonder at President [Brigham Young] saying he felt moved upon to call upon the Latter-day Saints to hurry up the building of these Temples. He felt the importance of the work; but now he has gone, it rests with us to continue it, and God will bless our labors and we will have joy therein. This is a preparation necessary for the second advent of the Savior; and when we shall have built the Temples now contemplated, we will then begin to see the necessity of building others, for in proportion to the diligence of our labors in this direction, will we comprehend the extent of the work to be done and the present is only a beginning. (*Deseret News: Semi-Weekly*, Mar. 26, 1878, 1)

Sacrifices

What the Book of 1 Chronicles Teaches Us

1 Chronicles 6:49 But Aaron and his sons offered upon the altar of the burnt offering, and on the altar of incense, and were appointed for all the work of the place most holy, and to make an atonement of Israel, according to all that Moses the servant of God had commanded.

What the Scriptures of the Restoration Teach Us

Alma 34:10–15 For it is expedient that there should be a great and last sacrifice; yea, not a sacrifice of man, neither of beast, neither of any manner of fowl; for it shall not be a human sacrifice; but it must be an infinite and eternal sacrifice.

Now there is not any man that can sacrifice his own blood which will atone for the sins of another. Now, if a man murdereth, behold will our law, which is just, take the life of his brother? I say unto you, Nay.

But the law requireth the life of him who hath murdered; therefore there can be nothing which is short of an infinite atonement which will suffice for the sins of the world.

Therefore, it is expedient that there should be a great and last sacrifice, and then shall there be, or it is expedient there should be, a stop to the shedding of blood; then shall the law of Moses be fulfilled; yea, it shall be all fulfilled, every jot and tittle, and none shall have passed away.

And behold, this is the whole meaning of the law, every whit pointing to that great and last sacrifice; and that great and last sacrifice will be the Son of God, yea, infinite and eternal.

And thus he shall bring salvation to all those who shall believe on his name; this being the intent of this last sacrifice, to bring about the bowels of mercy, which overpowereth justice, and bringeth about means unto men that they may have faith unto repentance.

Moses 5:6–8 And after many days an angel of the Lord appeared unto Adam, saying: Why dost thou offer sacrifices unto the Lord? And Adam said unto him: I know not, save the Lord commanded me.

And then the angel spake, saying: This thing is a similitude of the sacrifice of the Only Begotten of the Father, which is full of grace and truth.

Wherefore, thou shalt do all that thou doest in the name of the

Son, and thou shalt repent and call upon God in the name of the Son forevermore.

Record Keeping

What the Book of 1 Chronicles Teaches Us

1 Chronicles 9:1 So all Israel were reckoned by genealogies; and, behold, they were written in the book of the kings of Israel and Judah, who were carried away to Babylon for their transgression.

What the Scriptures of the Restoration Teach Us

1 Nephi 5:10–14 And after they had given thanks unto the God of Israel, my father, Lehi, took the records which were engraven upon the plates of brass, and he did search them from the beginning.

And he beheld that they did contain the five books of Moses, which gave an account of the creation of the world, and also of Adam and Eve, who were our first parents;

And also a record of the Jews from the beginning, even down to the commencement of the reign of Zedekiah, king of Judah;

And also the prophecies of the holy prophets, from the beginning, even down to the commencement of the reign of Zedekiah; and also many prophecies which have been spoken by the mouth of Jeremiah.

And it came to pass that my father, Lehi, also found upon the plates of brass a genealogy of his fathers; wherefore he knew that he was a descendant of Joseph; yea, even that Joseph who was the son of Jacob, who was sold into Egypt, and who was preserved by the hand of the Lord, that he might preserve his father, Jacob, and all his household from perishing with famine.

The Teachings of Inspired Church Leaders

President Joseph F. Smith:

The Spirit which moves the saints to work for the redemption of the dead is the planting in the hearts of the children the promises made to the fathers. This same spirit seems to be moving upon the hearts of honorable men of the earth who are spending their time and means in collecting and compiling genealogical records. . . . The saints should take advantage of every opportunity to obtain the records as far as possible of their ancestors, that their redemption through the ordinances of the House of God might be obtained. We commend the saints for their diligence in this most important and essential work. (In James R. Clark, comp., *Messages of the First Presidency of the Church of Jesus Christ of Latter-day Saints*, 6 vols. [1965–75], 4:193–94)

By Common Consent

What the Book of 1 Chronicles Teaches Us

1 Chronicles 13:1–4 And David consulted with the captains of thousands and hundreds, and with every leader.

And David said unto all the congregation of Israel, if it seem good unto you, and that it be of the Lord our God, let us send abroad unto our brethren every where, that are left in all the land of Israel, and with them also to the priests and Levites which are in their cities and suburbs, that they may gather themselves unto Us

And let us bring again the ark of our God to Us for we inquired not at it in the days of Saul.

And all the congregation said that they would do so: for the thing was right in the eyes of all the people.

What the Scriptures of the Restoration Teach Us

D&C 26:2 And all things shall be done by common consent in the church, by much prayer and faith, for all things you shall receive by faith. Amen.

Learning and Fulfilling Your Duty

What the Book of 1 Chronicles Teaches Us

1 Chronicles 15:13 For because ye did it not at the first, the Lord our God made a breach upon us, for that we sought him not after the due order.

What the Scriptures of the Restoration Teach Us

D&C 107:84, 99 Thus, none shall be exempted from the justice and the laws of God, that all things may be done in order and in solemnity before him, according to truth and righteousness.

Wherefore, now let every man learn his duty, and to act in the office in which he is appointed, in all diligence.

The Teachings of Inspired Church Leaders

George Albert Smith:

And then there are those who accept nominal membership in the Church but who seem to feel themselves exempt from rendering any kind of service. But sooner or later they find themselves uneasy in their hearts, and doubtful in their thoughts, as we all do when we fail to do what we know to be our full duty. A man who is living in accordance with the gospel of Jesus Christ is never in doubt about its success; but the man who neglects his duty, who fails to keep his covenants, loses the Spirit of the Lord, and then he begins to wonder what will become of Zion. ("Our Full Duty," *Improvement Era*, Mar. 1946, 141)

Psalms of Praise

What the Book of 1 Chronicles Teaches Us

1 Chronicles 16:9 Sing unto him, sing psalms unto him, talk ye of all his wondrous works.

What the Scriptures of the Restoration Teach Us

D&C 25:12 For my soul delighteth in the song of the heart; yea, the song of the righteous is a prayer unto me, and it shall be answered with a blessing upon their heads.

Abraham's Promise Coming to Pass

What the Book of 1 Chronicles Teaches Us

1 Chronicles 27:23 But David took not the number of them from twenty years old and under: because the Lord had said he would increase Israel like to the stars of the heavens.

What the Scriptures of the Restoration Teach Us

D&C 132:30 Abraham received promises concerning his seed, and of the fruit of his loins—from whose loins ye are, namely, my servant Joseph—which were to continue so long as they were in the world; and as touching Abraham and his seed, out of the world they should continue; both in the world and out of the world should they continue as innumerable as the stars; or, if ye were to count the sand upon the seashore ye could not number them.

Seek the Lord

What the Book of 1 Chronicles Teaches Us

1 Chronicles 28:9 And thou, Solomon my son, know thou the God of thy father, and serve him with a perfect heart and with a willing mind: for the Lord searcheth all hearts, and understandeth all the imaginations of the thoughts: if thou seek him, he will be found of thee; but if thou forsake him, he will cast thee off forever.

What the Scriptures of the Restoration Teach Us

D&C 6:16 Yea, I tell thee, that thou mayest know that there is none else save God that knowest thy thoughts and the intents of thy heart.

D&C 88:63 Draw near unto me and I will draw near unto you; seek me diligently and ye shall find me; ask, and ye shall receive; knock, and it shall be opened unto you.

Willing Offerings

What the Book of 1 Chronicles Teaches Us

1 Chronicles 29:9 Then the people rejoiced, for that they offered willingly, because with perfect heart they offered willingly to the Lord: and David the king also rejoiced with great joy.

What the Scriptures of the Restoration Teach Us

D&C 64:34 Behold, the Lord requireth the heart and a willing mind; and the willing and obedient shall eat the good of the land of Zion in these last days.

2 Chronicles

The Lord's Gift

What the Book of 2 Chronicles Teaches Us

2 Chronicles 1:7, 10 In that night did God appear unto Solomon, and said unto him, Ask what I shall give thee.

Give me now wisdom and knowledge, that I may go out and come in before this people: for who can judge this thy people, that is so great?

What the Scriptures of the Restoration Teach Us

3 Nephi 28:1–3 And it came to pass when Jesus had said these words, he spake unto his disciples, one by one, saying unto them: What is it that ye desire of me, after that I am gone to the Father?

And they all spake, save it were three, saying: We desire that after we have lived unto the age of man, that our ministry, wherein thou hast called us, may have an end, that we may speedily come unto thee in thy kingdom.

And he said unto them: Blessed are ye because ye desired this thing of me; therefore, after that ye are seventy and two years old ye shall come unto me in my kingdom; and with me ye shall find rest.

D&C 7:1–2 And the Lord said unto me: John, my beloved, what desiredst thou? For if you shall ask what you will, it shall be granted unto you.

And I said unto him: Lord, give unto me power over death, that I may live and bring souls unto thee.

The Teachings of Inspired Church Leaders

President John Taylor:

> I am reminded of my boyhood. At that early period of my life I learned
> to approach God. Many a time I have gone into the fields, and, con-
> cealing myself behind some bush, would bow before the Lord and call
> upon him to guide and direct me. And he heard my prayer. . . . My
> spirit was drawn out after God then; and I fell the same yet. (*The Gospel
> Kingdom*, sel. G. Homer Durham [1943], 343)

Interesting Information

This trust in God was evident in 1839 when then Elder Taylor left
with Elder Wilford Woodruff for a mission in the British Isles. Elder
Taylor became seriously ill on the journey from Nauvoo to New York,
where they were to take passage on a ship to England. Elder Woodruff
went ahead to New York and waited for Elder Taylor, who was delayed in
his journey due to his illness.

When Elder Taylor reached New York, Elder Woodruff was anxious to depart and immediately obtained his own passage to England.
Although Elder Taylor had no money, he told Elder Woodruff, "Well,
Brother Woodruff, if you think it best for me to go, I will accompany
you." Elder Woodruff inquired as to how Elder Taylor would obtain the
money for the journey, to which Elder Taylor answered: "Oh, there will
be no difficulty about that. Go and take a passage for me on your vessel,
and I will furnish you the means."

Hearing the conversation between Elder Taylor and Elder Woodruff,
a Brother Theodore Turley expressed a desire to accompany the Apostles on their journey and offered to cook for them, although he had no
money either. In response to Brother Turley's desire to be involved in the
work, Elder Taylor told Elder Woodruff to obtain a passage for Brother
Turley also.

In a short time, the Lord provided the means for the journey. Elder
B. H. Roberts of the Seventy recorded: "At the time of making these
arrangements Elder Taylor had no money, but the Spirit had whispered
[to] him that means would be forthcoming, and when had that still,
small voice failed him! In that he trusted, and he did not trust in vain.
Although he did not ask for a penny of anyone, from various persons in
voluntary donations he received money enough to meet his engagements

for the passage of himself and Brother Turley, but no more" (*The Life of John Taylor* [1963], 65–74).

Acceptance of the Temple

What the Book of 2 Chronicles Teaches Us

2 Chronicles 7:16 For now have I chosen and sanctified this house, that my name may be there for ever: and mine eyes and mine heart shall be there perpetually.

What the Scriptures of the Restoration Teach Us

D&C 110:7 For behold, I have accepted this house, and my name shall be here; and I will manifest myself to my people in mercy in this house.

Missing Scripture

What the Book of 2 Chronicles Teaches Us

2 Chronicles 9:29 Now the rest of the acts of Solomon, first and last, are they not written in the book of Nathan the prophet, and in the prophecy of Ahijah the Shilonite, and in the visions of Iddo the seer against Jeroboam the son of Nebat?

The Teachings of Inspired Church Leaders

President Joseph Smith:

From what we can draw from the Scriptures relative to the teachings of heaven, we are induced to think that much instruction has been given to man since the beginning which we do not possess now. This may not agree with the opinions of some of our friends who are bold to say that we have everything written in the Bible which God ever spoke to man since the world began, and that if he had ever said anything more we should certainly have received it. But we ask, does it remain for a people who never had faith enough to call down one scrap of revelation from heaven, and for all they have now are indebted to the faith of another people who lived hundreds and thousands of years before them, does it remain for them to say how much God has spoken and how much he has not spoken? We have what we have, and the Bible contains what it does contain: but to say that God never said anything more to man than is there recorded, would be saying at once that we have at last received a revelation; for it must require one to advance thus far, because it is nowhere said in that volume by the mouth of God, that He would not, after giving, what is there contained, speak again; and if any man has found out for a fact that the Bible contains all that God ever revealed to man he has ascertained it by an immediate revelation, other than has been previously written by the prophets and apostles. But through the kind providence of our Father a portion of His word which He delivered to His ancient saints, has fallen into our hands, is presented to us with a promise of a reward if obeyed, and with a penalty if disobeyed. That all are deeply interested in these laws of teachings, must admitted by all who acknowledge their divine authenticity. (In *History of the Church*, ed. B. H. Roberts [1932–51], 2:18)

Interesting Information

Joseph Smith's answer to an inquiry as recorded in the *Elders Journals*: "Is not the canon of scripture full? If it is, there is a great defect in the book [Bible], or else it would have said so" (*Elders Journal*, Nov. 1837. 2, 28–29).

The Lord commanded Oliver through Joseph Smith to satisfy himself for the time being to write for the prophet. In D&C 2:2 the Lord instructs Oliver that there are other records that he will give Oliver the power to translate. What other records could the Lord be referring to? We understand that a portion of the Book of Mormon is sealed. Could it be that the Lord had this in mind? Also, it was not too many years after this when Joseph Smith purchased the Egyptian mummies, which also included the Book of Abraham. So why didn't Oliver translate, even "other records"?

President Joseph F. Smith alludes to this when he commented that maybe we as a Church would have these other scriptures at our disposal, but since the general Church membership failed to follow the commandments as outlined in the Book of Mormon and the Doctrine and Covenants, these additional scriptures have been withheld. President Joseph F. Smith goes on to say it was because of Oliver's disobedience, by falling away from the Church for a time, that this ability to translate other scripture was taken away. Joseph Smith also experienced this at the time of Martin Harris's negligence in losing the 116 translated pages of the Book of Mormon. The difference between Joseph and Oliver is Joseph humbled himself and had his ability restored, whereas Oliver failed in his attempt to shed himself of pride (Joseph Fielding Smith, *Church History and Modern Revelation* [1949], 1:52–53)

It is possible the Lord had other scriptures in mind for Oliver to help translate, scriptures that were hidden deep in the heart of the Hill Cumorah:

Heber C. Kimball, *Journal of Discourses*, 28 September 1856

In response to a Brother Mills's statement about the handcart pioneers, Heber C. Kimball said:

"How does it compare with the vision that Joseph and others had, when they went into a cave in the hill Cumorah, and saw more records than ten men could carry? There were books piled up on tables, book upon book. Those records this people will yet have, if they accept of the Book of Mormon and observe its precepts, and keep the commandments." (As quoted in Cameron J. Packer, "Cumorah's Cave," *Journal of Book of Mormon Studies*, vol. 13, no.1–2 [2004], 52)

Elizabeth Kane Journal, 15 January 1873

Although not a member of the Church, Elizabeth Kane lived in St. George, Utah, and entertained the company of Brigham Young. She recorded the following discussion:

"I asked where the plates were now, and saw in a moment from the expression of the countenances around that I had blundered. But I was answered that they were in a cave; that Oliver Cowdery though now an apostate would not deny that he had seen them. He had been to the cave. . . . Brigham Young's tone was so solemn that I listened bewildered like a child to the evening witch stories of its nurse. . .

"Brigham Young said that when Oliver Cowdery and Joseph Smith were in the cave this third time, they could see its contents more distinctly than before. . . . It was about fifteen feet high and round its sides were ranged boxes of treasure. In the centre was a large stone table empty before, but now piled with similar gold plates, some of which lay scattered on the floor beneath. Formerly the sword of Laban hung on the walls sheathed, but it was now unsheathed and lying across the plates on the table; and One that was with them said it was never to be sheathed until the reign of Righteousness upon the earth." (As quoted in "Cumorah's Cave," *Journal of Book of Mormon Studies*, 53–54)

Missing Biblical Books as Identified in Both the Bible and the Book of Mormon:

The book of the War of the Lords—Numbers 21:14
The book of Jasher—Joshua 10:13; Samuel 1:18
The book of Acts of Solomon—1 Kings 11:41
Samuel the Seer, Gad the Seer, and Nathan the Prophet—1
    Chronicles 9:29; 29:29
The Visions of Iddo the Seer—2 Chronicles 9:29; 12:15;
    13:22
The book of Shemaiah—2 Chronicles 12:15
The book of Jehu—2 Chronicles 20:34
The Sayings of the Seers—2 Chronicles 33:19
The Prophecy of Ahijah the Shilonite—2 Chronicles 9:29
An epistle written by Paul to the Corinthians—1 Corinthians
    5:9 (This is another one over and beyond the current
    epistle we have in our current New Testament)
An epistle to the Church at Laodicea—Colossians 4:16
Prophecies of Enoch known to Jude—Jude 1:4
"The rest of the acts of Uzziah" written by Isaiah—2
    Chronicles 26:22
Writings of Zenock, Zenos, and Neum—1 Nephi 19:10;
    Jacob 5; Alma 33:3–17; 3 Nephi 19:10

Covenants

What the Book of 2 Chronicles Teaches Us

2 Chronicles 15:12 And they entered into a covenant to seek the Lord God of their fathers with all their heart and with all their soul.

What the Scriptures of the Restoration Teach Us

Mosiah 5:2, 5 And they all cried with one voice, saying: Yea, we believe all the words which thou hast spoken unto us; and also, we know of their surety and truth, because of the Spirit of the Lord Omnipotent, which has wrought a mighty change in us, or in our hearts, that we have no more disposition to do evil, but to do good continually.

And we are willing to enter into a covenant with our God to do his will, and to be obedient to his commandments in all things that he shall command us, all the remainder of our days, that we may not bring upon ourselves a never-ending torment, as has been spoken by the angel, that we may not drink out of the cup of the wrath of God.

The Teachings of Inspired Church Leaders

Wilford Woodruff:

There need be no fears if the Latter-day Saints will only be true to the covenants they have made with their God and strictly carry out the principles which He has told us must govern us in the building up of His Zion. . . .

If, however, we forget our covenants, and depart from and disregard the teachings which He has given us, then be assured, Latter-day Saints, our position is full of peril to us. God's purposes will not be thwarted; but we shall be scourged, and those who persist in this course will be rejected and be deprived of all share in the blessings promised to Zion. ("Epistle," *Woman's Exponent*, April 15, 1888, 174)

The Words of the Prophets

What the Book of 2 Chronicles Teaches Us

2 Chronicles 18:7 But the king of Israel [wicked king Ahab] said unto Jehoshaphat, There is yet one man, by whom we may inquire of the Lord: but I hate him; for he never prophesied good unto me, but always evil: the same is Micaiah the son of Imla. And Jehoshaphat said, Let not the king say so.

What the Scriptures of the Restoration Teach Us

Helaman 13:26 Behold ye are worse than they; for as the Lord liveth, if a prophet come among you and declareth unto you the word of the Lord, which testifieth of your sins and iniquities, ye are angry with him, and cast him out and seek all manner of ways to destroy him; yea, you will say that he is a false prophet, and that he is a sinner, and of the devil, because he testifieth that your deeds are evil.

The Teachings of Inspired Church Leaders

President Joseph F. Smith said, "Honor and praise be unto [President

Lorenzo Snow,] that instrument in the hands of God of establishing order in the midst of uncertainty, and certain rules by which we know our bearings" (In Conference Report, Oct. 1902, 87).

Interesting Information

Hiram Page claimed to have in his possession a seer stone that provided him with many revelations. Newell Knight records that when he arrived in Fayette for the second conference of the Church, "he [Hiram Page] had quite a roll of papers full of these revelations, and many in the Church were led astray by them. Even Oliver Cowdery and the Whitmer family had given heed to them, although they were in contradiction to the New Testament and the revelations of these last days." Newell Knight further adds that the Prophet was extremely concerned with the situation, so concerned in fact, that "the greater part of the night was spent in prayer and supplication" concerning what he should do to defuse the situation. It was during this time Joseph received section 28 of the Doctrine and Covenants. The next day at conference, the Prophet reasoned with those who had been swayed by Hiram Page's revelations and his stone. To the joy of all, the seer stone was renounced and peace prevailed for the remainder of the conference. (In Andrew Jenson, comp.,"26 September 1830," *Journal History of the Church of Jesus Christ of Latter-day Saints* vol. 1, 3.)

> **D&C 28:2** But, behold, verily, verily, I say unto thee, no one shall be appointed to receive commandments and revelations in this church excepting my servant Joseph Smith, Jun., for he receiveth them even as Moses.

The Lord Will Fight Israel's Battles

What the Book of 2 Chronicles Teaches Us

The prophet Jahaziel prophesies to Jehoshaphat, indicating to him that the Lord would fight the battle against the Ammonites.

> **2 Chronicles 20:15** And he said, Hearken ye, all Judah, and ye inhabitants of Jerusalem, and thou king Jehoshaphat, Thus saith the Lord unto you, Be not afraid nor dismayed by reason of this great multitude; for the battle is not yours, but God's.

What the Scriptures of the Restoration Teach Us

D&C 105:14 For behold, I do not require at their hands to fight the battles of Zion; for, as I said in a former commandment, even so will I fulfill—I will fight your battles.

Seeking God

What the Book of 2 Chronicles Teaches Us

2 Chronicles 26:5 And he [Uzziah] sought God in the days of Zechariah, who had understanding in the visions of God: and as long as he sought the Lord, God made him to prosper.

What the Scriptures of the Restoration Teach Us

2 Nephi 4:23 Behold, he hath heard my cry by day, and he hath given me knowledge by visions in the night-time.

Satan Will Not Support His Followers

What the Book of 2 Chronicles Teaches Us

2 Chronicles 28:23 For he [Ahaz] sacrificed unto the gods of Damascus, which smote him: and he said, Because the gods of the kings of Syria help them, therefore will I sacrifice to them, that they may help me. But they were the ruin of him and of all Israel.

What the Scriptures of the Restoration Teach Us

Alma 30:60 And thus we see the end of him who perverteth the ways of the Lord; and thus we see that the devil will not support his children at the last day, but doth speedily drag them down to hell.

Of One Heart

What the Book of 2 Chronicles Teaches Us

2 Chronicles 30:12 Also in Judah the hand of God was to give them one heart to do the commandment of the king and of the princes, by the word of the Lord.

What the Scriptures of the Restoration Teach Us

Moses 7:18 And the Lord called his people Zion, because they were of one heart and one mind, and dwelt in righteousness; and there was no poor among them.

The Teachings of Inspired Church Leaders

Wilford Woodruff:

Father Adam, Enoch, Moses, Noah, Abraham, Isaac and Jacob, and all those old patriarchs and prophets were obliged to have communion with God. They were under the necessity of seeking unto the Lord, for unless they had this communion they were not qualified to do their duty. They were dependent upon the Lord for revelation, for light, and for instruction to have power to carry out the commandments of God. This union that the Lord required of the ancient patriarchs and prophets, and which Jesus required of His Apostles, was required of Joseph Smith and his brethren. It has been required of all Saints of God from the foundation of the world till today. (*Deseret Weekly*, Aug. 30, 1890, 305)

The Danger of Falling Away

What the Book of 2 Chronicles Teaches Us

2 Chronicles 33:9–10, 12 So Manasseh made Judah and the inhabitants of Jerusalem to err, and to do worse than the heathen, whom the Lord had destroyed before the children of Israel.

And the Lord spake to Manasseh, and to his people: but they would not hearken.

And when he was in affliction, he besought the Lord his God, and humbled himself greatly before the God of his fathers.

What the Scriptures of the Restoration Teach Us

Alma 24:30 And thus we can plainly discern that after a people have been once enlightened by the Spirit of God, and have had great knowledge of things pertaining to righteousness, and then have fallen away into sin and transgression, they become more hardened, and thus their state becomes worse than though they had never known these things.

Alma 5:37 O ye workers of iniquity; ye that are puffed up in the vain things of the world, ye that have professed to have known the ways of righteousness nevertheless have gone astray, as sheep having no shepherd, notwithstanding a shepherd hath called after you and is still calling after you, but ye will not hearken unto his voice!

D&C 101:7–8 They were slow to hearken unto the voice of the Lord their God; therefore, the Lord their God is slow to hearken unto their prayers, to answer them in the day of their trouble.

In the day of their peace they esteemed lightly my counsel; but, in the day of their trouble, of necessity they feel after me.

Ezra

The Lord Requires That You Try

What the Book of Ezra Teaches Us

> **Ezra 4:21** Give ye now commandment to cause these men to cease, and that this city be not builded, until another commandment shall be given from me.

What the Scriptures of the Restoration Teach Us

> **D&C 124:49** Verily, verily, I say unto you, that when I give a commandment to any of the sons of men to do a work unto my name, and those sons of men go with all their might and with all they have to perform that work, and cease not their diligence, and their enemies come upon them and hinder them from performing that work, behold, it behooveth me to require that work no more at the hands of those sons of men, but to accept of their offerings.

Coming Out from among the Wicked

What the Book of Ezra Teaches Us

> **Ezra 6:21** And the children of Israel, which were come again out of captivity, and all such as had separated themselves unto them from the filthiness of the heathen of the land, to seek the Lord God of Israel, did eat.

What the Scriptures of the Restoration Teach Us

Alma 5:57 And now I say unto you, all you that are desirous to follow the voice of the good shepherd, come ye out from the wicked, and be ye separate, and touch not their unclean things; and behold, their names shall be blotted out, that the names of the wicked shall not be numbered among the names of the righteous, that the word of God may be fulfilled, which saith: The names of the wicked shall not be mingled with the names of my people.

D&C 133:5, 14 Go ye out from Babylon. Be ye clean that bear the vessels of the Lord.

Go ye out from among the nations, even from Babylon, from the midst of wickedness, which is spiritual Babylon.

Preparing for Spiritual Matters

What the Book of Ezra Teaches Us

Ezra 7:10 For Ezra had prepared his heart to seek the law of the Lord, and to do it, and to teach in Israel statutes and judgments.

What the Scriptures of the Restoration Teach Us

3 Nephi 17:3 Therefore, go ye unto your homes, and ponder upon the things which I have said, and ask of the Father, in my name, that ye may understand, and prepare your minds for the morrow, and I come unto you again.

D&C 29:8 Wherefore the decree hath gone forth from the Father that they shall be gathered in unto one place upon the face of this land, to prepare their hearts and be prepared in all things against the day when tribulation and desolation are sent forth upon the wicked.

D&C 132:3 Therefore, prepare thy heart to receive and obey the instructions which I am about to give unto you; for all those who have this law revealed unto them must obey the same.

Choosing Righteous Leaders

What the Book of Ezra Teaches Us

Ezra 7:25 And thou, Ezra, after the wisdom of thy God, that is in thine hand, set magistrates and judges, which may judge all the people that are beyond the river, all such as know the laws of thy God; and teach ye them that know them not.

What the Scriptures of the Restoration Teach Us

Mosiah 29:11, 25 Therefore I will be your king the remainder of my days; nevertheless, let us appoint judges, to judge this people according to our law; and we will newly arrange the affairs of this people, for we will appoint wise men to be judges, that will judge this people according to the commandments of God.

Therefore, choose you by the voice of this people, judges, that ye may be judged according to the laws which have been given you by our fathers, which are correct, and which were given them by the hand of the Lord.

D&C 134:3 We believe that all governments necessarily require civil officers and magistrates to enforce the laws of the same; and that such as will administer the law in equity and justice should be sought for and upheld by the voice of the people if a republic, or the will of the sovereign.

Fasting and Prayer

What the Book of Ezra Teaches Us

Ezra 8:21 Then I proclaimed a fast there, at the river of Ahava, that we might afflict ourselves before our God, to seek of him a right way for us, and for our little ones, and for all our substance.

What the Scriptures of the Restoration Teach Us

Alma 5:46 Behold, I say unto you they are made known unto me by the Holy Spirit of God. Behold, I have fasted and prayed many days that I might know these things of myself. And now I do know of myself

that they are true; for the Lord God hath made them manifest unto me
by his Holy Spirit; and this is the spirit of revelation which is in me.

The Teachings of Inspired Church Leaders

Brigham Young said, "In our fast-day meetings, the Saints meet
to express their feelings and to strengthen each other in their faith in
the holy Gospel" (*Discourses of Brigham Young*, comp. John A. Widtsoe
[1954], 262).

Nehemiah

The Wall Builder

What the Book of Nehemiah Teaches Us

Nehemiah 4:6 So built we the wall; and all the wall was joined together unto the half thereof: for the people had a mind to work.

What the Scriptures of the Restoration Teach Us

D&C 75:3 Behold, I say unto you that it is my will that you should go forth and not tarry, neither be idle but labor with your might.

Fear Not Man

What the Book of Nehemiah Teaches Us

Nehemiah 4:14 And I looked, and rose up, and said unto the nobles, and to the rulers, and to the rest of the people, Be not ye afraid of them: remember the Lord, which is great and terrible, and fight for your brethren, your sons, and your daughters, your wives, and your houses.

What the Scriptures of the Restoration Teach Us

D&C 122:9 Therefore, hold on thy way, and the priesthood shall remain with thee; for their bounds are set, they cannot pass. Thy days are known, and thy years shall not be numbered less; therefore, fear not what man can do, for God shall be with you forever and ever.

Leaders Earning Their Own Way

What the Book of Nehemiah Teaches Us

Nehemiah 5:14–15 Moreover from the time that I was appointed to be their governor in the land of Judah, from the twentieth year even unto the two and thirtieth year of Artaxerxes the king, that is, twelve years, I and my brethren have not eaten the bread of the governor.

But the former governors that had been before me were chargeable unto the people, and had taken of them bread and wine, beside forty shekels of silver; yea, even their servants bare rule over the people: but so did not I, because of the fear of God.

What the Scriptures of the Restoration Teach Us

Mosiah 2:12, 14 I say unto you that as I have been suffered to spend my days in your service, even up to this time, and have not sought gold nor silver nor any manner of riches of you;

And even I, myself, have labored with mine own hands that I might serve you, and that ye should not be laden with taxes, and that there should nothing come upon you which was grievous to be borne—and of all these things which I have spoken, ye yourselves are witnesses this day.

Teaching the Law of God

What the Book of Nehemiah Teaches Us

Nehemiah 8:8 So they read in the book in the law of God distinctly, and gave the sense, and caused them to understand the reading.

What the Scriptures of the Restoration Teach Us

Jacob 4:13 Behold, my brethren, he that prophesieth, let him prophesy to the understanding of men; for the Spirit speaketh the truth and lieth not. Wherefore, it speaketh of things as they really are, and of things as they really will be; wherefore, these things are manifested unto us plainly, for the salvation of our souls. But behold, we are not witnesses alone in these things; for God also spake them unto prophets of old.

Having a Knowledge of God

What the Book of Nehemiah Teaches Us

Nehemiah 10:28 And the rest of the people, the priests, the Levites, the porters, the singers, the Nethinims, and all they that had separated themselves from the people of the lands unto the law of God, their wives, their sons, and their daughters, every one having knowledge, and having understanding.

What the Scriptures of the Restoration Teach Us

Mosiah 18:26 And the priests were not to depend upon the people for their support; but for their labor they were to receive the grace of God, that they might wax strong in the Spirit, having the knowledge of God, that they might teach with power and authority from God.

The Teachings of Inspired Church Leaders

Brigham Young:

He gives a little to his humble followers today, and if they improve upon it, tomorrow he will give them a little more, and the next day a little more. He does not add to that which they do not improve upon, but they are required to continually improve upon the knowledge they already possess, and thus obtain a store of wisdom. (*Discourses of Brigham Young*, comp. John A. Widtsoe [1954], 138)

The Bishop's Responsibility

What the Book of Nehemiah Teaches Us

Nehemiah 11:16 And Shabbethai and Jozabad, of the chief of the Levites, had the oversight of the outward business of the house of God.

What the Scriptures of the Restoration Teach Us

D&C 107:68 Wherefore, the office of a bishop is not equal unto it [the High Priesthood]; for the office of a bishop is in administering all temporal things.

The Teachings of Inspired Church Leaders

Brigham Young said the following of the bishop's responsibilities:

Appoint good, wise, judicious men to go through your Ward, to find out what is in that Ward, and the situation of every family, whether they have money, flour, or costly clothing, or whether they are destitute and suffering[.] This is your business and calling. (In *Journal of Discourses*, 26 vols. [1854–86], 3:244)

Esther

Plain and Precious

The book of Esther is small (comprising 9 chapters) yet tells a story of a courageous woman who saved the Jews from destruction at the hands of a conniving individual. It is a story we see today. I'm sure in your workplace you have recognized that individual, the personality that craves power and does what it takes to get to the top. This is essentially the story shared in the book of Esther and what she did to save her people. It's also a plain and easily understood story in which little explanation is required from outside sources. With that being said, let's move on to Job.

Job

Reality of Job

What the Book of Job Teaches Us

> **Job 1:1** There was a man in the land of Uz, whose name was Job; and that man was perfect and upright, and one that feared God, and eschewed evil.

What the Scriptures of the Restoration Teach Us

There are those who believe that Job was not a real person, but rather a fictional character whose purpose is to teach a lesson. Latter-day Saints can put their minds to rest knowing that he is a historical figure and lived and breathed the same as you and me. Not only do the prophet Ezekiel (Ezekiel 14:14, 20) and the Apostle James (James 5:11) make reference to him, but we also have the definitive word of the Lord to the Prophet Joseph Smith:

> **D&C 121:7–10** My son, peace be unto thy soul; thine adversity and thine afflictions shall be but a small moment;
>
> And then, if thou endure it well, God shall exalt thee on high; thou shalt triumph over all thy foes.
>
> Thy friends do stand by thee, and they shall hail thee again with warm hearts and friendly hands.
>
> Thou art not yet as Job; thy friends do not contend against thee, neither charge thee with transgression, as they did Job.

The Teachings of Inspired Church Leaders

President Thomas S. Monson:

If any of us feels his challenges are beyond his capacity to meet them, let him or her read of Job. By so doing, there comes the feeling. "If Job could endure and overcome, so will I."

Job was a "perfect and upright" man who "feared God, and eschewed evil." Pious in his conduct, prosperous in his fortune, Job was to face a test which could have destroyed anyone. Shorn of his possessions, scorned by his friends, afflicted by his suffering, shattered by the loss of his family, he was urged to "curse God, and die." He resisted this temptation and declared from the depths of his noble soul, "Behold, my witness is in heaven, and my record is on high" (Job 16:19). "I know that my redeemer liveth" (Job 19:25).

Job became a model of unlimited patience. To this day we refer to those who are long-suffering as having the patience of Job. He provides an example for us to follow. ("Models to Follow," *Ensign*, Nov. 2002, 60)

I Shall See God

What the Book of Job Teaches Us

Job 19:26 And though after my skin worms destroy this body, yet in my flesh shall I see God.

The Teachings of Inspired Church Leaders

President Brigham Young:

To make this passage [Job 19:26] clearer to your comprehension, I will paraphrase it, Though my spirit leave my body, and though worms destroy its present organization, yet in the morning of the resurrection I shall behold the face of my Savior, in this same tabernacle; this is my understanding of the idea so briefly expressed by Job. (*Discourses of Brigham Young*, comp. John A. Widtsoe [1954], 566–67)

Psalms

Wicked Destroyed

What the Book of Psalms Teaches Us

Psalm 2:9 Thou shalt break them with a rod of iron; thou shalt dash them in pieces like a potter's vessel.

What the Scriptures of the Restoration Teach Us

D&C 19:15 Therefore I command you to repent—repent, lest I smite you by the rod of my mouth, and by my wrath, and by my anger, and your sufferings be sore—how sore you know not, how exquisite you know not, yea, how hard to bear you know not.

"What is man?"

What the Book of Psalms Teaches Us

Psalm 8:4 What is man, that thou art mindful of him? and the son of man, that thou visitest him?

What the Scriptures of the Restoration Teach Us

D&C 5:16 And behold, whosoever believeth on my words, them will I visit with the manifestation of my Spirit; and they shall be born of me, even of water and of the Spirit.

Ether 3:15 Seest thou that ye are created after mine own image? Yea, even all men were created in the beginning after mine own image.

The Teachings of Inspired Church Leaders

President Marion G. Romney:

Now the answer to this profound question—What is man that he should be of such inestimable worth?—comes only by direct revelation from heaven. So important is it that it is communicated to men by God himself and angels sent by him. It was thus revealed in the very beginning to Adam and Eve. In each succeeding gospel dispensation, it has been likewise revealed to "chosen vessels of the Lord" (Moroni 7:31)—that is, to his prophets. . . .

Man, being a child of God—who himself is a glorified, resurrected, immortal soul, enjoying eternal life—has, in harmony with the universal law of nature, the potentiality to reach, in full maturity, the high status of his Heavenly Father. ("The Worth of Souls," *Ensign*, Nov. 1978, online)

Slow to Hearken to the Lord

What the Book of Psalms Teaches Us

Psalm 10:1 Why standest thou afar off, O Lord? Why hidest thou thyself in times of trouble?

What the Scriptures of the Restoration Teach Us

D&C 101:7 They were slow to hearken unto the voice of the Lord their God; therefore, the Lord their God is slow to hearken unto their prayers, to answer them in the day of their trouble.

"Lift up your heads"

What the Book of Psalms Teaches Us

Psalm 24:7–10 Lift up your heads, O ye gates; and be ye lift up, ye everlasting doors; and the King of glory shall come in.

Who is this King of glory? The Lord strong and mighty, the Lord mighty in battle.

Lift up your heads, O ye gates; even lift them up, ye everlasting doors; and the King of glory shall come in.

Who is this King of glory? The Lord of hosts, he is the King of glory. Selah.

What the Scriptures of the Restoration Teach Us

Joseph Smith Translation—Psalm 24:7–10 Lift up your heads, O ye generations of Jacob; and by ye lifted up; and the Lord strong and mighty; the Lord mighty in battle, who is the king of glory, shall establish you forever.

And he will roll away the heavens; and will come down to redeem his people; to make you an everlasting name; to establish you upon his everlasting rock.

Lift up your heads, O ye generations of Jacob; lift up your heads, ye everlasting generations, and the Lord of hosts, the king of kings;

Even the king of glory shall come unto you; and shall redeem his people, and shall establish them in righteousness. Selah.

Waiting on the Lord

What the Book of Psalms Teaches Us

Psalm 27:14 Wait on the Lord: be of good courage, and he shall strengthen thine heart: wait, I say, on the Lord.

What the Scriptures of the Restoration Teach Us

D&C 98:2–3 Waiting patiently on the Lord, for your prayers have entered into the ears of the Lord of Sabaoth, and are recorded with this seal and testament—the Lord hath sworn and decreed that they shall be granted.

Therefore, he giveth this promise unto you, with an immutable covenant that they shall be fulfilled; and all things wherewith you have been afflicted shall work together for your good, and to my name's glory, saith the Lord.

The Teachings of Inspired Church Leaders

Elder Robert D. Hales said, "What, then, does it mean to wait upon the Lord? In the scriptures, the word *wait* means to hope, to anticipate, and to trust. To hope and trust in the Lord requires faith, patience, humility, meekness, long-suffering, keeping the commandments, and enduring to the end" ("Waiting upon the Lord: Thy Will Be Done," *Ensign*, Nov. 2011, online).

David's Misunderstanding of Sin

What the Book of Psalms Teaches Us

David grieves after committing adultery with Bathsheba.

Psalm 51:4 Against thee, thee only, have I sinned, and done this evil in thy sight: that thou mightest be justified when thou speakest, and be clear when thou judgest.

Interesting Information

Author and Bible commentator David Ridges shares this perspective: "That is not correct doctrine. David sinned against Bathsheba, against her husband, against his other wives and children, against the citizens of his kingdom, and so forth. It is often the claim of the sinner that he has done damage only to himself" (*The Old Testament Made Easier* [2009], 2:374).

Eyes Full of Greediness

What the Book of Psalms Teaches Us

Psalm 73:7 Their eyes stand out with fatness: they have more than heart could wish.

What the Scriptures of the Restoration Teach Us

D&C 68:31 Now, I, the Lord, am not well pleased with the inhabitants of Zion, for there are idlers among them; and their children are also growing up in wickedness; they also seek not earnestly the riches of eternity, but their eyes are full of greediness.

The Teachings of Inspired Church Leaders

President Gordon B. Hinckley said, "The Lord will open the windows of heaven according to our need, and not according to our greed" ("Tithing: An Opportunity to Prove Our Faithfulness" *Ensign*, May 1982, 40).

The Cup of Wrath

What the Book of Psalms Teaches Us

Psalm 75:8 For in the hand of the Lord there is a cup, and the wine is red; it is full of mixture; and he poureth out of the same: but the dregs thereof, all the wicked of the earth shall wring them out, and drink them.

What the Scriptures of the Restoration Teach Us

Mosiah 3:26 Therefore, they have drunk out of the cup of the wrath of God, which justice could no more deny unto them than it could deny that Adam should fall because of his partaking of the forbidden fruit; therefore, mercy could have claim on them no more forever.

The Teachings of Inspired Church Leaders

Elder Robert S. Wood of the Seventy:

Wrath is defined both as the righteous indignation of God and as the very human instances of impetuous ardor and deep or violent anger. The former arises from the concern of a loving Father whose children are often "without affection, and they hate their own blood," whereas the latter wrath arises from a people "without order and without mercy, . . . strong in their perversion." I fear the earth is experiencing both wraths, and I suspect the divine wrath is very much provoked by those who are stirring up the hearts of men to wickedness, slander, and violent hatreds. ("Instruments of the Lord's Peace" *Ensign*, May 2006, online)

Given to Prayer

What the Book of Psalms Teaches Us

Psalm 109:4 For my love they are my adversaries: but I give myself unto prayer.

What the Scriptures of the Restoration Teach Us

Joseph Smith Translation—Psalm 109:4 And, notwithstanding my love, they are my adversaries; yet I will continue in prayer for them.

Perfect in Knowledge

What the Book of Psalms Teaches Us

> **Psalm 138:8** The Lord will perfect that which concerneth me: thy mercy, O Lord, endureth for ever: forsake not the works of thine own hands.

What the Scriptures of the Restoration Teach Us

> **Joseph Smith Translation—Psalm 138:8** The Lord will perfect me in knowledge, concerning his kingdom. I will praise thee O Lord, forever; for thou art merciful, and wilt not forsake the works of thine own hands.

Proverbs

What the Book of Proverbs Teaches Us

Proverbs 2:10 When wisdom entereth into thine heart, and knowledge is pleasant unto thy soul.

What the Scriptures of the Restoration Teach Us

D&C 9:8 But, behold, I say unto you, that you must study it out in your mind; then you must ask me if it be right, and if it is right I will cause that your bosom shall burn within you; therefore, you shall feel that it is right.

Wickedness Is Darkness

What the Book of Proverbs Teaches Us

Proverbs 4:18–19 But the path of the just is as the shining light, that shineth more and more unto the perfect day.

The way of the wicked is as darkness: they know not at what they stumble.

The Teachings of Inspired Church Leaders

President Brigham Young:

The life of a Christian is said to be full of pain, tribulation, sorrow, and excruciating torments; of fightings without and fears within, of anxieties, despair, gloominess, and mourning. His path is supposed to be spread with gins [snares], pitfalls, and uncertainties, but this is a mistake, for "the path of the just is as the shining light, that shineth more and more unto the perfect day," while "the wicked is snared by the transgression of his lips, but the just shall come out of trouble."

The faith I have embraced has given me light for darkness, ease of pain, joy and gladness for sorrow and mourning, certainty for uncertainty, hope for despair. (In *Journal of Discourses*, 26 vols. [1854–86], 9:318)

Sparing the Rod

What the Book of Proverbs Teaches Us

Proverbs 13:24 He that spareth his rod hateth his son: but he that loveth him chasteneth him betimes.

The Teachings of Inspired Church Leaders

President Brigham Young:

Instead of using the rod, I will teach my children by example and by precept. I will teach them every opportunity I have to cherish faith, to exercise patience, to be full of long-suffering and kindness. It is not by the whip or the rod that we can make obedient children; but it is by faith and by prayer, and by setting a good example before them. (In *Journal of Discourses*, 11:117)

Soft Answers

What the Book of Proverbs Teaches Us

Proverbs 15:1 A soft answer turneth away wrath: but grievous words stir up anger.

The Teachings of Inspired Church Leaders

President Brigham Young:

In all our daily pursuits in life, of whatever nature and kind, Latter-day Saints, and especially those who hold important positions in the kingdom of God, should maintain a uniform and even temper, both when at home and when abroad. They should not suffer reverses and unpleasant circumstances to sour their natures and render them fretful and unsocial at home, speaking words full of bitterness and biting acrimony to their wives and children, creating gloom and sorrow in their habitations, making themselves feared rather than beloved by their families. Anger should never be permitted to rise in our bosoms, and words suggested by angry feelings should never be permitted to pass our lips. (In *Journal of Discourses*, 11:136)

Ignoring the Cries of the Poor

What the Book of Proverbs Teaches Us

Proverbs 21:13 Whoso stoppeth his ears at the cry of the poor, he also shall cry himself, but shall not be heard.

What the Scriptures of the Restoration Teach Us

Alma 34:28 And now behold, my beloved brethren, I say unto you, do not suppose that this is all; for after ye have done all these things, if ye turn away the needy, and the naked, and visit not the sick and afflicted, and impart of your substance, if ye have, to those who stand in need—I say unto you, if ye do not any of these things, behold, your prayer is vain, and availeth you nothing, and ye are as hypocrites who do deny the faith.

Interesting Information

The Church added to the "three-fold mission of the Church" the further important mission of "caring for the poor and needy." The handbook for administering for the Church now reads,

In fulfilling its purpose to help individuals and families qualify for exaltation, the Church focuses on divinely appointed responsibilities. These include helping members live the gospel of Jesus Christ, gathering Israel through missionary work, *caring for the poor and needy*, and enabling the salvation of the dead by building temples and performing vicarious ordinances. (Emphasis added) (*Handbook 2: Administering the Church* [2010], 2.2)

Ecclesiastes

The Preacher

What the Book of Ecclesiastes Teaches Us

Ecclesiastes 2:24 There is nothing better for a man, than that he should eat and drink, and that he should make his soul enjoy good in his labour. This also I saw, that it was from the hand of God.

Ecclesiastes 3:13 And also that every man should eat and drink, and enjoy the good of all his labour, it is the gift of God.

What the Scriptures of the Restoration Teach Us

D&C 59:18 Yea, all things which come of the earth, in the season thereof, are made for the benefit and the use of man, both to please the eye and to gladden the heart.

Animals in the Resurrection?

What the Book of Ecclesiastes Teaches Us

Ecclesiastes 3:21 Who knoweth the spirit of man that goeth upward, and the spirit of the beast that goeth downward to the earth?

In other words, will animals be a part of the resurrection?

What the Scriptures of the Restoration Teach Us

D&C 29:23–25 And the end shall come, and the heaven and the earth shall be consumed and pass away, and there shall be a new heaven and a new earth.

For all old things shall pass away, and all things shall become new, even the heaven and the earth, and all the fulness thereof, both men and beasts, the fowls of the air, and the fishes of the sea;

And not one hair, neither mote, shall be lost, for it is the workmanship of mine hand.

The Teachings of Inspired Church Leaders

President Brigham Young:

In the first place, matter is eternal. The principle of annihilation, of striking out of existence anything that has existed, or had a being, so as to leave an empty space which that thing occupied, is false, there is no such principle in all the *eternities*. What does exist? Matter is eternal. We grow our wheat, our fruit, and our animals, There they are organized, they increase and grow; but, after a while, they decay, dissolve, become disorganized, and return to their mother earth. No matter by what process, these are the revolutions which they undergo; but the elements of the particles of which they were composed, still do, always have, and always will exist, and through this principle of change, we have an eternal increase. (In *Journal of Discourses*, 26 vols. [1854–86], 1:116)

Gaining Spiritual Knowledge

What the Book of Ecclesiastes Teaches Us

Ecclesiastes 4:13 Better is a poor and a wise child than an old and foolish king, who will no more be admonished.

The Teachings of Inspired Church Leaders

President Brigham Young:

When I was baptized into this Church, it was in its infancy, although a considerable number had been baptized before me, and many of them were older when they were baptized than I was. They improved, their minds expanded, they received truth and intelligence, increased in the knowledge of the things of God, and bid fair to become full-grown men in Christ Jesus. But some of them, when they had gained a little spiritual strength and knowledge, apparently stopped in their growth. This was in the eastern country, and but a few years passed before the fruit-trees began to cease bearing fruit. . . . Like the fruit-trees, they have ceased to grow and increase and bear the fruits of the Spirit. (In *Journal of Discourses*, 7:335)

"Excellency of Knowledge"

What the Book of Ecclesiastes Teaches Us

Ecclesiastes 7:12 For wisdom is a defence, and money is a defence: but the excellency of knowledge is, that wisdom giveth life to them that have it.

What the Scriptures of the Restoration Teach Us

D&C 130:18–19 Whatever principle of intelligence we attain unto in this life, it will rise with us in the resurrection.

And if a person gains more knowledge and intelligence in this life through his diligence and obedience than another, he will have so much the advantage in the world to come.

The Race Is Not to the Swift

What the Book of Ecclesiastes Teaches Us

Ecclesiastes 9:11 I returned, and saw under the sun, that the race is not to the swift, nor the battle to the strong, neither yet bread to the wise, nor yet riches to men of understanding, nor yet favour to men of skill; but time and chance happeneth to them all.

The Teachings of Inspired Church Leaders

President Brigham Young:

The race is not to the swift, nor riches to men of wisdom. Do not fret, nor be so anxious about property, nor think that when you have gathered treasures, they alone will produce joy and comfort; for it is not so.

The race is not to the swift, nor the battle to the strong, nor riches to men of wisdom. The Lord gives the increase: he makes rich whom he pleases. You may inquire, "Why not make us rich?" Perhaps, because we would not know what to do with riches. (In *Journal of Discourses*, 7:241)

The Lord's Judgment is Imminent

What the Book of Ecclesiastes Teaches Us

Ecclesiastes 11:3 If the clouds be full of rain, they empty themselves upon the earth: and if the tree fall toward the south, or toward the north, in the place where the tree falleth, there it shall be.

The Teachings of Inspired Church Leaders

President Brigham Young said, "Ere long we will have to lay down these tabernacles and go into the spirit world. And I do know that as we lie down, so judgment will find us, and that is scriptural; 'as the tree falls so it shall lie,' or, in other words, as death leaves us so judgment will find us" (in *Journal of Discourses*, 4:52–53).

Songs of Solomon

What the Book of Songs of Solomon Teaches Us

Song of Solomon 1:1 The song of songs, which is Solomon's.

Interesting Information

You will notice in the cross references under the chapters a note for verse 1. The Joseph Smith Translation (JST) manuscript states that "The Songs of Solomon are not inspired writings." Enough said. We'll move on to Isaiah.

Isaiah

The Prophecies of Isaiah

What the Book of Isaiah Teaches Us

Isaiah 1:19–20 If ye be willing and obedient ye shall eat the good of the land:

But if ye refuse and rebel, you shall be devoured with the sword: for the mouth of the Lord hath spoken it.

What the Scriptures of the Restoration Teach Us

D&C 64:34–35 Behold, the Lord requireth the heart and a willing mind; and the willing and obedient shall eat the good of the land of Zion in these last days.

And the rebellious shall be cut off out of the land of Zion, and shall be sent away, and shall not inherit the land.

Trust in the Lord

What the Book of Isaiah Teaches Us

Isaiah 2:22 Cease ye from man, whose breath is in his nostrils: for wherein is he to be accounted of?

What the Scriptures of the Restoration Teach Us

2 Nephi 4:34 O Lord, I have trusted in thee, and I will trust in thee forever. I will not put my trust in the arm of flesh; for I know that cursed is he that putteth his trust in the arm of flesh. Yea, cursed is he that putteth his trust in man or maketh flesh his arm.

The Teachings of Inspired Church Leaders

President John Taylor:

If we will perform our part, the Lord will not fail to do His. Because others act foolishly we cannot afford to imitate them. We profess to be the Zion of God, the pure in heart. We profess to be men and women of integrity, of truth and virtue, and to have faith in God. It must not only be our profession, but our practice; we must carry out and [fulfill] the word and will and law of God. (*Deseret News: Semi-Weekly*, May, 15 1883, 1)

God's Love: A Cloud by Day and a Pillar by Night

What the Book of Isaiah Teaches Us

Isaiah 4:4–5 When the Lord shall have washed away the filth of the daughters of Zion, and shall have purged the blood of Jerusalem from the midst thereof by the spirit of judgment, and by the spirit of burning.

And the Lord will create upon every dwelling place of mount Zion, and upon her assemblies, a cloud and smoke by day, and the shining of a flaming fire by night: for upon all the glory shall be a defence.

The Teachings of Inspired Church Leaders

Elder Orson Pratt:

The time is to come when God will meet with all the congregation of his Saints, and to show his approval, and that he does love them, he will work a miracle by covering them in the cloud of his glory. I do not mean something that is invisible, but I mean that same order of things which once existed on the earth so far as the tabernacle of Moses was concerned, which was carried in the midst of the children of Israel as they journeyed in the wilderness. . . . But in the latter days there will be people so pure in Mount Zion, with a house established upon the tops of the mountains, that God will manifest himself, not only in their Temple and upon all their assemblies, with a visible cloud during the day, but when the night shall come, if they shall be assembled for worship, God will meet with them by his pillar of fire; and when they retire to their habitations, behold each habitation will be lighted up by the glory of God,—a pillar of flaming fire by night.

Did you ever hear of any city that was thus favored and blessed since the day that Isaiah delivered this prophecy? No, it is a latter-day work, one that God must consummate in the latter times when he begins to reveal himself, and show forth his power among the nations. (In *Journal of Discourses*, 26 vols. [1854–86], 16:82)

Interesting Information

It is thought that the Provo temple's architectural design was based on the concept of a "cloud by day" (the white base structure) and the "pillar by night" (the spire, which used to be gold). (See articles such as Alan Barnett, "Lessons in Mormon Modernism: Or, How I Learned to Love the Provo and Ogden Temples," https://www.sunstonemagazine.com/lessons-in-mormon-modernism-or-how-i-learned-to-love-the-provo-and-ogden-temples/.)

Our Merciful God

What the Book of Isaiah Teaches Us

Isaiah 10:4 Without me they shall bow down under the prisoners and they shall fall under the slain. For all this his anger is not turned away, but his hand is stretched out still.

What the Scriptures of the Restoration Teach Us

Jacob 6:4–5 And how merciful is our God unto us, for he remembereth the house of Israel, both roots and branches; and he stretches forth his hands unto them all the day long; and they are a stiffnecked and a gainsaying people; but as many as will not harden their hears shall be saved in the kingdom of God.

Wherefore, my beloved brethren, I beseech of you in words of soberness that ye would repent, and come with full purpose of heart, and cleave unto God as he cleaveth unto you. And while his arm of mercy is extended towards you in the light of the day, harden not your hearts.

The Rod and Stem of Jesse

What the Book of Isaiah Teaches Us

Isaiah 11:1 And there shall come forth a rod out of the stem of Jesse, and a Branch shall grow out of his roots.

What the Scriptures of the Restoration Teach Us

D&C 113:1–6 Who is the Stem of Jesse spoken of in the 1st, 2d, 3d, 4th, and 5th verses of the 11th chapter of Isaiah?

Verily thus saith the Lord: it is Christ.

What is the rod spoken of in the first verse of the 11th chapter of Isaiah, that should come of the Stem of Jesse?

Behold, thus saith the Lord: It is a servant in the hands of Christ, who is partly a descendant of Jesse as well as of Ephraim, or of the house of Joseph, on whom there is laid much power.

What is the root of Jesse spoken of in the 10th verse of the 11th chapter?

Behold, thus saith the Lord, it is a descendant of Jesse, as well as of Joseph, unto whom rightly belongs the priesthood, and the keys of the kingdom, for an ensign, and for the gathering of my people in the last days.

Interesting Information

George A. Horton Jr., who was associate director of the BYU Jerusalem Center for Near Eastern Studies, said,

Undoubtedly, the terms *rod* and *root*, like the term *Elias*, can be used to designate different people in different situations. Since they are symbols, the terms can also be applied to the same person. It is possible, therefore, that Joseph Smith is both the "rod" and the "root." Not only was he a descendant of Ephraim, of the house of Joseph, but he was probably a descendant of Jesse, King David's father, as well. ("Prophecies in the Bible about Joseph Smith", *Ensign,* Jan. 1989, online)

The Knowledge of God Will Cover the Earth

What the Book of Isaiah Teaches Us

Isaiah 11:9 They shall not hurt nor destroy in all my holy mountain: for the earth shall be full of the knowledge of the Lord, as the waters cover the sea.

The Teachings of Inspired Church Leaders

Elder Orson Pratt:

The knowledge of God will then cover the earth as the waters cover the mighty deep. There will be no place of ignorance, no place of darkness, no place for those that will not serve God. Why? Because Jesus, the Great Creator, and also the Great Redeemer, will be himself on the earth, and his holy angels will be on the earth, and all the resurrected Saints that have died in former dispensations will all come forth, and they will be on the earth. What a happy earth this creation will be, when this purifying process shall come, and the earth be filled with the knowledge of God as the waters cover the great deep! What a change! Travel, then, from one end of the earth to another, you can find no wicked man, no drunken man, no man to blaspheme the name of the Great Creator, no one to lay hold on his neighbor's goods, and steal them, no one to commit whoredoms—for all who commit whoredoms will be thrust down to hell, saith the Lord God Almighty, and all persons who commit sin will be speedily visited by the judgments of the Almighty! (In *Journal of Discourses*, 21:325)

The Highway from Assyria

What the Book of Isaiah Teaches Us

Isaiah 11:15–16 And the Lord shall utterly destroy the tongue of the Egyptian sea; and with his mighty wind shall he shake his hand over the river, and shall smite it in the seven streams, and make men go over dryshod.

And there shall be an highway for the remnant of this people, which shall be left, from Assyria; like as it was to Israel in the day that he came up out of the land of Egypt.

The Teachings of Inspired Church Leaders

Elder Parley P. Pratt:

We have also presented before us, in verse 15, the marvelous power of God, which will be displayed in the destruction of a small branch of the Red Sea, called the tongue of the Egyptian Sea, and also the dividing of the seven streams of some river, and causing me to go over dryshod; and lest any should not understand it literally, verse 16 says that "there shall be an highway for the remnant of his people, which shall be left, from Assyria; like as it was to Israel in the day that he came upon out of the land of Egypt." Now we have only to ask whether, in the days of Moses, the Red Sea was literally divided or whether it was only a figure? For as it was then, so it shall be again. (*Key to the Science of Theology; A Voice of Warning* [1978], 35)

The Worth of the Righteous

What the Book of Isaiah Teaches Us

Isaiah 13:11–12 And I will punish the world for their evil, and the wicked for their iniquity; and I will cause the arrogancy of the proud to cease, and will lay low the haughtiness of the terrible.

I will make a man more precious than fine gold; even a man than the golden wedge of Ophir.

What the Scriptures of the Restoration Teach Us

D&C 60:4 For I, the Lord, rule in the heavens above, and among the armies of the earth; and in the day when I shall make up my jewels, all men shall know what it is that bespeaketh the power of God.

D&C 101:3 Yet I will own them, and they shall be mine in that day when I shall come to make up my jewels.

The Sealed Book

What the Book of Isaiah Teaches Us

Isaiah 29:11–12 And the vision of all is become unto you as the words of a book that is sealed, which men deliver to one that is learned, saying, Read this, I pray thee: and he saith, I cannot; for it is sealed:

And the book is delivered to him that is not learned, saying, Read this, I pray thee: and he saith, I am not learned.

What the Scriptures of the Restoration Teach Us

Joseph Smith—History 1:65 He then said to me, "Let me see that certificate." I accordingly took it out of my pocket and gave it to him, when he took it and tore it to pieces, saying that there was no such thing now as ministering of angels, and that if I would bring the plates to him he would translate them. I informed him that part of the plates were sealed, and that I was forbidden to bring them. He replied, "I cannot read a sealed book." I left him and went to Dr. Mitchell, who sanctioned what Professor Anthon had said respecting both the characters and the translation.

The Teachings of Inspired Church Leaders

Elder Orson Pratt:

Now in regard to Joseph Smith's qualifications or attainments in learning, they were very ordinary. He had received a little education in the common country schools in the vicinity in which he had lived. He could read a little, and could write, but it was in such an ordinary hand that he did not venture to act as his own scribe, but had to employ sometimes one and sometimes another to write as he translated. This unlearned man did not make the same reply that the learned man did. For when the book was delivered to this unlearned youth and he was requested to read it, he replied, "I am not learned." I suppose he felt his weakness when the Lord told him to read this book; for he thought it was a great work. (In *Journal of Discourses*, 15:186)

All Shall Come to the Knowledge of the Truth

What the Book of Isaiah Teaches Us

Isaiah 29:24 They also that erred in spirit shall come to understanding, and they that murmured shall learn doctrine.

The Teachings of Inspired Church Leaders

Elder Orson Pratt:

Oh, how my heart has been pained within me when I have seen the blindness of the Christian world, and I knew that many of them were sincere! I knew they desired to know that truth, but they scarcely knew whether to turn to the right or to the left, so great were the errors that were taught in their midst, and so strong the traditions which they had imbibed, the fear of the Lord [being] taught them by the precepts of men instead of by inspiration and the power of the Holy Ghost. "They also that erred in spirit shall come to understanding" when this book come forth, and "they that murmur shall learn doctrine."

. . . But those who have read this book will bear me record that their minds have been forever set at rest in regard to doctrine, so far as the ordinances of the kingdom of God are concerned. Those who erred, and did not know whether sprinkling, pouring or immersion was the true method of baptism, now know? Why? Because the Book of Mormon reveals the mode as it was given to the ancient Nephites on this continent. So in regard to every other principle of the doctrine of Christ—it is set forth in such great plainness that it is impossible for any two persons to form different ideas in relation to it, after reading the Book of Mormon. (In *Journal of Discourses*, 15:188–89)

Preaching to the Spirits in Prison

What the Book of Isaiah Teaches Us

Isaiah 42:7 To open the blind eyes, to bring out the prisoners from the prison, and them that sit in darkness out of the prison house.

The Teachings of Inspired Church Leaders

President Joseph Smith:

Here then we have an account of our Savior preaching to the spirits in prison, to spirits that had been imprisoned from the days of Noah; and what did He preach to them? That they were to stay there? Certainly not! Let His own declaration testify. "He hath sent me to heal the broken hearted, to preach deliverance to the captives, and recovering of sight to the blind, to set at liberty them that are bruised." (Luke 4:18. Isaiah has it—"To bring out the prisoners from the prison, and them that sit in darkness from the prison house.") (Isaiah 42:7) It is very evident from this that He not only went to preach to them, but to deliver, or bring them out of the prison house. . . . Thus we find that God will deal with all the human family equally, and that as the antediluvians had their day of visitation, so will those characters referred to by Isaiah, have their time of visitation and deliverance, after having been many days in prison. (In *History of the Church*, ed. B. H. Roberts [1932–51], 4:596–97)

Be Ye Clean That Bear the Vessels of the Lord

What the Book of Isaiah Teaches Us

Isaiah 52:11–12 Depart ye, depart ye, go ye out from thence, touch no unclean thing; go ye out of the midst of her; be ye clean, that bear the vessels of the Lord.

For ye shall not go out with haste, nor go by flight: for the Lord will go before you; and the God of Israel will be your rearward.

What the Scriptures of the Restoration Teach Us

D&C 133:5, 14 Go ye out from Babylon. Be ye clean that bear the vessels of the Lord.

Go ye out from among the nations, even from Babylon, from the midst of wickedness, which is spiritual Babylon.

The Teachings of Inspired Church Leaders

John Taylor stated, "It is for us who hold the Holy Priesthood to be pure. 'Be ye pure that bear the vessels of the Lord'" (in *Journal of Discourses*, 24:272).

Charles W. Penrose:

Let us put away our follies and our errors. Let us not drink into the spirit of the world. Let us not pattern after the wickedness that is creeping into our midst. Come out from among them and be ye separate, and touch not the unclean thing! Be ye clean that bear the vessels of the Lord. It is only by the practice of righteousness and personal purity, that we will be made fit to dwell in the presence of the Lord. (In *Journal of Discourses*, 21:91)

The Sun Shall Lose Its Light

What the Book of Isaiah Teaches Us

Isaiah 60:19–20 The sun shall be no more thy light by day; neither for brightness shall the moon give light unto thee: but the Lord shall be unto thee an everlasting light, and thy God thy glory.

Thy sun shall no more go down; neither shall thy moon withdraw itself; for the Lord shall be thine everlasting light, and the days of thy mourning shall be ended.

The Teachings of Inspired Church Leaders

Elder Orson Pratt:

Zion will not need the sun when the Lord is there, and all the city is lighted up by the glory of his presence. When the whole heavens above are illuminated by the presence of his glory we shall not need those bright luminaries of heaven to give light, so far as the city of Zion is concerned. But there will be a great people round about, dwelling in other cities that will still have need of the light of the sun and the moon. (In *Journal of Discourses*, 14:355)

Jeremiah

The Prophecies of Jeremiah

What the Book of Jeremiah Teaches Us

Jeremiah 1:7–10 But the Lord said unto me, Say not, I am a child: for thou shalt go to all that I shall send thee, and whatsoever I command thee thou shalt speak.

Be not afraid of their faces: for I am with thee to deliver thee, saith the Lord.

Then the Lord put forth his hand, and touched my mouth. And the Lord said unto me, Behold, I have put my words in thy mouth.

See, I have this day set thee over the nations and over the kingdoms, to root out, and to pull down, and to destroy, and to throw down, to build, and to plant.

What the Scriptures of the Restoration Teach Us

D&C 1:38 What I the Lord have spoken, I have spoken, and I excuse not myself; and though the heavens and the earth pass away, my word shall not pass away, but shall all be fulfilled, whether by mine own voice or by the voice of my servants, it is the same.

Clay in the Potter's Hand

What the Book of Jeremiah Teaches Us

Jeremiah 18:1–10 The Parable of the Clay in the Potter's Hands.

The Teachings of Inspired Church Leaders

On Sunday, December 19, 1841, at Nauvoo, President Wilford Woodruff recorded the following:

> The subjoined minutes are from Elder Wilford Woodruff's journal—
>
> . . . Elder Heber C. Kimball preached at the house of President Joseph Smith, on the parable in the 18th chapter of Jeremiah, of the clay in the hands of the potter, that when it marred in the hands of the potter it was cut off the wheel and then thrown back again into the mill, to go in to the next batch, and was a vessel of dishonor; but all clay that formed well in the hands of the potter, and was pliable, was a vessel of honor; and thus it was with the human family, and ever will be: all that are pliable in the hands of God are obedient to His commands, are vessels of honor, and God will receive them. (In Joseph Smith, *History of the Church*, ed. B. H. Roberts [1932–51], 4:478)

A New Covenant

What the Book of Jeremiah Teaches Us

> **Jeremiah 31:31–34** Behold, the days come, saith the Lord, that I will make a new covenant with the house of Israel, and with the house of Judah:
>
> Not according to the covenant that I made with their fathers in the day that I took them by the hand to bring them out of the land of Egypt; which my covenant they brake, although I was an husband unto them, saith the Lord:
>
> But this shall be the covenant that I will make with the house of Israel; After those days, saith the Lord, I will put my law in their inward parts, and write it in their hearts; and will be their God, and they shall be my people.
>
> And they shall teach no more every man his neighbour, and every man his brother, saying, know the Lord: for they shall all know me, from the least of them unto the greatest of them, saith the Lord: for I will forgive their iniquity, and I will remember their sin no more.

The Teachings of Inspired Church Leaders

President Joseph Smith:

Christ in the days of His flesh, proposed to make a covenant with them, but they rejected Him and His proposals, and in consequence thereof, they were broken off, and no covenant was made with them at that time. But their unbelief has not rendered the promise of God of none effect: no, for there was another day limited in David, which was the day of His power; and then His people, Israel, should be a willing people;—and He would write His law in their hearts, and print it in their thoughts; their sins and their iniquities He would remember no more.

Thus after this chosen family had rejected Christ and His proposals, the heralds of salvation said to them, "Lo, we turn unto the Gentiles;" and the Gentiles received the covenant, and were grafted in from whence the chosen family were broken off; but the Gentiles have not continued in the goodness of God, but have departed from the faith that was once delivered to the Saints, and have broken the covenant in which their fathers were established. . . .

And now what remains to be done, under circumstances like these? I will proceed to tell you what the Lord requires of all people, high and low, rich and poor, male and female, ministers and people, professors of religion and non-professors, in order that they may enjoy the Holy Spirit of God to a fulness and escape the judgments of God, which are almost ready to burst upon the nations of the earth. Repent of all your sins, and be baptized in water for the remission of them, in the name of the Father, and of the Son, and of the Holy Ghost, and receive the ordinance of the laying on of the hands of him who is ordained and sealed unto this power, that ye may receive the Holy Spirit of God; and this is according to the Holy Scriptures, and the Book of Mormon; and the only way that man can enter into the celestial kingdom. These are the requirements of the new covenant. (In *History of the Church*, 1:313–14)

Lamentations

Mourning for the Wicked

What the Book of Lamentations Teaches Us

Lamentations 2:11 Mine eyes do fail with tears, my bowels are troubled, my liver is poured upon the earth, for the destruction of the daughter of my people; because the children and the sucklings swoon in the streets of the city.

What the Scriptures of the Restoration Teach Us

Mormon 6:17–22 O ye fair ones, how could ye have departed from the ways of the Lord! O ye fair ones, how could ye have rejected that Jesus, who stood with open arms to receive you!

Behold, if ye had not done this, ye would not have fallen. But behold, ye are fallen, and I mourn your loss.

O ye fair sons and daughters, ye fathers and mothers, ye husbands and wives, ye fair ones, how is it that ye could have fallen!

But behold, ye are gone, and my sorrows cannot bring your return.

And the day soon cometh that your mortal must put on immortality, and these bodies which are now moldering in corruption must soon become incorruptible bodies; and then ye must stand before the judgment-seat of Christ, to be judged according to your works; and if it so be that ye are righteous, then are ye blessed with your fathers who have gone before you.

O that ye had repented before this great destruction had come upon you. But behold, ye are gone, and the Father, yea, the Eternal

Father of heaven, knoweth your state; and he doeth with you according to his justice and mercy.

The Shedding of Just Blood

What the Book of Lamentations Teaches Us

Lamentations 4:13 For the sins of her prophets, and the iniquities of her priests, that have shed the blood of the just in the midst of her.

What the Scriptures of the Restoration Teach Us

Alma 14:9–11 And it came to pass that they took Alma and Amulek, and carried them forth to the place of martyrdom, that they might witness the destruction of those who were consumed by fire.

And when Amulek saw the pains of the women and children who were consuming in the fire, he also was pained; and he said unto Alma: How can we witness this awful scene? Therefore let us stretch forth our hands, and exercise the power of God which is in us, and save them from the flames.

But Alma said unto him: The Spirit constraineth me that I must not stretch forth mine hand; for behold the Lord received them up unto himself, in glory; and he doth suffer that they may do this thing, or that the people may do this thing unto them, according to the hardness of their hearts, that the judgments which he shall exercise upon them in his wrath may be just; and the blood of the innocent shall stand as a witness against them, yea, and cry mightily against them at the last day.

Turning to the Lord

What the Book of Lamentations Teaches Us

Lamentations 5:21 Turn thou us unto thee, O Lord, and we shall be turned; renew our days as of old.

What the Scriptures of the Restoration Teach Us

D&C 98:47 But if the children shall repent, or the children's children, and turn to the Lord their God, with all their hearts and with all their might, mind, and strength, and restore four-fold for all their trespasses wherewith they have trespassed, or wherewith their fathers have trespassed, or their father's fathers, then thine indignation shall be turned away.

The Teachings of Inspired Church Leaders

President Brigham Young:

Do you think that he has feeling for them? Yes, his mercy yearns over the nation that has striven for a score of years to rid the earth of the Priesthood of the Son of God and to destroy the last Saint. He has mercy upon them, he bears with them, he pleads with them by his Spirit, and occasionally sends his angels to administer to them. Marvel not, then, that I pray for every soul that can be saved. Are they yet upon saving ground? Many of them can yet be saved, if they will turn to the Lord. (In *Journal of Discourses*, 26 vols. [1854–86], 8:124)

Elder Donald L. Hallstrom:

"Hold on thy way" (D&C 122:9); giving up is not an option. And, without delay, turn to the Lord. Exercise all of the faith you have in Him. Let Him share your burden. Allow His grace to lighten your load. We are promised that we will "suffer no manner of afflictions, save it were swallowed up in the joy of Christ" (Alma 31:38). Never let an earthly circumstance disable you spiritually. ("Turn to the Lord," *Ensign*, May 2010, online)

Ezekiel

The Prophecies of Ezekiel

What the Book of Ezekiel Teaches Us

Ezekiel 1:4 And I looked, and, behold, a whirlwind came out of the north, a great cloud, and a fire infolding itself, and a brightness was about it, and out of the midst thereof as the colour of amber, out of the midst of the fire.

What the Scriptures of the Restoration Teach Us

It's interesting that in a number of places in the scriptures, that whenever the Lord has appeared to man, fire and amber are words used to describe the heavenly visitation in the narrative.

D&C 110:2 We saw the Lord standing upon the breastwork of the pulpit, before us; and under his feet was a paved work of pure gold, in color like amber.

The Teachings of Inspired Church Leaders

The Saints also experienced wind and fire at the time of the Kirtland Temple dedication.

President Joseph Smith:

Brother George A. Smith arose and began to prophesy, when a noise was heard like the sound of a rushing mighty wind, which filled the Temple, and all the congregation simultaneously arose, being moved upon by an invisible power; many began to speak in tongues and prophesy; others saw glorious visions; and I beheld the Temple was filled with angels, which fact I declared to the congregation. The people of the neighborhood came running together (hearing an unusual sound within, and seeing a bright light like a pillar of fire resting upon the Temple), and were astonished at what was taking place. (In *History of the Church*, ed. B. H. Roberts [1932–51], 2:428)

The Interpretation of Visions

What the Book of Ezekiel Teaches Us

Ezekiel 1:5 Also out of the midst thereof came the likeness of four living creatures. And this was their appearance; they had the likeness of a man.

The Teachings of Inspired Church Leaders

President Joseph Smith:

I make this broad declaration, that whenever God gives a vision of an image, or beast, or figure of any kind, He always holds Himself responsible to give a revelation or interpretation of the meaning thereof, otherwise we are not responsible or accountable for our belief in it. Don't be afraid of being damned for not knowing the meaning of a vision or figure, if God has not given a revelation or interpretation of the subject. (*Teachings of the Prophet Joseph Smith*, sel. Joseph Fielding Smith [2002], 291)

As of today, the Lord has not provided a revelation concerning Ezekiel's vision.

Condemnation if They Do Not Repent

What the Book of Ezekiel Teaches Us

Ezekiel 9:5–8 And to the others he said in mine hearing, Go ye after him through the city, and smite: let not your eye spare, neither have ye pity:
    Slay utterly old and young, both maids, and little children, and women: but come not near any man upon whom is the mark; and begin at my sanctuary. Then they began at the ancient men which were before the house.

And he said unto them, Defile the house, and fill the courts with the slain: go ye forth. And they went forth, and slew in the city.

And it came to pass, while they were slaying them, and I was left, that I fell upon my face, and cried, and said, Ah Lord God! Wilt thou destroy all the residue of Israel in thy pouring out of thy fury upon Jerusalem?

What the Scriptures of the Restoration Teach Us

D&C 97:25–27 Nevertheless, Zion shall escape if she observe to do all things whatsoever I have commanded her.

But if she observe not to do whatsoever I have commanded her, I will visit her according to all her works, with sore affliction, with pestilence, with plague, with sword, with vengeance, with devouring fire.

Nevertheless, let it be read this once to her ears, that I, the Lord, have accepted of her offering; and if she sin no more none of these things shall come upon her.

False Prophets

What the Book of Ezekiel Teaches Us

Ezekiel 13:1–3 And the word of the Lord came unto me, saying,

Son of man, prophesy against the prophets of Israel that prophesy, and say thou unto them that prophesy out of their own hearts, Hear ye the word of the Lord;

Thus saith the Lord God; Woe unto the foolish prophets, that follow their own spirit, and have seen nothing!

What the Scriptures of the Restoration Teach Us

Helaman 13:26–28 Behold ye are worse than they; for as the Lord liveth, if a prophet come among you and declareth unto you the word of the Lord, which testifieth of your sins and iniquities, ye are angry with him, and cast him out and seek all manner of ways to destroy him; yea, you will say that he is a false prophet, and that he is a sinner, and of the devil, because he testifieth that your deeds are evil.

But behold, if a man shall come among you and shall say: Do this, and there is no iniquity; do that and ye shall not suffer; yea, he will say: Walk after the pride of your own hearts; yea, walk after the pride of your eyes, and do whatsoever your heart desireth—and if a man shall come among you and say this, ye will receive him, and say that he is a prophet.

Yea, ye will lift him up, and ye will give unto him of your substance; ye will give unto him of your gold, and of your silver, and ye will clothe him with costly apparel; and because he speaketh flattering words unto you, and he saith that all is well, then ye will not find fault with him.

The Teachings of Inspired Church Leaders

Elder M. Russell Ballard:

Regardless of which particular false doctrines they teach, false prophets and false teachers are an inevitable part of the last days. "False prophets," according to the Prophet Joseph Smith, "always arise to oppose the true prophets" (*Teachings of the Prophet Joseph Smith*, sel. Joseph Fielding Smith [2002], 365).

However, in the Lord's Church there is no such thing as a "loyal opposition." One is either for the kingdom of God and stands in defense of God's prophets and apostles, or one stands opposed. ("Beware of False Prophets and False Teachers," *Ensign*, Nov. 1999, online)

President Brigham Young:

And you know that false prophets were to arise in the last days, and, if possible, deceive the very elect, and that many false shepherds would come and pretend to be the true shepherds. Now, be sure to get the spirit of revelation, so that you can tell when you hear the true Shepherd's voice, and know him from a false one; for if you are the elect, it would be a great pity to have you led astray to destruction. (In *Journal of Discourses*, 26 vols. [1854–86], 6:45)

The Blossoming of a New Twig

What the Book of Ezekiel Teaches Us

Ezekiel 17:1–21 The Parable of the Branch of the Cedar.

The Teachings of Inspired Church Leaders

Elder Orson Pratt:

When Zedekiah, king of Judah, was carried away captive into Babylon, the Lord took one of his sons, whose name was Mulok [Mulek] with a company of those who would hearken unto His words, and brought them over the ocean, and planted them in America. This was done in fulfillment of the 22nd and 23rd verses of the seventeenth chapter of Ezekiel, which read thus "Thus saith the Lord God, I will also take of the highest branch of the high cedar, and will set it: I will crop off from the top of his young twigs a *tender one*, and will plant it upon an high mountain and eminent; in the mountain of the height of Israel will I plant it; and it shall bring forth boughs, and bear fruit and, be a goodly cedar; and under it shall dwell all fowl of every wing; in the shadow of the branches thereof shall they dwell." By reading this chapter, it will be seen that the Jews were the "high cedar," that Zedekiah the king was the "highest branch," that the "tender one" cropped off from the top of his young twigs, was one of his sons, whom the Lord brought out and planted him and his company upon the choice land of America, which He had given unto a remnant of the tribe of Joseph for an inheritance, in fulfillment of the blessing of Jacob and Moses upon the head of that tribe. (*Orson Pratt's Works on the Doctrines of the Gospel* [1945], 280–81)

The Saints Will Not Escape Suffering

What the Book of Ezekiel Teaches Us

Ezekiel 21:4 Seeing then that I will cut off from thee the righteous and the wicked, thereof shall my sword go forth out of his sheath against all flesh from the south to the north.

What the Scriptures of the Restoration Teach Us

Alma 60:13 For the Lord suffereth the righteous to be slain that his justice and judgment may come upon the wicked; therefore ye need not suppose that the righteous are lost because they are slain; but behold, they do enter into the rest of the Lord their God.

The Teachings of Inspired Church Leaders

President Joseph Smith:

It is a false idea that the Saints will escape all the judgments, whilst the wicked suffer; for all flesh is subject to suffer, and "the righteous shall hardly escape;" still many of the Saints will escape, for the just shall live by faith; yet many of the righteous shall fall prey to disease, to pestilence, etc., by reason of the weakness of the flesh, and yet be saved in the Kingdom of God. So that it is an unhallowed principle to say that such and such have transgressed because they have been preyed upon by disease or death, for all flesh is subject to death; and the Savior had said, "Judge not, lest ye be judged." (In *History of the Church*, 4:11)

The Stick of Judah and Joseph

What the Book of Ezekiel Teaches Us

Ezekiel 37:16–17 Moreover, thou son of man, take thee one stick, and write upon it, For Judah, and for the children of Israel his companions: then take another stick, and write upon it, For Joseph, the stick of Ephraim, and for all the house of Israel his companions:

And join them one to another into one stick; and they shall become one in thine hand.

What the Scriptures of the Restoration Teach Us

2 Nephi 29:10–14 Wherefore, because that ye have a Bible ye need not suppose that it contains all my words; neither need ye suppose that I have not caused more to be written.

For I command all men, both in the east and in the west, and in the north, and in the south, and in the islands of the sea, that they shall write the words which I speak unto them; for out of the books which shall be written I will judge the world, every man according to their works, according to that which is written.

For behold, I shall speak unto the Jews and they shall write it; and I shall also speak unto the Nephites and they shall write it; and I shall also speak unto the other tribes of the house of Israel, which I have led away, and they shall write it; and I shall also speak unto all nations of the earth and they shall write it.

And it shall come to pass that the Jews shall have the words of the Nephites, and the Nephites shall have the words of the Jews; and the Nephites and the Jews shall have the words of the lost tribes of Israel; and the lost tribes of Israel shall have the words of the Nephites and the Jews.

And it shall come to pass that my people, which are of the house of Israel, shall be gathered home unto the lands of their possessions; and my word also shall be gathered in one. And I will show unto them that fight against my word and against my people, who are of the house of Israel, that I am God, and that I covenanted with Abraham that I would remember his seed forever.

Ezekiel Enwrapped in Vision

What the Book of Ezekiel Teaches Us

Ezekiel 40:2–4 In the visions of God brought he me into the land of Israel, and set me upon a very high mountain, by which was as the frame of a city on the south.

And he brought me thither, and, behold, there was a man, whose appearance was like the appearance of brass, with a line of flax in his hand, and a measuring reed; and he stood in the gate.

And the man said unto me, Son of man, behold with thine eyes, and hear with thine ears, and set thine heart upon all that I shall shew thee; for to the intent that I might shew them unto thee art thou brought hither: declare all that thou seest to the house of Israel.

The Teachings of Inspired Church Leaders

Elder James E. Talmage:

In the twenty-fifth year of the Babylonian captivity, while yet the people of Israel were in exile in a strange land, the word of the Lord came to the prophet Ezekiel; the power of God rested upon him; and he saw in vision a glorious Temple, the plan of which he minutely described. As to whether the prophet himself considered the design so shown as one to be subsequently realized, or as but a grand yet unattainable ideal, is not declared. Certain it is that the Temple of the vision has not yet been builded.

In most of its essential features Ezekiel's ideal followed closely the plan of Solomon's Temple; so close, indeed, is the resemblance, that many of the details specified by Ezekiel have been accepted as those of the splendid edifice destroyed by Nebuchadnezzar. A predominant characteristic of the Temple described by Ezekiel was the spaciousness of its premises and the symmetry of both the Holy House and its associated buildings. The area was to be a square of five hundred cubits, walled about and provided with a gateway and arches on each of three sides; on the west side the wall was to be unbroken by arch or portal. At each of the gateways were little chambers regarded as lodges, and provide with porches. In the tower court were other chambers. The entire area was to be elevated, and a flight of steps led to each gateway. In the inner court was seen the great altar, standing before the House, and occupying the center of a square of one hundred cubits. Ample provision was made for every variety of sacrifice and offering, and for the accommodation of the priests, the singers, and all engaged in the holy ritual. The main structure comprised a Porch, a Holy Place, and an inner sanctuary or Most Holy Place, the last named elevated above the rest and reached by steps. The plan provided for even greater exclusiveness than had characterized the sacred area of the Temple of Solomon; the double courts contributed to this end. The service of the Temple was prescribed in detail; the ministry of the Levites, the regulations governing oblations and feasts were all set forth.

The immediate purpose of this revelation through the vision of the prophet appears to have been that of awakening the people of Israel to a realization of their fallen state and a conception of their departed glory. (*House of the Lord* [1968], 37–38)

Daniel

The Prophecies of Daniel

What the Book of Daniel Teaches Us

Daniel 2:44–45 And in the days of these kings shall the God of heaven set up a kingdom, which shall never be destroyed: and the kingdom shall not be left to other people, but it shall break in pieces and consume all these kingdoms, and it shall stand for ever.

Forasmuch as thou sawest that the stone was cut out of the mountain without hands, and that it brake in pieces the iron, the brass, the clay, the silver, and the gold; the great God hath made known to the king what shall come to pass hereafter: and the dream is certain, and the interpretation thereof sure.

The Teachings of Inspired Church Leaders

President Brigham Young:

The Lord God Almighty has set up a kingdom that will sway the sceptre of power and authority over all the kingdoms of the world, and will never be destroyed, it is the kingdom that Daniel saw and wrote of. It may be considered treason to say that the kingdom which that Prophet foretold is actually set up; that we cannot help, but we know it is so, and call upon the nations to believe our testimony. The kingdom will continue to increase, to grow, to spread and prosper more and more. Every time its enemies undertake to overthrow it, it will become more extensive and powerful; instead of its decreasing, it will continue to increase, it will spread the more, become more wonderful and conspicuous to the nations, until it fills the whole earth. (In *Journal of Discourses*, 26 vols. [1854–86], 1:202–3)

President Joseph Smith:

The second special Scripture to which I have promised a separate consideration is the prophecy of Daniel relative to the succession of the great earth empires; and the final establishment of the Kingdom of God, which in "the last days" shall fill the whole earth and remain for ever. By an error on the part of Christian writers Daniel's Prophecy concerning the Kingdom of God to be set up in "the last days" is supposed to have been fulfilled by the founding of "The Spiritual Kingdom of Christ" in the days of Messiah's earthly ministry; and therefore the conclusion is drawn that those days were "the last days," and the dispensation then ushered in, the final dispensation of the Gospel. It is my purpose here to refute that error.

The prophecy in question is familiar, and comes from Daniel's interpretation of the King of Babylon's dream of the great image, whose "brightness was excellent, whose form was terrible." The head of the image was of gold; his breast and arms were of silver; the body and thighs of brass; the legs of iron; and the feet and the toes part of iron and part of clay. The king in his dream also saw a little stone cut out of the mountain without hands, that smote the image upon the feet of mixed clay and iron, and broke it to pieces—until it became like the chaff of the summer threshingfloor, and the wind of heaven carried it away, that no place was found for it: but the little stone cut from the mountain without hands, which smote the image on the feet and ground it to dust, became a great mountain and filled the whole earth. . . .

As understood by the learned, Daniel's interpretation stands thus

"(1) The *Golden Head*—the Assyrio-Babylonish monarchy (the 6th and 5th century, B.C.);

"(2) The *Silver Breast and Arms*—the Medo-Persian empire (from 538 B.C. to about 330 B.C.);

"(3) The *Brazen Belly and Thighs*—the Greco-Macedonian kingdom, especially after Alexander, those of Egypt and Syria (from about 330 B. C. to 160 B. C.);

"(4) The *Legs of Iron*—the power of Rome, bestriding the east and west, but broken into a number of states, the ten toes, which retained some of its warlike strength (the iron), mingled with elements of weakness (the soft potter's clay), which rendered the whole imperial structure unstable.

"(5) The *Stone* cut without hands out of the *Living Rock*, dashing down the image, becoming a great mountain, and filling all the earth—*The Spiritual Kingdom of Christ*."

The last phrase—"The Spiritual Kingdom of Christ"—meaning of course the "Christian churches" which have existed from the time of Christ, and that now exist, and which, taken together, form Christ's spiritual kingdom.

On the foregoing exegesis, which is the one commonly accepted by orthodox Christians, I make the following several observations: . . .

First: The phrase with reference to the little Stone, "cut out of the Living Rock," is one introduced by Dr. Smith, from whose Old Testament History the above analysis of Daniel's interpretation is taken. The language of the Bible is "cut out of the mountain without hands." Why it is changed by the Doctor one may not conjecture, unless it is to lay the foundation of an argument not warranted by the text of Daniel's interpretation. It is enough here to note that the change in phraseology is wholly gratuitous and unwarranted.

Second: The claim that the "little Stone cut from the mountain without hands," is the "Spiritual Kingdom of Christ"—if by that "spiritual kingdom" is meant not a real kingdom, actually existing, visible and tangible—is an assumption of the Doctor's. It is not the language of the Bible, nor is there any evidence in Scripture for believing that the "kingdom," represented by "the stone cut out of the mountain without hands," is any less a material kingdom than those which preceded it. The differences between this kingdom of God and the other kingdoms of the vision are not in the kingdom being "spiritual," but in these; (1) that the kingdom which God shall set up will never be destroyed; (2) never left to another people; (3) will break in pieces and consume all other kingdoms; (4) it shall fill the whole earth; (5) and stand forever. We are warranted in the belief, however, that it will be a tangible, bona fide government of God on earth, consisting of a king; subordinate officers; laws; subjects; and the whole earth for its territory—for its dominion. The coming forth of such a government, the founding of such a kingdom, is in harmony with all the hopes of all the saints, and the predictions of all the prophets who have touched upon the subject. It is the actual reign of Christ on earth with His Saints, in fulfillment of the hopes held out to them in every dispensation of the Gospel. It is to be the burden of the song of the redeemed out of every kindred, and tongue, and people, and nation, that Christ has made them unto their God kings and priests—"and we shall reign on the earth." "It is to be the chorus in heaven—the kingdoms of this world are [to] become the kingdoms of our Lord, and of His Christ; and He shall reign for ever and ever." And the elders in heaven shall say: [(Rev. 11:17–18)] . . .

And still again: [(Rev 20:6)] . . .

It should be observed respecting the last passage and the one preceding it, that "the reign on earth" of the kingdom of God is connected with the resurrection of the righteous saints; so that it will be the "last days" indeed—not in the days of the Roman empire. And this reign of the saints on earth, this kingdom of God which they shall constitute shall be a reign of righteousness, but a veritable kingdom nevertheless.

Third: The orthodox exegesis under consideration omits one important matter of fact, viz., that instead of four great dominant political powers symbolized in the image which Nebuchadnezzar saw, and which Daniel interpreted, there are five: viz., (1) The Head of Gold—Babylonish Kingdom; (2) the Chest and Arms of Silver—the Medo-Persian Monarchy; (3) the Brazen Belly and Thighs—the Greco-Macedonian Empire; (4) the Legs of Iron—Rome; (5) the Feet and Toes Mixed of Iron and Clay—the modern kingdoms and states of the world.

This failure to recognize the fifth political power represented by the feet and toes of Daniel's image leads to serious errors with respect to this prophecy. It had led to the theologians to assign the setting up of God's kingdom spoken of in the prophecy to the wrong period of the world's history. They say the kingdom represented by the stone cut from the mountain without hands is "the spiritual kingdom of Christ;" and that the said kingdom was set up in the days of Messiah's earthly ministry in the meridian of time. This, however, cannot be correct; for the Church which Jesus established by His personal ministry and which, it is granted, is sometime spoken of as the Kingdom of God was founded in the days of the Roman empire, the fourth world power of Daniel's prophecy; and at a time, too, when imperial Rome was at the very zenith of her glory and power. Whereas the terms of Daniel's prophecy require that the kingdom which God shall establish, and which was represented by the stone cut from the mountain without hands, shall be set up in the days of the fifth political world power—in the days of the kingdom represented by the pieces of iron and clay in the feet and toes of the image. The language of the prophecy on this point is: "And whereas thou sawest the feet and toes, part of potter's clay, and part of iron, the kingdom [i.e. the political power so represented, and that succeeds the fourth power or Roman empire,] shall be divided; but there shall be in it of the strength of the iron, forasmuch as thou sawest the iron mixed with miry clay. And as the toes of the feet were part of iron, and part of clay, ***they [i.e., the kingdom represented by the pieces of iron and clay,] shall mingle themselves with the seed of men: but they shall not cleave one to another even as iron is not mixed with clay. And in the days of *these kings* [not in the days of the Roman empire]—*in the days of these kings* shall the God of heaven set up a kingdom, which never shall be destroyed. (In *History of the Church*, ed. B. H. Roberts [1932–51], 1:xxxiv–xxxix)

Elder Daniel H. Wells:

I have often been asked the question, "When will the kingdom be given into the hands of the Saints of the most high God;" and I have always answered it in this way: just so soon as the Lord finds that He has a people upon the earth who will uphold and sustain that kingdom, who shall be found capable of maintaining its interests and of extending its influence upon the earth. When he finds that he has such a people, a people who will stand firm and faithful to him, a people that will not turn it over into the lap of the devil, then, and not until then, will he give "the kingdom" into the hands of the Saints of the most high, in its power and influence when it shall fill the whole earth. . . . It depends, in a great measure, upon the people themselves, as to how soon the kingdom spoken of by Daniel shall be given into the hands of the Saints of God. When we shall prove ourselves faithful in every emergency that may arise, and capable to contend and grapple with every difficulty that threatens our peace and welfare, and to overcome every obstacle that may tend to impede the progress of the Church and kingdom of God upon the earth, then our heavenly Father will have confidence in us, and then he will be able to trust us. (*Journal of Discourses*, 23:305)

The Prophecy of Daniel Continued

What the Book of Daniel Teaches Us

Daniel 7:3 And four great beasts came up from the sea, diverse one from another.

The Teachings of Inspired Church Leaders

President Joseph Smith:

The revelations do not give us to understand anything of the past in relation to the kingdom of God. What John saw and speaks of were things which he saw in heaven; those which Daniel saw were on and pertaining to the earth.

I am now going to take exceptions to the present translation of the Bible in relation to these matters. Our latitude and longitude can be determined in the original Hebrew with far greater accuracy than in the English version. There is a grand distinction between the actual meaning of the prophets and the present translation. The prophets do not declare that they saw a beast or beasts, but that they saw the image or figure of a beast. Daniel did not see an actual bear or a lion, but the images or figures of those beasts. The translation should have been rendered "image" instead of "beast," in every instance where beasts are mentioned by the prophets. But John saw the actual beast in heaven, showing to John that beasts did actually exist there, and not to represent figures of things on the earth. When the prophets speak of seeing beasts in their visions, they mean that they saw the images, they being types to represent certain things. At the same time they received the interpretation as to what those images or types were designed to represent. (In *History of the Church*, 5:342)

Hosea

Prophecies of Hosea

Imagery of a marriage is used in this book in the form of a parable. The Lord covenanted and the covenant children of Israel promised, but, like the unfaithful spouse, they severed that promise through their wickedness and adopting of the customs and practices of a heathen nation (the Canaanites).

What the Book of Hosea Teaches Us

Hosea 5:15 I will go and return to my place, till they acknowledge their offence, and seek my face: in their affliction they will seek me early.

What the Scriptures of the Restoration Teach Us

D&C 101:8 In the day of their peace they esteemed lightly my counsel; but, in the day of their trouble, of necessity they feel after me.

The Lament of the Wicked

What the Book of Hosea Teaches Us

Hosea 7:14 And they have not cried unto me with their heart, when they howled upon their beds: they assemble themselves for corn and wine, and they rebel against me.

What the Scriptures of the Restoration Teach Us

Mormon 2:11–13 Thus there began to be a mourning and a lamentation in all the land because of these things, and more especially among the people of Nephi.

And it came to pass that when I, Mormon, saw their lamentation and their mourning and their sorrow before the Lord, my heart I did begin to rejoice within me, knowing the mercies and the long-suffering of the Lord, therefore supposing that he would be merciful unto them that they would again become a righteous people.

But behold this my joy was vain, for their sorrowing was not unto repentance, because of the goodness of God; but it was rather the sorrowing of the damned, because the Lord would not always suffer them to take happiness in sin.

The Teachings of Inspired Church Leaders

Elder Erastus Snow:

But the time will come when the fainthearted and the wicked, whose knees tremble and who cannot endure the contradiction of the ungodly world, and choose rather to hide their heads and retire, making lies their refuge, will lift up their eyes in hell, being in torment: they will look back, and they will try to repent as it were in sackcloth and ashes: they will seek repentance carefully with tears, but will not find it, because there will be no chance left for them to regain what they have lost. If the Lord has compassion upon them and hears their cries, their weeping, and their bitter lamentation in the day of their degradation and misery, it will be to give them the privilege of becoming, in a future day, the servants of those who maintained their integrity. (In *Journal of Discourses*, 26 vols. [1854–86], 6:92)

The Result of Wickedness

What the Book of Hosea Teaches Us

Hosea 8:7 For they have sown the wind, and they shall reap the whirl-wind: it hath no stalk: the bud shall yield no meal: if so be it yield, the strangers shall swallow it up.

What the Scriptures of the Restoration Teach Us

Mosiah 7:30 And again, he saith: If my people shall sow filthiness they shall reap the chaff thereof in the whirlwind; and the effect thereof is poison.

Our Offering to the Lord

What the Book of Hosea Teaches Us

Hosea 14:2 Take with you words, and turn to the Lord: say unto him, Take away all iniquity, and receive us graciously: so will we render the calves of our lips.

What the Scriptures of the Restoration Teach Us

D&C 59:8 Thou shalt offer a sacrifice unto the Lord thy God in righteousness, even that of a broken heart and a contrite spirit.

Joel

The Prophecies of Joel

What the Book of Joel Teaches Us

Joel 2:28–32 And it shall come to pass afterward, that I will pour out my spirit upon all flesh; and your sons and your daughters shall prophesy, your old men shall dream dreams, your young men shall see visions:

And also upon the servants and upon the handmaids in those days will I pour out my spirit.

And I will shew wonders in the heavens and in the earth, blood, and fire, and pillars of smoke.

The sun shall be turned into darkness, and the moon into blood, before the great and the terrible day of the Lord come.

And it shall come to pass, that whosoever shall call on the name of the Lord shall be delivered: for in mount Zion and in Jerusalem shall be deliverance, as the Lord hath said, and in the remnant whom the Lord shall call.

The Teachings of Inspired Church Leaders

President Joseph Smith:

Of the special passages before referred to, and which I said would receive separate consideration, the first is Peter's quotation from the Prophet Joel concerning the outpouring of the Spirit of God upon "all flesh in the last days." This quotation from Joel is regarded as identifying the days in which the Apostle was speaking, as "the last days"; and the dispensation in which he was living as the Dispensation of the last

303

Days and of the Fulness of Times. The conditions existing when Peter was speaking, and the prophecy of Joel, however, admit of no such interpretation. The circumstances were as follows: The Holy Ghost in an extraordinary manner rested upon the Apostles and gave them the power of speaking in other languages than those they had learned. Some in the listening multitude attributed this singular manifestation to drunkenness, whereupon the Apostle Peter arose and refuted the slander, saying: "These are not drunken, as ye suppose, seeing it is but the third hour of the day. But this is that which was spoken by the Prophet Joel;" [Acts 2:15–21 the same as Joel 2:28–32]. . . . "For," to finish the passage as it stands in Joel, but which is not in Peter's quotation, "For in Mount Zion and in Jerusalem shall be deliverance, as the Lord hath said, and in the remnant whom the Lord shall call."

Because Peter, referring to the Spirit that was then resting upon the Twelve Apostles, said, "this is that which was spoken by the Prophet Joel," etc., the very general opinion prevails that Joel's prophecy was then fulfilled; and hence the last days were come. This is an entire mis-apprehension of the purpose of Peter in making the quotation; as also of the quoted passage itself. Beyond all controversy Peter meant only: This Spirit which you now see resting upon these Apostles of Jesus of Nazareth, is that same Spirit which your Prophet Joel says will, in the last days, be poured out upon all flesh, Obviously he did not mean that this occasion of the Apostles receiving the Holy Ghost was a com-plete fulfillment of Joel's prediction. To insist upon such an exegesis would be to charge the chief of the Apostles with palpable ignorance of the meaning of Joel's prophecy. On the occasion in question the Holy Ghost was poured out upon the Twelve Apostles, who were given the power to speak in various tongues; Joel's prophecy for its complete fulfillment requires that the Spirit of the Lord, the Holy Ghost, shall be poured out upon all flesh, and undoubtedly refers to that time which shall come in the blessed millennium when the enmity shall not only cease between man and man, but even between the beasts of the forests and of the fields; and between man and beast, as described by Isaiah in the following language:

"The wolf also shall dwell with the Lamb, and the leopard shall lie down with the kid; and the calf and the young lion and the fatling together; and a little child shall lead them. And the cow and the bear shall feed; their young ones shall lie down together; and the lion shall eat straw like the ox. And the suckling child shall play on the hole of the asp, and the weaned child shall put his hand on the cockatrice den. They shall not hurt nor destroy in all my holy mountain; for the earth shall be full of the knowledge of the Lord, as the waters cover the sea." [Isaiah 11:6–9]

Compare these conditions so vividly described with what Joel himself says of the period when the Spirit of the Lord shall be poured out upon all flesh, and it will at once be clear that the two Prophets are dealing with the same period, and not only dealing with the same period, but that the period itself is certainly far beyond, in time, the days of Peter; in fact is still in the future; for the sun has not yet been turned into blackness; nor the moon into blood; nor have the stars withdrawn their shining. It is obvious that the events upon the day of Pentecost did not fulfill the terms of this prophecy, except in those particulars already pointed out. The mention in this prophecy, however, of those special signs which Jesus refers to as immediately preceding His own second and glorious coming, clearly demonstrate that Joel was speaking of the last days indeed, and not of a circumstance that occurred in connection with a period more properly designated as the Dispensation of the Meridian of Time. Immediately following the prediction of the outpouring of God's Spirit upon all flesh, Joel represents the Lord as saying: "And I will show wonders in the heavens and in the earth, blood, and fire, and pillars of smoke. The sun shall be turned into darkness and the moon into blood, before the great and the terrible day of the Lord comes." And later: "The sun and the moon shall be darkened, and the stars shall withdraw their shining. The Lord also shall roar out of Zion, and utter his voice from Jerusalem; and the heavens and the earth shall shake; but the Lord will be the hope of his people, and the strength of the children of Israel.

Compare this with the Savior's description of conditions in the earth that will precede His own second coming:

"Immediately after the tribulation of those days shall the sun be darkened, and the moon shall not give her light, and the stars shall fall from heaven, and the powers of the heavens shall be shaken: and then shall appear the sign of the Son of Man in heaven: and then shall all the tribes of the earth mourn, and they shall see the Son of Man coming in the clouds of heaven with power and great glory. And he shall send his angels with a great sound of a trumpet, and they shall gather together his elect from the four winds, from one end of heaven to the other." [Matthew 24:29–31]

The same wonders in heaven and earth; the same changes in sun and moon, and stars; the same promises of the gathering of God's people as are found in the prophecy of Joel. There can be no question, then, but that the prophecy of Joel refers to the same "last days" that Jesus here alludes to—the days of the coming of the Son of Man—and not to the days of Peter and the other Apostles in the Meridian of time.

The sum of the matter then is, that Peter was not living in the "last days"; that the prophecy of Joel was not in its entirety fulfilled in the outpouring of God's Spirit upon the Apostles on the day of Pentecost; that at no time subsequent to the days of the Apostles has there existed such conditions in the earth as amount to a complete fulfillment of Joel's prophecy; therefore at some time future from the days of the Apostles, we may look forward to a universal outpouring of God's Holy Spirit upon all flesh, resulting in a universal peace and widespread knowledge of God, brought about, unquestionably, by a subsequent dispensation from that in which Peter wrought—the Dispensation of the Fulness of Times, in which God promises to "gather together in one all things in Christ, both which are in heaven and which are in earth; even in Him." [Ephesians 1:10] (In *History of the Church*, ed. B. H. Roberts [1932–51], 1:xxxi–xxxiv)

Interesting Information

The evening the angel Moroni appeared to Joseph Smith, the young prophet wrote, "He also quoted the second chapter of Joel, from the twenty eighth verse to the last. He also said that this was not yet fulfilled, but was soon to be" (in *History of the Church*, 1:13).

The following event took place June or July of 1830:

Meantime, and notwithstanding all the rage of our enemies, we had much consolation, and many things occurred to strengthen our faith and cheer our hearts.

After our departure from Colesville, after the trial, the Church there were very anxious, as might be expected, concerning our again visiting them, during which time Sister Knight, wife of Newel Knight, had a dream, which enabled her to say that we would visit them that day, which really came to pass, for a few hours afterwards we arrived; and thus was our faith much strengthened concerning dreams and visions in the last days, foretold by the ancient Prophet Joel. (Joseph Smith, in *History of the Church*, 1:101)

Amos

The Prophecies of Amos

What the Book of Amos Teaches Us

Amos 3:7 Surely the Lord God will do nothing, but he revealeth his secret unto his servants the prophets.

The Teachings of Inspired Church Leaders

Christians understand the role of biblical prophets and the function they played in leading, for the most part, a hard-hearted people. But what about today? Our Christian neighbors will tell you that the heavens are sealed, that the Lord is now quiet, that there isn't a need for prophets today. They believe this, because the Bible, the way it is currently written, gives no evidence that the Lord communicates with man today. As Latter-day Saints, we know that there are prophets who continue to receive revelation as indicated by Amos, but also, that he reveals his will to each individual who seeks guidance for his own life.

President Joseph Smith:

The Melchizedek High Priesthood was no other than the Priesthood of the Son of God; that there are certain ordinances which belong to the Priesthood from which flow certain results; and the Presidents or Presidency are over the Church; and revelations of the mind and will of God to the Church, are to come through the Presidency. This is the order of heaven, and the power and privilege of this Priesthood. It is also the privilege of any officer in this Church to obtain revelations, so far as relates to his particular calling and duty in the Church. All are bound by the principles of virtue and happiness, but one great privilege of the Priesthood is to obtain revelation of the mind and will of God. (In *History of the Church*, ed. B. H. Roberts [1932–51], 2:477)

Those Who Are Snared by Satan

What the Book of Amos Teaches Us

Amos 6:3–7 Ye that put far away the evil day, and cause the seat of violence to come near;

That lie upon beds of ivory, and stretch themselves upon their couches, and eat the lambs out of the flock, and the calves out of the midst of the stall;

That chant to the sound of the viol, and invent to themselves instruments of musick, like David;

That drink wine in bowls, and anoint themselves with the chief ointments: but they are not grieved for the affliction of Joseph.

Therefore now shall they go captive with the first that go captive, and the banquet of them that stretched themselves shall be removed.

What the Scriptures of the Restoration Teach Us

2 Nephi 28: 21–25 And others will he pacify, and lull them away into carnal security, that they will say: All is well in Zion; yea, Zion prospereth, all is well—and thus the devil cheateth their souls, and leadeth them away carefully down to hell.

And behold, others he flattereth away, and telleth them there is no hell; and he saith unto them: I am no devil, for there is none—and thus he whispereth in their ears, until he grasps them with his awful chains, from whence there is no deliverance.

Yea, they are grasped with death, and hell; and death, and hell, and the devil, and all that have been seized therewith must stand before the throne of God, and be judged according to their works, from whence they must go into the place prepared for them, even a lake of fire and brimstone, which is endless torment.

Therefore, wo be unto him that is at ease in Zion!

Wo be unto him that crieth: All is well!

Obadiah

The Prophecies of Obadiah

What the Book of Obadiah Teaches Us

Obadiah 1:3 The pride of thine heart hath deceived thee, thou that dwellest in the clefts of the rock, whose habitation is high; that saith in his heart, Who shall bring me down to the ground?

What the Scriptures of the Restoration Teach Us

D&C 101:42 He that exalteth himself shall be abased, and he that abaseth himself shall be exalted.

Saints to Judge

What the Book of Obadiah Teaches Us

Obadiah 1:21 And saviours shall come up on mount Zion to judge the mount of Esau; and the kingdom shall be the Lord's.

What the Scriptures of the Restoration Teach Us

D&C 64:37–38 Behold, I, the Lord, have made my church in these last days, like unto a judge sitting on a hill, or in a high place, to judge the nations.

For it shall come to pass that the inhabitants of Zion shall judge all things pertaining to Zion.

The Teachings of Inspired Church Leaders

President Joseph F. Smith:

Read your Bible, for there it is written that the Saints shall "judge angels," and also they shall "judge the world." And why? Because the resurrected, righteous man has progressed beyond the pre-existent or disembodied spirits, and has risen above them, having both spirit and body as Christ has, having gained the victory over death and the grave, and having power over sin and Satan; in fact, having passed from the condition of the angels to that of a God. (*Gospel Doctrine: Selections from the Sermons and Writings of Joseph F. Smith* [1959], 18–19)

Jonah

Reality of Jonah

What the Book of Jonah Teaches Us

Jonah 1:17 Now the Lord had prepared a great fish to swallow up Jonah. And Jonah was in the belly of the fish three days and three nights.

The Teachings of Inspired Church Leaders

President Joseph Fielding Smith:

Are we to reject it as being an impossibility and say that the Lord could not prepare a fish, or whale, to swallow Jonah?. . . .

I believe . . . the story of Jonah. My chief reason for so believing is not in the fact that it is recorded in the Bible, . . . but in the fact that Jesus Christ, our Lord believed it.

"He answered and said unto them, An evil and adulterous generation seeketh after a sign; and there shall no sign be given to it, but the sign of the Prophet Jonas: For as Jonas was three days and three nights in the whale's belly; so shall the Son of man be three days and three nights in the heart of the earth." [Matthew 12:39–40] (*Doctrines of Salvation*, comp. Bruce R. McConkie, 3 vols. [1954–56], 2:314–15)

Nineveh Repents

What the Book of Jonah Teaches Us

Jonah 3:10 And God saw their works, that they turned from their evil way; and God repented of the evil, that he had said that he would do unto them; and he did it not.

What the Scriptures of the Restoration Teach Us

Joseph Smith Translation—Jonah 3:10 And God saw their works that they turned form their evil way and repented; and God turned away the evil that he had said he would bring upon them.

As strange as it may seem, and for whatever reason, Jonah felt that the people's repentance should not be accepted by the Lord. However, one lesson that Jonah failed to understand is that God's ways are not man's ways (Isaiah 55:8–9). God does a better job at looking on the heart, whereas with man, judgment is more severe because of our nature to look at the outward expression of the individual.

Micah

The Prophecies of Micah

What the Book of Micah Teaches Us

Micah 1:4 And the mountains shall be molten under him, and the valleys shall be cleft, as wax before the fire, and as the waters that are poured down a steep place.

What the Scriptures of the Restoration Teach Us

D&C 133:40–41 Calling upon the name of the Lord day and night, saying: O that thou wouldst rend the heavens, that thou wouldst come down, that the mountains might flow down at thy presence.

And it shall be answered upon their heads; for the presence of the Lord shall be as the melting fire that burneth, and as the fire which causeth the waters to boil.

The Mountain of the Lord

What the Book of Micah Teaches Us

Micah 4:1–2 But in the last days it shall come to pass, that the mountain of the house of the Lord shall be established in the top of the mountains, and it shall be exalted above the hills; and people shall flow unto it.

And many nations shall come and say, Come, and let us go up to the mountain of the Lord, and to the house of the God of Jacob; and he will teach us of his ways, and we will walk in his paths: for the law shall go forth of Zion, and the word of the Lord from Jerusalem.

What the Scriptures of the Restoration Teach Us

Part of preparing ourselves spiritually for the celestial world is to go to the "mountain of the Lord" and to the "house of Jacob" (the temple).

D&C 78:7 For if you will that I give unto you a place in the celestial world, you must prepare yourselves by doing the things which I have commanded you and required of you.

The Teachings of Inspired Church Leaders

Elder LeGrand Richards, speaking of the mountain of the Lord being established in the tops of the mountains: "How literally that has been fulfilled, in my way of thinking, in this very house of the God of Jacob right here on this block! This temple, more than any other building of which we have any record, has brought people from every land to learn of his ways and walk in his paths." ("In the Mountain of the Lord's House," *Ensign*, June 1971, online)

President Heber J. Grant:

I believe that if I can find the time to go to the temple and to do temple work once a week, there is hardly a man in the entire Church of Jesus Christ of Latter-day Saints but that can find time if he wishes to plan his work accordingly. . . . I do not know of any one that is any busier than I am, and if I can do it they can, if they will only get the spirit in their hearts and souls of wanting to do it. The trouble with so many people is they do not have the desire. (*Power from On High: A Lesson Book for Fourth Year Junior Genealogical Classes* [1937], 26; see also *Teachings of Presidents of the Church—Heber J. Grant* [2002], 55))

Nahum

The Prophecies of Nahum

What the Book of Nahum Teaches Us

> **Nahum 1:10** For while they be folden together as thorns, and while they are drunken as drunkards, they shall be devoured as stubble fully dry.

What the Scriptures of the Restoration Teach Us

Moroni said essentially the same thing when he visited Joseph Smith on the evening of September 21, 1823.

> **Joseph Smith—History 1:37** For behold, the day cometh that shall burn as an oven, and all the proud, yea, and all that do wickedly shall burn as stubble; for they that come shall burn them, saith the Lord of Hosts, that it shall leave them neither root nor branch.

"How Beautiful Are the Feet . . ."

What the Book of Nahum Teaches Us

> **Nahum 1:15** Behold upon the mountains the feet of him that bringeth good tidings, that publisheth peace! O Judah, keep thy solemn feasts, perform thy vows; for the wicked shall no more pass through thee; he is utterly cut off.

What the Scriptures of the Restoration Teach Us

> **Mosiah 15:18** And behold, I say unto you, this is not all. For O

how beautiful upon the mountains are the feet of him that bringeth good tidings, that is the founder of peace, yea, even the Lord, who has redeemed his people; yea, him who has granted salvation unto his people.

The Teachings of Inspired Church Leaders

Elder Mark E. Petersen:

Have you ever asked yourselves who these people are, who preach the gospel of peace and whose feet are so beautiful upon the mountains?

Abinadi, in the Book of Mormon, gives us the explanation.

These people are the prophets of God—they who preach the gospel of the Prince of Peace, the Lord Jesus Christ. . . . [See Mosiah 15: 13–18]

The prophets, then, are the servants of Jesus Christ and have been from the beginning of time. And because they are his servants and preach his gospel of peace, behold, how beautiful upon the mountains are their feet. ("Another Prophet Now Has Come!" *Ensign*, Jan. 1973, online)

Elder Orson Hyde:

Now go and take this, ye swift messengers, you faithful agents, in vessels of bulrushes, pipe-ships, or, in other words, steam-ships, and be messengers of glad tidings to the poor, and wretched, and oppressed, and meek of the earth. It is an honor to be a messenger, bearing to them the means of taking them out of their poverty, wretchedness, and oppression. He says to them, "I have come to bring you to the family of God; to rescue you from the land of your oppression and poverty, and put you in a position where you may be blessed temporally and spiritually." Is not he who bears these tidings blessed? "How beautiful upon the mountains are the feet of him that bringeth good tidings, that publisheth peace; that bringeth good tidings of good, that publisheth salvation; that saith unto Zion, Thy God reigneth." This messenger goes and brings them to his place by the means that is put into his hands. (In *Journal of Discourses*, 26 vols. [1854–86], 2:66)

Habakkuk

O God, Where Art Thou?

What the Book of Habakkuk Teaches Us

Habakkuk 1:2 O Lord, how long shall I cry, and thou wilt not hear! even cry out unto thee of violence, and thou wilt not save!

What the Scriptures of the Restoration Teach Us

D&C 121:1–2 O God, where art thou? And where is the pavilion that covereth thy hiding place?

How long shall thy hand be stayed, and thine eye, yea thy pure eye, behold from the eternal heavens the wrongs of thy people and of thy servants, and thine ear be penetrated with their cries?

The Teachings of Inspired Church Leaders

Elder Robert D. Hales:

In my life I have learned that sometimes I do not receive an answer to a prayer because the Lord knows I am not ready. When He does answer, it is often "here a little and there a little" because that is all that I can bear or all I am willing to do. . . .

We may not know when or how the Lord's answers will be given, but in His time and His way, I testify, His answers will come. For some answers we may have to wait until the hereafter. . . . Let us not give up on the Lord. His blessings are eternal, not temporary. ("Waiting upon the Lord: Thy Will Be Done," *Ensign*, Nov. 2011, online)

No Man Knows the Hour

What the Book of Habakkuk Teaches Us

> **Habakkuk 2:3** For the vision is yet for an appointed time, but at the end it shall speak, and not lie: though it tarry, wait for it; because it will surely come, it will not tarry.

What the Scriptures of the Restoration Teach Us

> **D&C 39:21** For the time is at hand; the day or the hour no man knoweth; but it surely shall come.

Zephaniah

The Prophecies of Zephaniah

What the Book of Zephaniah Teaches Us

Zephaniah 1:2 I will utterly consume all things from off the land, saith the Lord.

What the Scriptures of the Restoration Teach Us

1 Nephi 22:23 For the time speedily shall come that all churches which are built up to get gain, and all those who are built up to get power over the flesh, and those who are built up to become popular in the eyes of the world, and those who seek the lusts of the flesh and the things of the world, and to do all manner of iniquity; yea, in fine, all those who belong to the kingdom of the devil are they who need fear, and tremble, and quake; they are those who must be brought low in the dust; they are those who must be consumed as stubble; and this is according to the words of the prophet.

Punishment of the Wicked

What the Book of Zephaniah Teaches Us

Zephaniah 1:8 And it shall come to pass in the day of the Lord's sacrifice, that I will punish the princes, and the king's children, and all such as are clothed with strange apparel.

What the Scriptures of the Restoration Teach Us

Mormon 8:36–37 And I know that ye do walk in the pride of your hearts; and there are none save a few only who do not lift themselves up in the pride of their hearts, unto the wearing of very fine apparel, unto envying, and strifes, and malice, and persecutions, and all manner of iniquities; and your churches, yea, even every one, have become polluted because of the pride of your hearts.

For behold, ye do love money, and your substance, and your fine apparel, and the adorning of your churches, more than ye love the poor and the needy, the sick and the afflicted.

Haggai

The Prophecies of Haggai

What the Book of Haggai Teaches Us

Haggai 1:7–8 Thus saith the Lord of hosts; Consider your ways.

Go up to the mountain, and bring wood, and build the house; and I will take pleasure in it, and I will be glorified, saith the Lord.

What the Scriptures of the Restoration Teach Us

D&C 124:31, 40, 55 But I command you, all ye my saints, to build a house unto me; and I grant unto you a sufficient time to build a house unto me; and during this time your baptisms shall be acceptable unto me.

And verily I say unto you, let this house be built unto my name, that I may reveal mine ordinances therein unto my people;

And again, verily I say unto you, I command you again to build a house to my name, even in this place, that you may prove yourselves unto me that ye are faithful in all things whatsoever I command you, that I may bless you, and crown you with honor, immortality, and eternal life.

The Glory of the Lord Will Rest on the Temple

What the Book of Haggai Teaches Us

Haggai 2:7 And I will shake all nations, and the desire of all nations shall come: and I will fill this house with glory, saith the Lord of hosts.

What scriptures of the restoration teach Us

D&C 97:15 And inasmuch as my people build a house unto me in the name of the Lord, and do not suffer any unclean thing to come into it, that it be not defiled, my glory shall rest upon it.

The Teachings of Inspired Church Leaders

President Daniel H. Wells:

Treasure up the words of wisdom that we hear from time to time, and be cleanly in our persons and in our habitations; for the Holy Ghost will not dwell in unholy temples. It is an insult to the Holy Spirit for us to be filthy, and it may be grieved away if we do not observe cleanliness. Be careful to treasure these things up in your minds. Keep the commandments of God; do not take His name in vain; do not be seen loafing about at the corners of the streets, and spending your time in idleness. When you go to plough and plant, ask God to bless the ground and the seed, and let us have His blessing on all that we do, and have our faith centred upon the things that we are called upon to perform, and we shall be blessed and prospered, and will see the work of the Almighty roll forth with might and power, even until we shall redeem Zion and build a temple upon the consecrated spot, where it is said that the glory of God shall rest upon it as a cloud by day, and a pillar of fire by night. (In *Journal of Discourses*, 26 vols. [1854–86], 5:44)

Zechariah

Servants of the Lord

What the Book of Zechariah Teaches Us

Zechariah 4:10 For who hath despised the day of small things? for they shall rejoice, and shall see the plummet in the hand of Zerubbabel with those seven; they are the eyes of the Lord, which run to and fro through the whole earth.

What the Scriptures of the Restoration Teach Us

Joseph Smith Translation—Zechariah 4:10 Joseph Smith changed, "they are the eyes of the Lord," to "they are the servants of the Lord."

The Teachings of Inspired Church Leaders

Elder Bruce R. McConkie:

We are the servants of the Lord, and he has sent us to deliver a message to the world.

The Lord has a message for people today, and he has revealed it to us. We are commanded to go forth, in his name and by his power, and tell all men everywhere what lies ahead and what the Lord wants them to do about it. ("The Lord God of the Restoration," *Ensign*, Nov. 1980, online)

Many to Seek the Lord

What the Book of Zechariah Teaches Us

Zechariah 8:20–23 Thus saith the Lord of hosts; It shall yet come to pass, that there shall come people, and the inhabitants of many cities:

And the inhabitants of one city shall go to another, saying, Let us go speedily to pray before the Lord and to seek the Lord of hosts: I will go also.

Yea, many people and strong nations shall come to seek the Lord of hosts in Jerusalem, and to pray before the Lord.

Thus saith the Lord of hosts; In those days it shall come to pass, that ten men shall take hold out of all languages of the nations, even shall take hold of the skirt of him that is a Jew, saying, We will go with you: for we have heard that God is with you.

What the Scriptures of the Restoration Teach Us

2 Nephi 30:2 For behold, I say unto you that as many of the Gentiles as will repent are the covenant people of the Lord; and as many of the Jews as will not repent shall be cast off; for the Lord covenanteth with none save it be with them that repent and believe in his Son, who is the Holy One of Israel.

The Command to Obey the Feast of the Tabernacles

What the Book of Zechariah Teaches Us

Zechariah 14:16–19 And it shall come to pass, that every one that is left of all the nations which came against Jerusalem shall even go up from year to year to worship the King, the Lord of hosts, and to keep the feast of tabernacles.

And it shall be, that whoso will not come up of all the families of the earth unto Jerusalem to worship the King, the Lord of hosts, even upon them shall be no rain.

And if the family of Egypt go not up, and come not, that have no rain; there shall be the plague, wherewith the Lord will smite the heathen that come not up to keep the feast of tabernacles.

This shall be the punishment of Egypt, and the punishment of all nations that come not up to keep the feast of tabernacles.

The Teachings of Inspired Church Leaders

President Joseph Smith:

While in conversation at Judge Adams' during the evening, I said, Christ and the resurrected Saints will reign over the earth during the thousand years. They will not probably dwell upon the earth, but will visit it when they please, or when it is necessary to govern it. There will be [wicked] men on the earth during the thousand years. The heathen nations who will not come up to worship will be visited with the judgments of God, and must eventually be destroyed from the earth. (*Teachings of the Prophet Joseph Smith*, sel. Joseph Fielding Smith [2002], 268–69)

Malachi

The Prophecies of Malachi

What the Book of Malachi Teaches Us

Malachi 4:5–6 Behold, I will send you Elijah the prophet before the coming of the great and dreadful day of the Lord:

And he shall turn the heart of the fathers to the children, and the heart of the children to their fathers, lest I come and smite the earth with a curse.

The Teachings of Inspired Church Leaders

It was on the evening of September 21, 1823, after the Smith family retired for the night, that the angel Moroni appeared to Joseph Smith and shared this verse of scripture. At this point during the young Joseph's life, it may have been possible that he might not have read this scripture, and if he had, maybe not have comprehended the complete significance of the message. It was of such import that with each subsequent visit by Moroni that evening, he repeated what he had shared with Joseph on his previous appearances. As the prophet was taught from heaven and matured spiritually, later in life, just prior to his martyrdom, he was able to shed new light on the words of Malachi:

President Joseph Smith:

Now, the word *turn* here should be translated bind, or seal. But what is the object of this important mission? or how is it to be fulfilled? The keys are to be delivered, the spirit of Elijah is to come, the Gospel to be established, the Saints of God gathered, Zion built up, and the Saints to come up as saviors on Mount Zion.

But how are they to become saviors on Mount Zion? By building their temples, erecting their baptismal fonts, and going forth and receiving all the ordinances, baptisms, confirmations, washings, anointing, ordinations and sealing powers upon their heads, in behalf of all their progenitors who are dead, and redeem them that they may come forth in the first resurrection and be exalted to thrones of glory with them; and herein is the chain that binds the hearts of the fathers to the children, and the children to the fathers, which fulfills the mission of Elijah. And I would to God that this temple was now done, that we might go into it, and go to work and improve our time, and make use of the seals while they are on earth.

The Saints have not too much time to save and redeem their dead, and gather together their living relatives, that they may be saved also, before the earth will be smitten, and the consumption decreed falls upon the world.

I would advise all the Saints to go to with their might and gather together all their living relatives to this place, that they may be sealed and saved, that they may be prepared against the day that the destroying angel goes forth; and if the whole Church should go to with all their might to save their dead, seal their posterity, and gather their living friends, and spend none of their time in behalf of the world, they would hardly get through before night would come, when no man can work; and my only trouble at the present time is concerning ourselves, that the Saints *will be divided, broken up, and scattered*, before we get our salvation secure; for there are so many fools in the world for the devil to operate upon, it gives him the advantage often times. (In *History of the Church*, ed. B. H. Roberts [1932–51], 6:183–84)

Sources

Ballard, M. Russell. "Beware of False Prophets and False Teachers." *Ensign*, November 1999, http://www.lds.org/ensign/1999/11/ beware-of-false-prophets-and-false-teachers?lang=eng.

Barlow, Ora H. *The Israel Barlow Story and Mormon Mores*. Salt Lake City: Publishers Press, 1968.

Barnett, Alan. "Lessons in Mormon Modernism: Or, How I Learned to Love the Provo and Ogden Temples." *Sunstone*, no. 168 (September 20, 2012), https://www.sunstonemagazine.com/lessons-in-mormon-modernism-or-how-i-learned-to-love-the-provo-and-ogden-temples/.

Benson, Ezra T. *The Teachings of Ezra Taft Benson*. Salt Lake City: Bookcraft, 1988.

———. "What I Hope You Will Teach Your Children about the Temple." *Ensign*, August 1985, http://www.lds.org/ensign/1985/08/ what-i-hope-you-will-teach-your-children-about-the-temple.

Black, Susan Easton. "*St. Louis Luminary*: The Latter-day Saint Experience at the Mississippi River, 1854–1855," *BYU Studies* 49, no. 4 (2010): 165–66.

Brown, Victor L. "Is There Not a Cause?" *Ensign*, November 1974.

Church History in the Fulness of Times Student Manual, 2nd ed. Salt Lake City: The Church of Jesus Christ of Latter-day Saints, 1989.

Church Archives. Patriarchal Blessings 1833–2005. The Church of Jesus Christ of Latter-day Saints.

Clark, James R., comp. *Messages of the First Presidency of The Church of Jesus Christ of Latter-day Saints.* 6 vols. Salt Lake City: Bookcraft, 1965–75.

Corrill, John. *A Brief History of The Church of Christ of Latter-day Saints (Commonly Called Mormons;) including an Account of their Doctrine and Discipline, with the Reasons of the Author for Leaving the Church.* St. Louis: printed for author, 1839.

Cowley, Matthias. *Wilford Woodruff: History of His Life and Labors as Recorded in His Daily Journals.* Salt Lake City: Bookcraft, 1970.

Daniell, David. *The Bible in English: Its History and Influence.* New Haven: Yale University Press, 2003.

Dibble, Philo. "Early Scenes in Church History." In *Four Faith Promoting Classics.* Salt Lake City: Bookcraft, 1968.

Doctrine and Covenants Student Manual, 2nd ed. Salt Lake City: The Church of Jesus Christ of Latter-day Saints, 2001.

Donaldson, Lee, V. Dan Rogers, and David Rolph Seely. "I Have a Question." *Ensign*, February 1994.

Encyclopedia of Mormonism. Edited by Daniel Ludlow. 5 vols. New York: Macmillan, 1992.

England, Eugene. "George Laub's Nauvoo Journal." *BYU Studies* 18, no. 2 (1978): 25, https://byustudies.byu.edu/PDFLibrary/18.2EnglandGeorge-03639c50-48a5-4a79-bc09-09d24fa06ef5.pdf.

Grant, Heber J. In The Church of Jesus Christ of Latter-day Saints, *Power from On High: A Lesson Book for Fourth Year Junior Genealogical Classes*, 1937.

———. *Gospel Standards*. Compiled by G. Homer Durham. Salt Lake City: Deseret Book, 1976, first published 1969.

———. "The President Speaks." *Improvement Era*, November 1936, https://archive.org/details/improvementera.

Gunn, Stanley R. *Oliver Cowdery: Second Elder and Scribe*. Salt Lake City: Bookcraft, 1962.

Gygi, Alma E. "Is It Possible That Shem and Melchizedek Are the Same Person?" *Ensign*, November 1973.

Hancock, Mosiah. *Autobiography of Mosiah Hancock*, typescript, BYU-S, http://www.boap.org/.

Handbook 2: Administering the Church. Salt Lake City: The Church of Jesus Christ of Latter-day Saints, 2010, http://www.lds.org/handbook/handbook-2-administering-the-church/priesthood-principles?lang=eng#22.

Hales, Robert D. "Waiting upon the Lord: Thy Will Be Done." *Ensign*, November 2011, http://www.lds.org/general-conference/2011/10/waiting-upon-the-lord-thy-will-be-done?lang=eng.

Hallstrom, Donald L. "Turn to the Lord." *Ensign*, May 2010, http://www.lds.org/ensign/2010/05/turn-to-the-lord?lang=eng.

Hinckley, Gordon B. "Overpowering the Goliaths in Our Lives." *Ensign*, May 1983, http://www.lds.org/ensign/1983/05/overpowering-the-goliaths-in-our-lives?lang=eng.

———, "Tithing: An Opportunity to Prove Our Faithfulness." *Ensign*, May 1982.

———, "Women of the Church." *Ensign*, November 1996.

Horton, George A., Jr., "Prophecies in the Bible about Joseph Smith." *Ensign*, January 1989, http://www.lds.org/ensign/1989/01/prophecies-in-the-bible-about-joseph-smith?lang=eng.

Jenson, Andrew, comp. "26 September 1830," *Journal History of The Church of Jesus Christ of Latter-day Saints* vol. 1, http://eadview.lds.org/findingaid/CR%20100%20137.

Jolley, JoAnn. "News of the Church." *Ensign*, May 1983, http://www.lds.org/ensign/1983/05/news-of-the-church?lang=eng.

Josephus, Flavius. *Antiquities of the Jews.* In *The Life and Works of Flavius Josephus.* Translated by William Whiston. Philadelphia: John C. Winston, 1957.

Journal of Discourses. 26 vols. London: Latter-day Saints' Book Depot, 1854–86.

Kimball, Spencer W. *Miracle of Forgiveness.* Salt Lake City: Bookcraft, 1969.

Lee, Harold B. *"But Arise and Stand upon Thy Feet"—and I Will Speak with Thee.* Brigham Young University Speeches of the Year, Provo, February 7, 1956, http://speeches.byu.edu/.

Litchman, Kristin E. "Deborah and the Book of Judges." *Ensign*, January 1990, https://www.lds.org/ensign/1990/01/deborah-and-the-book-of-judges?lang=eng.

Maxwell, Neal A. "Teaching Opportunities from the Old Testament." *Ensign*, April 1981.

McConkie, Bruce R. "Christ and the Creation." *Ensign*, June 1982.

———. "The Lord God of the Restoration." *Ensign*, November 1980, http://www.lds.org/ensign/1980/11/the-lord-god-of-the-restoration?lang=eng.

———. *The Millennial Messiah.* Salt Lake City: Deseret Book, 1982.

———. *Mormon Doctrine.* 2d ed. Salt Lake City: Bookcraft, 1966.

———. *The Promised Messiah—The First Coming of Christ.* Salt Lake City: Bookcraft, 1978.

McKay, David O. *Gospel Ideals: Life's Surest Anchor.* In Brigham Young University Devotional speech, October 30, 1956, http://speeches.byu.edu/.

Minutes. Salt Lake City School of the Prophets. October 11, 1883. In "Remarks Of Zebede Coltrin on Kirtland, Ohio, History of the Church," www.boap.org/LDS/Early-Saints/ZebC.html.

Monson, Thomas S. "Crisis at the Crossroads." *New Era*, November 2002, http://www.lds.org/new-era/2002/11/crisis-at-the-crossroads?lang=eng

———. "Models to Follow." *Ensign*, November 2002.

———. "They Showed the Way." *Ensign*, May 1997.

———. "Your Future Awaits." BYU College of Engineering and Technology Convocation, April 25, 2003.

Nibley, Hugh. *Abraham in Egypt.* Salt Lake City: Deseret Book, 1981.

Oaks, Dallin H. "The Great Plan of Happiness." *Ensign*, November 1993.

Old Testament Student Manual: Genesis–2 Samuel, 3rd ed. Salt Lake City: The Church of Jesus Christ of Latter-day Saints, 2003.

Packer, Cameron J. "Cumorah's Cave." *Journal of Book of Mormon Studies* 13, number 1–2 (2004): 50–57, 170–71, http://publications.maxwellinstitute.byu.edu/publications/jbms/13/1/S00006-50be6ae14ef1b5Packer.pdf.

Petersen, Mark E. "Another Prophet Now Has Come!" *Ensign*, January 1973, http://www.lds.org/ensign/1973/01/another-prophet-now-has-come?lang=eng.

———, *Moses: Man of Miracles.* Salt Lake City: Deseret Book, 1978.

———. *Noah and the Flood.* Salt Lake City: Deseret Book, 1982.

Phelps, W. W. *Deseret Almanac*, no. 2. Salt Lake City: W. Richards Printer, 1852, https://archive.org/details/deseretalmanacfo02phel.

———. *Deseret Almanac*, no. 3. Salt Lake City: W. Richards Printer, 1853, https://archive.org/details/deseretalmanacfo03phel.

———. Times and Seasons, 5:578.

Pratt, Orson. *Orson Pratt's Works on the Doctrines of the Gospel*. Salt Lake City: Deseret News Press, 1945.

Pratt, Parley P. *Key to the Science of Theology; A Voice of Warning*. Salt Lake City: Deseret Book, 1978.

Rabinowitz, Abraham Hirsch. "Commandments, The 613." *Encyclopedia Judaica*. Edited by Michael Berenbaum and Fred Skolnik. 2nd ed., Vol. 5. Detroit: Macmillan Reference USA, 2007, 73–85. *Gale Virtual Reference Library*. Web. Accessed Oct. 25, 2013, http://go.galegroup.com/ps/i.do?id=GALE%7CCCX2587504542&v=2.1&u=imcpl1111&it=r&p=GVRL&sw=w&asid=dbd5e71e288dd5fbdd05 83a1a72d8535.

Rector, Hartman, Jr. "Live above the Law to Be Free." *Ensign*, January 1973.

Richards, LeGrand. "In the Mountain of the Lord's House." *Ensign*. June 1971, http://www.lds.org/ensign/1971/06/in-the-mountain-of-the-lords-house.

Ridges, David J. *The Old Testament Made Easier*. 3 vols. Springville, UT: Cedar Fort, 2009.

Roberts, B. H. *A Comprehensive History of The Church of Jesus Christ of Latter-day Saints*. Provo, UT: Brigham Young University Press, 1965.

———. *The Life of John Taylor*. Salt Lake City: George Q. Cannon & Sons, 1963. First published 1892.

Romney, Marion G. *Jesus Christ, Man's Greatest Exemplar.* Brigham Young University Speeches of the Year, Provo, Utah, 9 May 1967, http://speeches.byu.edu/.

———, "The Worth of Souls." *Ensign*, November 1978, http://www.lds.org/ensign/1978/11/the-worth-of-souls?lang=eng.

Satterfield, Rick. "Adam-ondi-Ahman Temple," http://www.ldschurch-temples.com/adamondiahman/.

Smith, George Albert. In Conference Report, April 1942.

———. "Our Full Duty." *Improvement Era*, March 1946, https://archive.org/details/improvementera.

Smith, Joseph. *Elders Journal* 1, no. 2, November 1837.

———. *History of The Church of Jesus Christ of Latter-day Saints.* Edited by B. H. Roberts. 2d ed. rev., 7 vols. Salt Lake City: The Church of Jesus Christ of Latter-day Saints, 1932–51.

———. "The Last Days." *Evening and Morning Star*, February 1833.

———. *Teachings of the Prophet Joseph Smith.* Selected by Joseph Fielding Smith. Salt Lake City: Covenant Communications, 2002.

———. *Times and Seasons*, 3:781–82.

Smith, Joseph F. In Conference Report, October 1902.

———. *Deseret News: Semi-Weekly*, August 9, 1898, 1.

———. *Gospel Doctrine: Selections from the Sermons and Writings of Joseph F. Smith.* Salt Lake City: Deseret Book, 1959. First published 1919, https://archive.org/details/gospeldoctrinese00smitrich.

———. "Marriage God-ordained and Sanctioned." *Improvement Era*, July 1902, https://archive.org/details/improvementera.

———. "Modern Revelation." *Improvement Era*, August 1902, https://archive.org/details/improvementera.

———."Reason and the Scriptures." *The Juvenile Instructor*, April 1912.

———. "Restoration of the Melchizedek Priesthood." *Improvement Era*, October 1904, https://archive.org/details/improvementera.

———. "Trust in God." *Improvement Era*, November 1903, https://archive.org/details/improvementera.

Smith, Joseph Fielding. *Church History and Modern Revelation*. Salt Lake City: Deseret Book, 1949.

———. *Doctrines of Salvation*. Compiled by Bruce R. McConkie. 3 vols. Salt Lake City: Bookcraft, 1954–56.

———. *Improvement Era*, 717.

———. *Man, His Origin and Destiny*. Salt Lake City: Deseret Book, 1969. First published 1954.

———, "Was the Fall of Adam Necessary?" *Improvement Era*, April 1962, https://archive.org/details/improvementera.

Smith, Lucy Mack. *History of Joseph Smith By His Mother*. edited by Scot Facer Proctor and Maurine Jensen Proctor. Salt Lake City: Deseret Book, 1996.

Snow Smith, Eliza R. *Biography and Family Record of Lorenzo Snow: One of the Twelve Apostles of the Church of Jesus Christ of Latter-day Saints*. Salt Lake City: Deseret Book, 1884.

"Statement of the First Presidency." *Church News*, March 20, 1983.

Stuy, Brian H., comp. *Collected Discourses Delivered by Wilford Woodruff, His Two Counselors, the Twelve Apostles, and Others*. 5 vols. Burbank, CA: B. H. S. Publishing, 1987–92.

Talmage, James E. *Articles of Faith*. Salt Lake City: Deseret Book, 1981.

———. *House of the Lord*. Salt Lake City: Deseret Book, 1968.

———. *Jesus the Christ*. Salt Lake City: Deseret Book, 1916.

Tanner, John S. "The King James Bible in America; Pilgrim, Prophet, President, Preacher." *BYU Studies* 50, no. 3 (2011): 13–14.

Taylor, John. *Deseret News: Semi-Weekly*, April 18, 1882, 1.

———. *Deseret News: Semi-Weekly*, May 15, 1883, 1.

———. *The Gospel Kingdom: Selections from the Writings and Discourses of John Taylor, Third President of The Church of Jesus Christ of Latter-day Saints*. Selected by G. Homer Durham. Salt Lake City: Bookcraft, 1943.

———. *Items on the Priesthood: Presented to the Latter-day Saints*. Salt Lake City: George Q. Cannon & Sons, 1881.

———. *The Mediation and Atonement*. Salt Lake City: Deseret News, 1882.

Taylor, Moses. In "Stories and Counsel of President Taylor." *Young Woman's Journal*, May 1905.

Teaching, No Greater Call: A Resource Guide for Gospel Teaching. Salt Lake City: The Church of Jesus Christ of Latter-day Saints, 1999.

The Church of Jesus Christ of Latter-day Saints. *Scripture Stories*. Salt Lake City: The Church of Jesus Christ of Latter-day Saints.

Todd, Jay M. "Gondwanaland: What it Means to Latter-day Saints." *New Era*, March 1971, http://www.lds.org/new-era/1971/03/gondwanaland-what-it-means-to-latter-day-saints.

Uchtdorf, Dieter F. "Brother, I'm Committed." *Ensign*, July, 2011, http://www.lds.org/ensign/2011/07/brother-im-committed?lang=eng.

United Country Real Estate. "LISTING #35340," American Treasures: Your Source for Missouri Historic Homes & Vintage Property for Sale. Accessed Oct. 25, 2013, http://www.unitedcountry.com/HistoricProperty/Missouri/Kidder%20%20Missouri-24022-35340.htm.

Webster's Dictionary, 1828. In Donaldson, Lee, V. Dan Rogers, and David Rolph Seely, "I Have a Question." *Ensign*, February 1994.

Whitmer, David. *Millennial Star* 40 (May 2, 1878): 772–73.

Whitney, Orson F. *Life of Heber C. Kimball*. Salt Lake City: Bookcraft, 1992.

Wilson, J. Tuzo, comp. *Continents Adrift: Readings from Scientific American*. San Francisco: W. H. Freeman, 1970.

Wirthlin, Joseph B. "Come What May, and Love It." *Ensign*, November 2008.

———. "Lessons Learned in the Journey of Life." *Ensign*, December 2000.

Wood, Robert S. "Instruments of the Lord's Peace." *Ensign*, May 2006, http://www.lds.org/ensign/2006/05/instruments-of-the-lords-peace?lang=eng.

Woodruff, Wilford. In Conference Report, April 1898.

———. *Deseret News: Semi-Weekly*, March 26, 1878, 1.

———. *Deseret Weekly*, 823.

———. *Deseret Weekly*, August 30, 1890, 305.

———. *The Discourses of Wilford Woodruff*. Selected by G. Homer Durham. Salt Lake City: Bookcraft, 1995. First published 1946.

———. "Epistle." Woman's Exponent 16, no. 22 (April 15, 1888): 174, http://contentdm.lib.byu.edu/cdm/compoundobject/collection/WomansExp/id/38160/rec/382.

Young, Brigham. *Discourses of Brigham Young*. Compiled by John A. Widtsoe. Salt Lake City: Deseret Book, 1954.

———. *Manuscript History of Brigham Young*, 1847–1850. Edited by William S. Harwell. Salt Lake City: Collier's, 1997.

Notes

ABOUT THE AUTHOR

Born in Kalispell, Montana, Dan enjoyed a farmer's life until he was four when his parents moved to Calgary, Alberta, and made a city slicker out of him.

Dan had the privilege of spending the "best two years" of his life in the Massachusetts Boston Mission. He currently serves as the second assistant in his high priest group. (However, he occasionally skips Sunday School to be with Kate and play with the kids in the nursery.)

Dan and Kate married thirty-two years ago in the Cardston Alberta Temple and have six great children and soon-to-be fifteen grandchildren.

He never forgot his country roots. Always wishing for the outdoors, Dan graduated from Utah State University with a bachelor of science and enjoyed a brief career in forestry. He is now currently employed with Nestles.

Barker is the author of *Leaders, Managers, and Blue Collar Perceptions*; *Unique Stories & Facts from LDS History*; *Mormon History 101*; and *Little-Known Stories about the Doctrine and Covenants*. Dan welcomes reader feedback. Visit his blog at www.danbarkerldsauthor.com and answer a new Church history question every day! You may contact him through his blog or his email: dknkids@comcast.net.